D1598612

The
Greatest
Circus Stories
Ever Told

The Greatest Circus Stories Ever Told

Amazing Stories of Life Under the Big Top

STEPHEN VINCENT BRENNAN

THE LYONS PRESS
Guilford, Connecticut
An imprint of The Globe Pequot Press

The Lyons Press is an imprint of The Globe Pequot Press.

10 9 8 7 6 5 4 3 2 1

Printed in the United States of America

Library of Congress Cataloging-in-Publication Data

Brennan, Stephen J., 1951–
The greatest circus stories ever told : amazing stories of life under the big top /
Stephen Brennan.
    p. cm.
  ISBN 1-59228-740-9
  1. Circus—Miscellanea. 2. Circus—Fiction. I. Title.
GV1801.B74 2005
791.3—dc22
                                        2005027535

CONTENTS

Introduction

Maybe at last, being but a broken man,
I must be satisfied with my heart, although
Winter and summer till old age began
My circus animals were all on show,
Those stilted boys, that burnished chariot,
Lion and woman and Lord knows what.

—W. B. Yeats
"The Circus Animals Desertion"

About thirty years ago I left off what I was doing—which was nothing particular at the moment, and did a couple seasons as a clown
with one of America's largest big-top, three-ring circuses. I won't say
which, there are probably some of us still living. We played pretty
much all over the lower forty-eight states, chasing the good weather;
late winter and spring we played in the South, summer in the North
and East, autumn in the Southwest, finishing up the year in California before going into winter-quarters near San Francisco. We
claimed to be "The Greatest Show Under Canvas," and to my mind
we were, sometimes. When the crowds came, and the weather was
fair, and the planets all lined up just right, and God smiled, we had a
shot at greatness. But I get ahead of myself.

The first time I ever saw a circus I was in it. And it was a revelation to me.
Like so many people, I reckoned I knew all about the circus, though I'd

never actually been to one. What I knew, or thought I knew, I'd learned from the movies and TV and books; from"Circus Boy" on late 1950s TV, and "Toby Tyler" the classic Boy's Book by James Otis and the hit Disney movie. There were other films too: "The Greatest Show on Earth" and "Peck's Bad Boy with the Circus," and even the awful John Wayne/Rita Hayworth "Circus World." As a kid, I discovered C. R. Cooper's books in our village library, and for a short time read nothing else. In college I studied circus arts, and saw Chaplin's "The Circus" and Fellini's "The Clowns." Most importantly, I shared in, partook of, a kind of American circus *geist,* a notion of an ideal circus, a mix of lore, pop-culture and my own dreams. But none of this had prepared me for the reality of circus life; the excitement, the hard work, the numbing three-a-day grind, the constant travel from place to place, and all the strange and ordinary people of the show. It delighted me (and amused my friends and family) that I was re-enacting the old cliche of running away and joining the circus. And there I was in the ring, for the first time, stumbling through a routine I had first rehearsed only an hour before. I can mark the day of my first performance exactly, it was the day Nixon resigned.

Only three days earlier I had opened my hometown newspaper and discovered that the Circus had come to a nearby town. Not only that, but I read, that very night it was to leave this nearby town, and go to some faraway town. (Circuses are always doing this, they don't seem to be able to help themselves.) I borrowed the family car, but by the time I arrived on the lot, the last performance was almost over, and it took some while to locate the Owner. This is never an easy thing to do. Circus owners, as a rule, greatly value, prize their invisibility. But finally, I hunted him down, (or is it up?) and after some modest enlarging of the truth as to my prior experience as a clown, and to my real surprise, I got hired on. It just so happened that at that moment this show was one clown short. "Join us in Utica in three days," was all he said, and "Go introduce yourself to Johnny, he's Boss Clown."

Minutes later Johnny shook my hand, warily, and asked me what shows I'd worked before. I looked him straight in the eye and told him the truth. I was a theater clown, I said. I had studied mime (Decroux), and I had just returned from living in London where I had played a lot of roles. I named a few of them, including a couple of Shakespeare's clowns. Ah, Shakespeare—there was a name he'd heard. His eyelids flickered at me, and I hurried on to tell him, earnestly, "My ambition is to be a circus clown. I will work hard, I will do what you tell me. I am prepared. I have a clown *character* (this *was* true) and a clown costume (this was *not*) and I even have a few ideas for scenes."

He looked at me quizzically. "Scenes?" he asked.

"Yeah, scenes," I said, "situations, conflicts!"

"I know about bits and gags and blow-offs, but I don't know about scenes." He grinned slyly at me. "Maybe you can teach me." Was he putting me on? Had I blown the whole thing?

"Look," I told him with what I hoped was a manly forthrightness, "I'll do a good job. I'll make you proud."

"All right," Johnny said, in a tone that suggested he didn't know what all the fuss was about. Before I left him, he outlined my duties: Spec, short for Grand Spectacular, really a parade that opens the show; two set clown routines in the first half; first-half closing procession; second-half opening; another set clown routine; finale and "walk-arounds when I tell you." He patted my shoulder, shook my hand and said "See you in Utica."

I was in a daze. I couldn't believe my luck, if luck it was. Instead it was Johnny who needed to worry about *his* luck. My first few weeks on the show I was a handful, his cross to bear. Often times we'd leave the ring, Johnny shaking his head and muttering "You must be a theater clown, because you sure ain't a circus clown." But Johnny was patient and I worked hard, and in a few weeks I had the rudiments of clowning under canvas down. I saw clowning as an art, took it as such, applied myself, and in time got to be pretty good. If this is boasting—well then, I boast.

This book then, for me, is an opportunity to remember, and to have a conversation with myself; and each of these selections, these stories, have their twin in my experience. And because the circus is not one thing, one ideal, as I once imagined, but rather a many faceted wonder, I have sought to represent as many different aspects of circus life as I might. And if I introduce each selection in a manner, that's what?—a little unorthodox, then at least I've been forthright about the things I saw and the people I knew, more than thirty years ago, when my circus animals were on show.

There's a kind of ideal circus moment I've often dreamed; or awake, thought I'd dreamed. No doubt each dream was different, one from the other, but the setting is always the same. It is just before the beginning of the last performance of the day, and all of us have gathered outside the back door of the big-top for *spec*. If we are lucky it is one of those early evenings in midsummer when the heat of the day throws up it's hands and surrenders, and the whole world cools in a riot of new washed smells. The daylight, now horizontal, has suddenly rendered the whole world in different colors, and you see things you never noticed before. There is just enough wind to make the the sidewalls flap. And there we all are, the whole show assembled. In just a few moments the band will start the overture that will bring on the Ringmaster who will begin *"Ladies and gentlemen! Boys and girls! Families of America!"* And all of us, the bull handlers and their charges, the jugglers, clowns, acrobats and aerialists, the liberty horses and the dancing donkeys, the mean-tempered camels and the docile llamas, the big cat on her perch, and the seals atop their rolling balls, all of us, will begin the show.

Stephen Vincent Brennan
New York, 2005

The
Greatest
Circus Stories
Ever Told

Fifty Years with a Menagerie

BY DAN RICE

Dan Rice was your all purpose showman; an actor, dancer, clown, an entrepreneur, an animal trainer and acrobat. In his own lifetime he was a huge celebrity and was said to be Abraham Lincoln's favorite comedian. Rice began his career as a clown in the early 1840s with Spalding's American Circus. By 1848, partnering with a brother-in-law of Spalding, he had formed a show of his own. This circus traveled by steamboat, playing up and down the Mississippi and Ohio rivers. In those days most traveling circuses were ad hoc affairs. Usually they played in one ring, under canvas, or at any rate behind it; frequently the "tent" was only a round corral of canvas siding, and t'hell with the rain. Many of these shows were built upon a single exotic act or animal. (A man in possession of a rhinoceros, say, would likely do well, if he could keep the beast docile, alive and in some fettle to troupe.) Or you might build your show around a single Star or some Personality, he might be ringmaster and clown and rope-dancer, and even present the featured animal act, all in one show. This was the case with Rice, and in the decade leading to the Civil War he became famous, and infamous as well. Remarkably, as his career advanced, his popularity declined. His style of clowning was described as "Shakespearean," by which I take to mean that his clown was a specific character, and that his act involved quite a lot of verbal give and take with the other performers and with the audience. It may be that all the alcohol clouded his judgment, he drank way too much. It may be that he felt certain things so deeply that it was impossible that his art not partake of or express these convictions. Or it may be that his style or mode of clowning

3

required that half the audience be made angry or upset. Whatever the case, politics, and moreover partisan-politics became more and more a feature of his show, and this was poison at the box office. Before long it was impossible to take his circus South, and too dangerous to play many cities and towns in the North, and the circus failed. A performer and entrepreneur the rest of his life, he retained a kind of celebrity, largely becoming a caricature of himself. Which after all, is what clowns do.

At one point he set down various tales of his eccentricities and adventures, a few of which I give you here.

○ ○ ○

SOME FAMOUS PIGS, DOGS, AND MONKEYS.

During my long life as a showman I made the acquaintance of many interesting animals, gained the friendship of some, and was much attached to others, but never became quite so devoted to any one as to my educated pig, Patsy, whose memory must still be cherished by many who were boys and girls when we performed together. As "Patsy, the Peerless Pig," I think of him after nearly forty years, and I reflect sorrowfully on the fate to which his one failing led him.

Patsy was not the first educated pig I possessed, for I began my public career with a porker so accomplished that it was scarcely flattery to call him "the Professor," as I did. With him I toured the Middle States until I had made money enough to start out with a travelling show on a scale so large that my duties separated me from him. He was wise, he was capable of great things, but he was grim and lacking the engaging qualities of Patsy, who was presented to me many years later—together with a lot of his little brothers and sisters, of a good Jersey Red family.

From the litter I chose Patsy as the most lively and promising, placed him apart, and put him through a thorough course of training to become my ring partner during the coming circus season. Then I was a jester, or more vulgarly, a clown.

I trained the dear, clever little creature with such sympathy, patience, firmness and kindness that he was very well educated in two brief months—save for a little dullness, excusable in a pig, in his Greek and Latin, and some slowness in figures. He would answer all my questions by grunts, two for "yes" and one for "no," the key-word for the former when desired being "now."

When I rejoined the circus a great shout arose, for at my heels, like a dog, was Patsy, wearing an embroidered scarlet blanket and a blue bow upon his tiny, curly tail. He made a great hit with the public, and we were a star attraction in every town, but it was at first exasperating when he would dash wildly out of the street parade to devour potatoes, and so forth, displayed in front of stores. However, I soon turned even this to account by following him on a trick donkey, and bringing him back into line with the light lash of a tiny whip.

In the ring he felt his responsibilities, and his conduct was above reproach. After the grand *entrée* of the mounted company, Patsy, in tinsel and spangles, would open the performance by squatting upon his haunches, closing his eyes as if in meditation, and burying his muzzle between his paws, which were placed upon a little stool. From this attitude he would not change until I gave the word.

Patsy had been carefully trained to applaud at times by shrill squeals that rang out above the cheers of the multitude. He would also join occasionally in the choruses of some of my popular songs. He regularly brought me a bouquet of imitation cabbage-leaves at a certain part of each performance.

Always when Mademoiselle Celeste, a clever rider, came on, she was greeted with enthusiastic applause from Patsy, for she invariably brought him a potato, apple, or other tidbit. He would tell the time of day, the name of his father and his brother, and who would be the next governor of the state or President of the Union when I indicated the number or name by pronouncing the magic key-word, "Now."

But he had one great failing—a lamentable weakness for raw onions. It used to amuse audiences greatly to hear me lecture him on his numerous indulgences in that forbidden vegetable, or tell him to turn away his head when addressing me because of his breath, or gravely say that he would bring me to an early grave if he continued on his downward career.

To such remarks the pig would respond by going to his little stool, putting his head down between his paws in shame, and keeping it there until I gave him the word of forgiveness.

But cunning little Patsy went from bad to worse. Besides frequent onion sprees, he fell to staying out late nights, after the show, and was often seen with evil porcine companions. At last, at Louisville, Kentucky, he absented himself entirely from an afternoon performance, and only came back to the circus at sunset in a most disreputable plight. I talked with him about this gross wrongdoing, and he seemed heartily penitent. But the next day Patsy could not be found. Vainly was the city searched for him. I was distressed; I felt that I had been too severe in my lecture.

Four days later Patsy was picked up dead in the Mississippi. We were in doubt whether he had deliberately ended his life, or met death by assault, and after forty years I am unable to feel sure on this matter.

So many people know how to educate dogs that I will not discourse on the subject, except to tell of a very remarkable instance of canine sagacity in Louisiana in the early fifties. With my circus that season were Harry Guest and his dog-show. He was a kindly fellow, whom everyone liked, and his dogs were cleverer than any others I have seen; so it can be imagined with what consternation I learned that Guest had been found dead one morning in his room at a hotel in Shreveport—murdered by knife or dagger.

Behind a net door in an adjoining room poor Harry's dogs, which must have seen the killing, bayed mournfully until the crime was discovered by those who came to ascertain what ailed them.

The assassin had left no trace of identity for the detectives. Not a person could be found who had seen any one with Guest after his return from the show on the fatal night. That robbery was the criminal's motive seemed plain, for the victim's gold watch and expensive jewelry had been taken.

Although I at once offered a large reward for the arrest of the criminal, the mystery continued for several weeks, until we arrived in New Orleans.

There it was learned that, on the day of the arrival of my show, Harry Guest's gold watch had been pledged at a pawnbroker's by a white man, but the detectives searched in vain for a man to fit the pawnbroker's description. At last, however, he was strangely discovered.

After Harry Guest's death the management of the dog-show had devolved upon his brother Joe. Now the "star" dog was Nellie, a lustrous-eyed, long-haired Newfoundland. One afternoon Joe Guest, accompanied by Nellie, was passing down the street on his way to the menagerie, when he met one of my "candy butchers," named Ward.

No sooner did Nellie see Ward than she sprang for his throat, and bore him to the ground. Had she not been muzzled, the New-foundland, usually so gentle; would doubtless have soon seriously, if not fatally, wounded the man, from whom Joe Guest dragged her by force. After an apology for the assault, Joe and the excited dog hurried on to the show.

When I was told of Nellie's fierce attack upon Ward, I at once suspected the truth. As the closest inquiry failed to disclose that the candy man had ever done anything in the least to annoy the dog, I concluded that she knew he had been concerned in the death of her master.

I sent at once for the chief of detectives, who, upon seeing Ward in the candy-wagon, declared that he answered the description of the man who had pawned poor Harry's watch. Accordingly he was arrested and taken to police headquarters, where he was confronted by the pawnbroker, who fully identified him.

When ordered to take off his clothes and don another suit furnished by the police, Ward completely broke down and began weeping freely. And no wonder, for upon examination there were found carefully sewn into the seams of his clothing some notes, two diamond pins, a diamond stud and a ring, all of which jewelry had been the property of the murdered man.

In course of time Patrick Ward was convicted on evidence which was circumstantial, but yet as unerring as God's law that punishment shall follow sin and crime. At last he made a full confession, with such signs of remorse and repentance as, I have always trusted, may have been of avail before the Almighty.

○ ○ ○

Although cats have been trained to perform in public, they are intractable, artful creatures compared with dogs and pigs. It is not that pussy lacks intelligence; indeed, I think the shrewdness and will-power of cats keep them so much out of "the profession."

The cat seems to know that if she "just won't," the effort to train her will be given up soon, and as she likes her ease and cares naught for the hollow reward of human applause, she usually "just doesn't." Hence I have little to tell of cat performers—although I once trained a "cat orchestra." I now mention the tribe only because I want to tell of a family of cats at Long Branch that is worthy to perform before enlightened audiences, although they are not in the profession.

These cats are one "Malty" and her two children; they belong to Mr. William Seaman of Branchport. Once or twice each sunny day they go to a float beside his boathouse. Seating themselves at the edge of the float, they patiently await the coming of a shoal of minnows, and when the tiny fish approach within easy reach, each cat darts a paw into the water and endeavors to throw some out upon the float, which they usually succeed in doing. Then they devour their catch. Alas! the three frequently fight over the largest of the catch, and Mr. Seaman is made to feel ashamed that Malty has not instructed her children in the graces of deportment!

"Malty's fishing school" daily attracts a throng of deeply interested idlers. For my part, I watch the pussies and the crowd, and wonder that some young showman, as enterprising as I believe I was forty years ago, does not try to give, under canvas, an exhibition of cats catching minnows.

That would be pleasanter than one of a cat catching monkeys which I once saw—but the cat was a tiger in this case. It was when my menagerie was in winter quarters.

The cages of animals were ranged on a platform around a large hall, in the center of which were tied two camels. In order to make needed repairs, it became necessary to remove a large Bengal tiger from one cage to another.

This task I entrusted to the chief keeper, a very competent man. He placed the empty cage upon the platform close against the cage which contained the tiger, and two men were stationed on top of each to raise and close the respective doors, which slid up and down.

When the two doors were raised the tiger, being prodded with rods to force it from one cage to the other, started forward and put a paw across the narrow space between the two cages; but instead of placing it within the doorway of the empty cage he put it against the first bar on the side of its door and pushed, thus slightly shoving the cage away. The chief keeper had been negligent in not having lashed the cages together.

The men at once tried to hasten the tiger through the door, but it angrily continued to push back the new cage, all the time gradually getting out of the one but not into the other one.

The man on the roof of the old cage tried to shove down the door and pin the tiger under it, but the door jammed and could not be moved, so the beast continued to force its way to liberty.

The man on the roof of the empty cage continued to hold its door open, hoping the tiger would enter, when he would quickly close it and make it fast; but the tiger continued to push until there was room for it to spring out, which it did, just as I arrived in the hall. I instantly ordered the camels to be taken outside the building, for I knew that the tiger would pounce upon them in preference to a human being.

"Stripes" was then the master of the menagerie for a time, and he started to explore the hall for something good to eat. As nobody wished to become his meat, all got out of his way while, with waving tail and glaring eye, he moved on his tour of discovery.

At a monkey cage he paused and glared blood-thirstily at its inmates, which were greatly frightened, and beat a hurried retreat to the perches arranged across the farther side of the cage.

The tiger pounced forward, thrust one long paw hastily into the cage, and grasped a small monkey whose flight had been too slow. If ever I heard a cry of terror it was that given by the little captured creature, which was then dragged between the bars as a shapeless mass and at once ravenously devoured.

After licking its chops with great gusto the tiger repeatedly rushed from side to side and end to end of the cage in a vain attempt to capture another monkey, for monkey flesh is greatly liked by carnivorous animals. During this very exciting time I decided upon a way to capture the tiger.

I clambered down from the top of an animal cage upon which I, with my employees, had sought refuge. While the great Bengal man-eater's whole attention was on the monkeys at the farther end of the building, I rushed out of the hall. In the corridor I found the closed meat-cart, and the menagerie butcher busily preparing food for the animals.

While I informed him of the escape of the tiger I threw a huge piece of meat into the cart, and closed the lid down securely upon it. Hastily to wash the top of the cart and remove the scent of blood from it was but the work of a minute. Then pushing the cart forward a few feet, I quietly swung the door ajar, and made a quick but anxious survey of the hall preparatory to my entrance.

Fortunately the tiger was still at the monkey cage. Noiselessly I rolled the rubber-tyred meat-cart into the hall without distracting the tiger's attention from the monkeys. At the empty cage I halted, opened the lid of the cart, and with a quick move, threw the large and bloody piece of meat into the narrow, barred compartment of the empty cage. Then I scrambled for my life upon its top.

An instant later the tiger, scenting the bloody beef, came bounding down the hall, and with an awful cry rushed into the cage and began to devour the meat. To close and fasten the door required but an instant, and my Bengal tiger was again a captive.

A year later, in a menagerie in Great Britain, "Big" Cooper, a famous animal-tamer, tried to capture an escaped lion in the same manner, but he was not quick enough in reaching a place of security, and the lion overtook and killed him.

Tigers, as I have said, love monkey flesh, but tigers have affectionate streaks in their nature; hence one of the most incongruous affairs I ever saw—the adoption of a Brazilian monkey by a Bengal tigress.

One day while touring the Middle States my attention was attracted by the loud and angry talk of Seth Loper, the manager of my menagerie. Going to him I found that some employee had taken one of a litter of very valuable young monkeys from its mother, and placed it in a cage alone with Minnie, our largest and most valuable tigress.

No wonder Loper was angry, for we all felt certain that the tigress would soon devour the little monkey, unless we should somehow manage to lure it from the cage. Accordingly we resorted to every wile to entice the monkey out, but all to no avail. We dared not resort to force lest the tigress should be roused to wrath and immediate destruction.

Sorely vexed I turned away and shouted:

"Fifty dollars' reward for information who put the Brazilian in that cage!"

"Plank down the money, Colonel Rice, for I know who did it." The speaker was a tall, muscular canvasman, very witty and popular.

I counted out five ten-dollar bills, which I held in my hand.

"Go on," said I.

"I put the monk in the cage," the canvasman blandly said. "I was hard up for money, and knew that you would pay to know who did it. That's all there is to it."

"I'll keep my word, anyhow," said I, in great surprise, as I thrust the money into his hands. "But, Murphy, if I were big enough, I would give you the worst thrashing of your life."

He coolly took one bill from the roll of money, thrust it into his pocket, and returned the rest to me, saying:

"Ten dollars was all I needed."

I turned away with the remark that I should offer no more rewards of that sort.

At the close of the afternoon performance I visited the menagerie with Loper, and was delighted to find the monkey soundly sleeping and snuggled close to the breast of the tigress.

"What do you think of it, Loper?" I asked in amazement.

"Simply and purely a case of adoption, strange as it is," said Loper. "Now the menagerie will have an attraction such as never before was exhibited."

So it proved. The little Brazilian was duly christened "Miss Murphy," and the strangely assorted pair became a great attraction of my show.

Little Miss Murphy and her foster-mother became deeply attached. For hours at a time the monkey would sit on the back of the tigress; when she left that seat occasionally to dash from end to end of the cage, or to climb to the top of the bars, she evidently gave no little anxiety to her foster-parent. And one day the tigress was so horrified, as well as scandalized, when Miss Murphy dropped from the top of the cage and hung by her tail to a newly improvised perch, that she arose, and with her eyes steadfastly besought her ward to desist from her alarming conduct.

Little Miss Murphy, as she grew older, spent much time in combing her adopted mother's fur with a comb provided for that purpose, and brushing it until it fairly shone, which made the tigress appear the best-groomed animal in the menagerie.

As the monkey grew older it gave birth to a litter of little ones, which were tenderly welcomed and faithfully guarded by the tigress. As they grew large and lively there was great fun in the tigress's cage, where they romped merrily all day long; but the happy family had to be broken when "Minnie" had children of her own. Then all the monkeys were taken from her cage.

○ ○ ○

MONKEY MUSIC—AN ELEPHANT STAMPEDE— FRANCONELLI AND THE LION.

It may surprise many persons to learn that monkeys, despite their cleverness, are not enduringly susceptible to the influences of "higher education," for infinite is their innate depravity. I found them ready enough to learn, but persistent in refusal to display their knowledge when required to do so by their patient teacher. This peculiar side of monkey nature was forcibly impressed on me when I tried to form an orchestra, or string band, among the simians of my menagerie.

We were in winter quarters, and as it was my custom to devote my spare time during the cold term to taming and training wild animals for the next season, I had a family of monkeys confined in an apartment adjoining my reading- smoking- and music-room.

One morning upon nearing the cottage my ears were greeted by the sound of my 'cello. I paused, wondering what visitor had provoked my rich-toned instrument to such unseemly discord. Then I approached closely, and through a window saw a laughable scene.

Seated upon a chair, with a smoking-cap on his head, spectacles on his nose, and meerschaum pipe in his mouth, was Joe, the largest monkey of the menagerie, sawing away at the 'cello with bow in hand. Several of the smaller monkeys were in postures of surprise and delight at Joe's performance. I had omitted to lock the door of the monkey-room, and that accounted for the intrusion on my sanctum.

Highly entertained, I stood for a time a silent spectator, until seen by a little monkey, who notified its fellows of my presence with a sharp cry. In a twinkling the animals dashed from the room—Joe, minus cap, spectacles and pipe, bringing up the rear and carefully closing the door behind him. Upon entering the house I found all the monkeys safely ensconced in their proper room, and looking as innocent as lambs, while the old ringleader was snoring, and apparently sound asleep. From this occurrence the idea of trying to form an orchestra of monkeys came into my mind, for I well knew that such a troupe, even if it produced anything but melody, would be a strange attraction.

I began by securing small violins for four of my most promising young monkeys, reserving for old Joe, whom I rechristened Wagner, the exclusive right to play upon the 'cello. As I could play upon a violin perhaps well enough to teach a monkey to make a noise on one, I began by taking all the members of the proposed orchestra into a room by themselves, and enabling them to see how I held the instrument when playing.

Vigorously I began, after a time spent in tuning, to play a bar or two of "When the corn is waving, Annie dear," after which I passed a tiny violin and bow to a monkey whom I called Franz Liszt. He snatched the instrument from my hand, placed it under his chin, as his instructor had done, and extracted from it a torturing wail or two. Then, to my astonishment, he grasped the screws at the head of the violin and began to tighten the strings one by one, as his instructor had done, but with the result that two of them were snapped.

He treated a second violin in like manner before eliciting from it a series of most untuneful notes, and he closed his performance by evoking from the strings a fiendish shriek. At this the other monkeys, startled, fled to the backs of chairs and other places of presumed safety, except Joe, who continued to saw away vindictively upon the 'cello.

Somewhat disconcerted, I speedily restored order and gave a violin and bow to Beethoven, who promptly began to tune up his instrument in the same way and with a similar result. Each of the other monkeys in turn was given an opportunity to play a violin, and each imitated his predecessor by first tuning it up and then breaking strings.

For four weeks I patiently endeavored to teach the animals how to "fiddle." It was of no use; and at our last rehearsal old Joe, becoming angry, broke all the small violins and tried to burn up the fragments during my brief absence from the room.

At one time in the early fifties rival showmen spread the libelous report that the monkeys with Dan Rice's circus were killing themselves rather than have to witness the performances. Indeed, their deaths were very strange.

Early one morning a messenger informed me that one of my most promising young male monkeys had been found dead at the end of the night's journey. The little Brazilian, which was of the variety known as tail-hangers, had apparently hanged itself by passing its long tail over its perch, and then, after fastening the end of the tail tightly about its neck, had thrown itself deliberately off to its death.

This tragedy, a wholly new one in the world of monkeys, created a decided sensation among my showmen. Sam McGee, then the oldest animal-dealer in America, said it was the first monkey suicide of which he had heard. Joe O'Connor, a great joker, whom the boys of my staff had dubbed "Coroner," held an "inquest," and decided that the suicide was due to disgust with the Darwinian theory that monkeys are the ancestors of men.

After the dead monkey had been buried little more was thought of the tragedy until, four days later, another young monkey was found hanging dead by his tail from the same perch from which the first had hanged himself!

Three more days, and then another young monkey was found similarly hanging dead. This third death, which "Coroner" O'Connor ascribed to "sorrow for Dan Rice's heavy business losses," reduced my stock of monkeys to nine. Resolved to prevent its further depletion, I ordered a man to stay continually in the cage at night, trusting the mischievous monkeys to keep him awake.

This they did for several nights, teasing and tormenting him in every conceivable and many inconceivable ways whenever his drooping eyelids indicated a time ripe for mischief. But at the end of a week's time they had become accustomed to his nightly presence, and ceased to annoy him, so he slept.

Upon awaking after his nap in the cage, he was horrified to see another youthful monkey hanging from the same perch where his three former companions had been found dead.

This man suggested a new and most plausible theory of the tragedies. The victims had been all males. From this he inferred that each had been cruelly murdered by an older, stronger and jealous male. Acting at once on the suggestion of the watchman, I had Azariah, the grey old grandfather of the monkey family, and Zachariah, his son, the father of the victims, removed, greatly against their wish, to a cage by themselves. There were no more deaths by suicide or murder among the monkeys of that menagerie.

I have always believed that Azariah, the grandfather, was the criminal, and that while the young monkeys slept he would spring upon them and choke them to death. Then to divert suspicion he would craftily hang the victim to the perch, where it was subsequently found. Of course this line of reasoning demolished the theory of suicide, and confirmed my belief that monkeys are clever, and some of them quite fiendish.

Turning now from small to great, let me tell you that a thing greatly dreaded by showmen is a stampede of the elephants, and one of the most notable of such stampedes occurred while I was touring in the Eastern States.

One day word reached me that Tim, our performing elephant, and Sadie, his mate, had become terrified for some unknown reason, and had broken loose, upsetting the cages of lions and other fierce beasts before running away.

I hurried to the menagerie, and found everything in the wildest confusion. Lions were roaring, camels crying piteously, and hyenas howling with fear, raising such a bedlam as I had never before known.

The keepers soon succeeded in quieting the lions and tigers, and order ruled when I rode away at the head of a mounted posse to capture the fugitive elephants. In his flight Tim had taken Jock, the trick monkey, with him on his back, and I greatly feared that the little Brazilian would be injured or lost. The elephants had nearly an hour's start of us, but as we rode rapidly down the turnpike we hoped to overtake them soon.

At one little house we were tearfully informed that "two big black brutes" had stopped there to get drinks of water, the elephants obligingly taking turns in pumping for each other. Farther down the road we came to a creek, where the fugitives had stopped to bathe. Near the village one of the elephants had crushed a bulldog that had rushed out to bark at the strange visitors.

Putting our horses to the gallop, we dashed into the village and learned that the elephants had halted and rifled a fruit-stand; frightened a woman into convulsions by stopping and thrusting their trunks into an open window; and then, leisurely passing on, had caused three teams of horses to run away. Far down the street they had overthrown a garden fence in order to steal pears and pluck flowers.

Half an hour further on the fugitives had turned aside to raid an orchard of apples and wreck a pigsty. After assuring the owners that I would pay all damages we hurried onward, but not before learning that Jock, the monkey, or as the farmer said, "a queer little man in red clothes," was riding on Tim's back when the elephants were last seen.

As we approached a second village we intercepted a team of runaway horses hitched to a farm wagon. Soon after this we saw where the elephants had paused to tear down a fence, enter a field, and steal a lot of turnips. At every dwelling the frightened inmates told us of the fearsome passage of the great animals, which ran with uplifted trunks.

Now they were not more than ten minutes ahead of us, so on we hastened, in much perplexity as to a method of effecting their capture. The chief keeper's plan was to head them off, if possible, and endeavor to drive them back over the seven miles of road. But the elephant is a very fast traveller, and I doubted our ability to carry out the suggestion.

Soon we saw a throng of people in a side street, and galloped thither. There, in the middle of the thoroughfare, at some distance beyond the crowd, was Tim, dancing merrily, as he was used to dance in the ring, before a small house, with the monkey still perched on his back, and with Sadie looking admiringly on. The music of a fiddle within doors could be plainly heard, and this had caused Tim to pause and dance.

My keepers dismounted and quietly captured both elephants before the fiddler was aware that he had so extraordinary an audience. I rewarded his playing, sent my men back with the elephants, and paused frequently on the way home to pay damages.

As owner of menageries I made it my business to qualify for almost any vacancy that might occur among my performers, and eventually I essayed the rôle of lion-tamer under the tutelage of the celebrated Franconelli. Strange to say, he, though fearless among wild beasts, was the most arrant coward before threatening men.

I first entered a lion's cage with him at Vincennes, Indiana, in the days "befo' de wah." In the den was Richard III, the largest and fiercest African lion ever taken to America. This was at an afternoon performance, and not a very perilous venture, for the brute was afraid of its trainer and noticed my presence only by a long growl.

Embodied by the plaudits of the audience, I resolved to enter the cage alone at the evening performance, and Franconelli assented to my proposition. When, amid an outburst of music, I swung open the grated door and entered, the fierce Numidian seemed to pay me not the slightest attention; but fortunately for me, a blazing furnace containing red-hot iron rods had been placed under the cage!

The lion seemed to notice my presence even less than at the afternoon performance, and growled only when I patted its huge head. But when I began backing toward the exit, the great brute almost imperceptibly began to raise its body from the floor, and the next moment hurled itself full upon me.

Down I went, and must have been killed, had not my men with the red-hot irons forced the savage beast to the farther end of the cage, while I emerged with a tattered tinsel jacket, two severely lacerated shoulders, and shaken nerves. Though the occurrence was valuable to me in an advertising way, I never again ventured into a lion's den.

The next day Franconelli entered the cage of Richard III as if nothing unusual had occurred. He was a remarkable man, who habitually entered the dens of strange lions without a moment of preparatory acquaintance; but he was attacked by a caged beast at last.

Our canvas was then stretched in the city of Havana, prior to our departure for the United States. Everybody was well, money had been made, and the menagerie seemed likely to return home in good condition. But a day or two before our departure Richard III appeared to be in an angry mood. This worried me so much that I urged Franconelli to "dope"—that is, drug—the fierce beast before each performance. He only laughed and said he feared no lion in captivity.

On the last morning in Havana the Numidian was so "ugly" that I besought Franconelli not to enter the creature's den that day; but he insisted on carrying out his contract. Then I endeavored to "dope" the lion, but he refused to eat the drugged meat.

It was with dread of impending evil that I saw the fearless Frenchman appear in the ring, and bow with courtly grace to the large afternoon audience. Bravely he swung open the door and entered the cage, to be greeted with an awful roar by Richard III, who at once arose and lashed his sides with his tail.

I instantly moved to the edge of the platform, beneath which I had concealed a rifle.

Franconelli, calm as a summer's morn, advanced. The great lion wrathfully backed to the farther end of the cage, and my employees prepared to control him with red-hot irons.

The intrepid trainer kept his eyes steadily upon Richard III, and omitted his usual graceful salute to the audience preparatory to leaving the cage. Then he stealthily began his retreat backward. He had made but two steps when the huge, tawny brute sprang upon him, knocked him to the floor and buried its cruel fangs in his throat. While the attendants pressed the red-hot irons ineffectually to the lion's head and sides, I raised my rifle to my shoulder, took hasty aim at the heart of Richard III, and fired.

The great brute rolled over on the floor. When we opened the door of the cage Richard III was dead, but alas! so was poor Franconelli!

The audience was wild with excitement, and shouted vociferously. Had they been Americans an appalling panic would doubtless have ensued; but to the Spanish-Cuban crowd the tragedy was simply a magnificent performance. Sadly we buried the brave Franconelli in the suburbs of Havana, and with sore hearts left the Pearl of the Antilles.

Those Press Agents!

BY C. R. COOPER

No bird ever flew on one wing. You can have the greatest show on earth, or something near to it. You may feature the most exotic animals, or the most death-defying acts of bravery and skill. Your big cats may be the fiercest in captivity, your clowns the drollest, or your spectacles the most rousing; but if the people don't come, none of this matters, your bird don't fly. Getting the people to come is the job of the press agents, or as we call them today: publicists. They plan your press campaign and they orchestrate your media buys. They're always on the lookout for angles, even in the circular space of our now global consciousness. The best of them are master manipulators and spinners. Their aim is to get a buzz going and often they can make the difference between a successful stand and disaster for your show.

I heard a story from an old man who'd worked with elephants, on one circus or another, pretty much his whole life. As a kid he'd been on a show that had come upon hard times. This was smack in the middle of the Depression, and following a series of busted dates, this circus found itself stranded somewhere right in the middle of America's heartland. There was no money, not to pay the acts, or for feed for the animals, or even to buy gasoline. The banks weren't interested. This show was stuck. Their one hope was to make enough money playing right where they were, to get themselves down the road to some population center, where there was some chance of repairing their luck. But how were they to get the people to come? Their "target" audience was dispersed over several farm counties and they couldn't afford newspaper adverts or radio. On top of everything else, one of the stars of the show, and old elephant by the name of Judy, had "gone crazy" and would have to be put down. Enter the Press Agent. Why not, he suggested, invite the customers to participate in putting Judy down. The poor old girl had to be killed anyway. Why not announce an elephant shoot? Let anyone with their own gun and ammo join in. This was sure to get people talking. Who in America ever gets the chance to plug an elephant? It worked—for days it was all people talked about, and the bleachers were full every show.

It must have been an awful thing to see. Old Judy staked out in the open field, picked out of the darkness by the headlights of a hundred farm pickups and family sedans. The muster of fathers and their sons, and their daughters too, all awaiting permission to fire. A few words of eulogy, or perhaps consecration spoken by the Ringmaster, then the signal, and everybody lets go. Did she raise her trunk and cry to heaven as all that shot thwapped into her? I dunno, I don't know. But it saved the circus, or so that old man told me. And I believed him.

O O O

Once upon a time, there was an elephant which objected to going into a cage. Because of that fact, a million dollars or so was made, and he ceased to be "just an elephant." He formed a forerunner of national advertising, and a synonym for everything that is big. He lives today, nearly thirty years after his death, in Jumbo peanuts, Jumbo soap, Jumbo shoes, Jumbo bananas, Jumbo this, that and the other thing. All because a press agent "slipped it over."

To you who are not familiar with the inside workings of a newspaper, let it be known that there is but one person in the entire newspaper world who is to be feared. Public officials must either walk the straight and narrow path, or be shown up for their misdeeds. The rich and powerful "influence" may exert his czarism over a newspaper office for a certain length of time, but sooner or later, the newspaper exposes him, and sets him right—or wrong—in the eyes of the people. For everything there is a remedy, except for the press agent, the man who is employed by amusement enterprises, hotels, railroads, and other forms of trade which live through the constant interest of the public, to arouse that interest by more closely personal means than the ordinary methods of the advertising columns. The press agent has but one duty, one desire, one god,—to outwit the newspaper. What's more, he does it.

Incidentally, a press agent isn't what his fiction description would have him. He neither wears a checked suit and red vest, nor talks in a loud voice. Too often he is a college bred man, with a brain which measures up to his salary. He is the high-finance artist of newspaper-dom, and his methods are as diversified as the colors of the rainbow. All too often he does not appear; when he is unseen and unnoticed, then he is doing his hardest work. He is the general in command of the forces of an endless contest, and his army of ideas changes with the moods of the public. The last time you ate a Jumbo peanut, you paid homage to a press agent who played his trick more than a quarter of a century ago!

All of which does not mean that the press agent is a menace. Often he is a power for good. But a newspaper likes to believe that it is printing facts, not the output of an imagination. It likes to believe that its news is legitimate and that it is not some carefully concocted affair designed to make persons hurry to a certain playhouse or a certain circus. Therefore when an actress is robbed of her jewels, the city editor cynically throws the story, which has come through the regular channels of a report to the police, into the wastebasket. When a wildly dishevelled young lady hurries to headquarters to tell of her suffering in the secret harem of some modern Bluebeard, a reporter is assigned rather hastily to discover whether a motion picture of that sort is to be exhibited soon. When a society burglar begins to operate in town, leaving peculiar notes behind him, there is the question as to whether it is the forerunner of a publicity plan for a Raffles drama. Behind all this sort of thing, all too often, is to be found some keen-witted young man who never even goes near a newspaper, whose name often is not known, who chuckles at his success, and whom the city editor cusses long and enthusiastically when the game works. It is a joyful battle which never ends, which is carried on in good nature—for the simple reason that there's no other way to combat it—and in which the honors are even. Sometimes it is the newspaper which wins, with the result that months of work are lost. Sometimes it is the press agent who is victorious,—with the result that history is made. In the light of which you may remember the name of "Death Valley Scotty," who was supposed to own a mysterious mine in the heat-ridden regions of Death Valley. Scotty wanted to get rid of some of his surplus wealth. He made a record-breaking trip across the country on a special train, threw money from the rear platform, turned Broadway upside down, making his name—and the name of the railroad which carried him across country—known to every person in the United States. But Scotty couldn't do it again.

All for the reason that hundreds of visages would become sour. Hundreds of directing minds of newspapers would remember the trip which Scotty made once before and the delight of the publicity department of a certain railroad. Hundreds of lips would grunt: "Press-agent stuff!" and throw the dispatch in the wastebasket.

But to return to the elephant which didn't care to get into a cage, for it was then that the press agent really started. Before that time he had been a person who would glide into a newspaper office, leave his "press stuff?", buy the editor a drink and give him a few complimentary tickets to the circus or the play, whichever it happened to be. Sometimes too, just for the publicity it would cause, he would engage in a duel with an opposing press agent, or perpetrate some minor exploit which would get the name of his show into the paper. But all thought of national and even international publicity was beyond him. Then an elephant lay down and refused to budge; and the whole world sat up as a result of it!

His name was Jumbo, which, at that time, meant nothing. A tremendous pachyderm of the African species, he had been exhibited for years at the London Zoological Gardens. Naturally, being an elephant, Jumbo was a favorite with the children, who gathered about him on every exhibition day, to feed him peanuts and to watch his lumbering, ungainly antics. That was the end of their interest. Then along came P. T. Barnum.

No circus in America, at that time, ever had possessed a menagerie that could be featured. In fact, until this time—it was at the beginning of the 80s—the freak had been the main advertising attraction. Three-legged calves, double-headed ladies, the "Horse with his Tail where his Head Should Be," and other exhibits of this nature had been looked upon as the very last word in circus exhibits. Even the "Cardiff Giant"—which was the invention of George Hull, who lived at Binghamton, New York, and who carved the "prehistoric man" from a solid block of stone, dotted him with pores, buried him for two years, and then "discovered" him while making an excavation—had become common enough for various enterprising side-show attraction purveyors to advertise "Cardiff Giants, guaranteed against cracking, peeling or blistering," at a very reasonable price. The circus business, in fact, needed a rejuvenation, and Barnum sent emissaries to Europe with instructions to buy menagerie features, such as "twenty camels, thirty ostriches, and other big stuff." Naturally, one of the agents saw Jumbo and cabled Barnum regarding him. The reply was an order to buy.

In Jumbo there was nothing unusual—to the circus man—except that he was to be advertised as the biggest elephant in the world. To carry this thought, his name on the advertising bills had been changed to "Mastodon," and the posters already printed. The directors of the Zoölogical Society had set the price and agreed to the sale. The brief announcement had been made in the London newspapers that Jumbo, a favorite with the children at the Zoölogical Gardens, had been sold to P. T. Barnum, the widely known American circus man. There was nothing more to the transaction. Jumbo was going to America, and while a great many children felt sorry, that was the end of it. Then the unexpected happened!

Jumbo had been accustomed to a life of ease and tranquillity. His quarters had been—to an elephantine mind, at least—spacious and exceedingly comfortable. Therefore, when strange men attempted to prod him into the big, barred cage in which he was to be confined on the journey to America, Jumbo did exactly what any petted, pampered elephant would do under the circumstances. He refused to enter. More, when they sought to force him, he flopped to the floor and with pachydermic grunts announced that if he was going into that cage, he'd have to be carried. Which was no small job, considering the fact that Jumbo measured his weight by the ton. Then came the inspiration.

That afternoon, school children found themselves listening to a tearful tale by a mournful appearing gentleman, who told them in sympathetic fashion how Jumbo, the pet elephant, had refused to leave the little children whom he loved so well. Wasn't it cruel that a circus man should take away a loving, kind-hearted pet like Jumbo? Poor old Jumbo, who loved the children so that he could not bring himself to leave them! Nice old Jumbo, who even now was trumpeting and bellowing and resisting all efforts to place him in the cage that would remove him forever from his little playmates! It was just about this time that the children began to realize how much they loved Jumbo,—that Jumbo, in fact, had been a great, wonderful thing in their lives. A few of them cried for pity. It was the beginning of the end.

Would the dear little children care to circulate petitions asking for the retention of their dear old playmate? Of course, it was none of the affable stranger's business; he really didn't care, one way or the other, what happened to Jumbo. But he really did hate to see a money-grabbing circus man break up such a wonderful friendship as had existed between dear old Jumbo and all the childhood of London. Naturally, the fact that the London Zoölogical Society had been glad to part with the beast for the simple reason that its African blood made it intractable, often surly, and sometimes dangerous, was not mentioned. Nor the very apparent truth that Jumbo's refusal to enter that cage easily could be traced to a streak of ugly temper. The very soft-hearted men who went about London, interesting children, teachers—and of course, parents—in the sad fate of Jumbo, and the blank lives of London's childhood once the pachyderm had been kidnapped from their midst by a cold-hearted, calloused circus man who didn't and couldn't understand the tenderness of an elephant's heart, said nothing to indicate that they were connected in any manner with the brutal circus man whom they berated. Child after child took the petitions and began to circulate them. Boys and girls who never had seen even a picture of Jumbo wept over the elephant's fate,—and circulated more petitions. Teachers began to talk about the horrible affair and wonder where they were to take their wards on holidays when Jumbo, dear old Jumbo, was torn from them forever. Parents, excited by the red eyes and woeful mien of their offspring, began writing letters to the papers, and every day the circus men tried and tried and tried to get dear old Jumbo into the cage. But Jumbo wouldn't go; he loved the little children with such fervor that he simply refused to leave the old home fireside. Strangely enough, the circus men used very crude and uncouth methods. They pushed Jumbo and struck him and mistreated him and cursed him. Hard-hearted circus men!

By this time, the newspapers had placed Jumbo in the position of honor upon the first page. They had been forced to it. Jumbo had become news, real news. The Humane Society had begun to fight the cruel circus men, impelled by influences which had back of them those same hard-hearted beasts who were trying to tear Jumbo from his happy home. Suits were started, in the effort to gain injunctions against the removal of the pachyderm. Guiding spirits appeared, who suggested that there should be parades of children in protestation against the removal of the beast. They were held. The whole city of London now was in a ferment over Jumbo. More, what interested London at that time, interested the whole world, with the result that the cables soon were carrying their burden of the troubles of "the biggest elephant on earth."

Back in America printing orders hastily were rescinded and remodeled. The name of "Mastodon" now meant nothing. The word "Jumbo" had become a household affair; day after day the cables carried the news of London's uproar. Day after day passed without the circus men succeeding in getting Jumbo into his cage.

The directors of the Zoölogical Garden were attacked and threatened with removal from office. The sadness of Jumbo's departure even found its way into Parliament, where a speech was made, full of tears and pleading, in the hope that something might be done to prevent the removal of the most beloved thing of childhood, the dear old elephant Jumbo. Even Queen Victoria was appealed to, in the hope that she might be able to devise some way to save the mammoth elephant. More, the Queen even took the time to give her views on the subject, to sympathize both with the children and with the elephant,—but Jumbo was sold. Into slavery he must go.

But this was not the end. Jumbo had a wife—Alice. Soon the cables were buzzing with sympathetic stories regarding her. Every sob sister that London possessed was at work on the Jumbo story now;

every organization which was interested in the slightest manner in dumb animals was protesting, petitioning, even threatening. Nor could the repeated assertion of the Zoölogical directors to the effect that they had sold Jumbo because he was intractable, unmanageable and possibly dangerous make the slightest patter in the sea of disapproval. Day after day,—then the circus men took inventory of their accomplishments.

To date, figured at space rates, the Jumbo excitement had brought them exactly a half million dollars in advertising. The peak had been reached. The decision was made to transport Jumbo. And strangest of the strange! Once that decision came, Jumbo entered his cage! The circus men simply changed his food from its accustomed place to the shipping den, and in went Jumbo. But even then London didn't awaken.

They followed him to the docks, thousands of children, and as many women and men. Banners were carried protesting, even to the minute of the ship's sailing. The cables that day buzzed the news that Jumbo had been taken away just in time to evade the mob spirit and to escape a concerted attack of thousands which would have resulted in bloodshed—and the retention of Jumbo in London, thus leading to international complications and a possibility of diplomatic correspondence— over an elephant! When Jumbo landed in America, the police reserves were needed to keep clear the docks. Such is the value of publicity.

Is it any wonder therefore, that even today Jumbo is a trade name in a hundred diversified branches? Jumbo did a good many things for national advertising. More, he gave one of the first great lessons in a good name properly exploited. Yet Jumbo was the result of a press-agent inspiration! More, the strangest part of it all is the fact that years later, Jumbo lived up to the high-mindedness and spirit of good-heartedness with which he had been credited. He died a hero!

It was at a grade crossing, and the circus was "loading out." Jumbo, slightly in the lead of a baby elephant, had crossed a railroad track, then turned just in time to see that the life of the calf was endangered by the swift approach of a switch engine. The great beast turned; with head lowered, he butted the baby out of the way of the engine and into a zone of safety, only to be struck himself and killed,—while saving a life! But this really wonderful thing brought but little publicity. Jumbo was dead; the press agents were busy on more live and more useful things.

Thus goes the story of the press agent; look behind some of the best remembered things of America, and you will find him pulling the strings. For instance, even today it is a common expression to say that a person has a white elephant on his hands. It came from a press agent. More, the really queer thing about it was the fact that the man who had the white elephant really and truly on his hands possessed a genuine white pachyderm, while the one who caused the trouble had only—

Perhaps the whole story can be repeated. It is known only to showmen, and it is the story of a fight between a genuine white elephant and one which—well, which wasn't. Again Barnum was one of the participants, while on the other end of the contest was Adam Forepaugh, a rival circus owner. Both were to exhibit in Philadelphia at the same time, and for that exhibition, Barnum had saved his greatest trump. He had actually procured the thing which, at that time, was the dream of every circus owner,—a sacred white elephant from India. Almost simultaneously there came a dispatch from Algiers saying that the Barnum elephant was a leprous imitation, and that the real white elephant of sacred descent was being shipped, not to Barnum, but to Adam Forepaugh. It was the beginning of a white elephant war.

Again did elephants become news. The city was plastered with posters, while billposters engaged in fist fights and the police patrols were kept busy. The curiosity of the public had become aroused. The papers did the only possible thing,—printed the news. The rival exhibitions came, with the result that both shows did an overwhelming business. The Barnum circus displayed an elephant with a cream-colored blaze down its trunk and light spotted legs, as real a white elephant as ever a white elephant could be. But at the other show was "The Light of Asia," a great beast covered by a large velvet-spangled cloth, with a head, trunk and legs of purest white. Moreover, the audience was invited to step up and touch it! Which the audience did.

In the performance, "The Light of Asia" was brought in, stripped of its velvet trappings and placed on a large stage, where a "professor" lectured upon its life, history and habits, meanwhile dodging dexterously that the affectionate beast might not rub against him.

The head and trunk and legs of the beast had been carefully enameled, but that was as far as the risk could be taken. More enameling might have clogged the pores of the skin and killed the beast; hence the rest of the body had been kalsomined only. But to the public, this was the real white elephant, while the other, possessed by Barnum, was only a poor imitation. The result was that when interest in white elephants waned, Adam Forepaugh washed the paint from his pachyderm and again became the owner of an ordinary elephant. Barnum wasn't as lucky. Nature had given his beast its coloring, with the result that he had "a white elephant on his hands," about which the public cared nothing, because it was considered only a poor imitation!

Nor is this the only time when the real has been forgotten and the bogus become the real. Nor the only instance when an elephant has figured in "press stuff." For in a certain portion of the Middle West, the name of Rajah is a household affair, while in the newspaper offices of that section of the country the same name recalls some pleasure and a good measure of chagrin. Rajah formed the basis of many a column of free publicity, which explains much, especially why the press agent exists, why the newspaper editor cocks his head and narrows his eyes at the slightest hint of "press stuff?", and why the actress who loses her jewels doesn't get her name in the paper. It is what might be called "insidious promotion."

When a newspaper prints an advertisement stating certain things, and displayed in advertising type and in an advertising manner, the person who reads it knows it to be an advertisement and takes the statement as that of an interested person who desires to sell his wares. Naturally, he understands that this person wants to sell what he offers and that he is telling its good points to the exclusion of all else. It is an equitable affair in which the seller talks to the buyer through the medium of print.

But when a press-agent story is printed, the basis is different. Now, it is not the seller who is striving to arouse interest; it is the newspaper itself which is speaking as a third party. The seller himself has ceased to exist. An outside person is doing the talking, and in a confidential manner which causes more interest than all the advertising in the world. More, that newspaper is responsible, and the person who reaps the benefit isn't. Hence the press agent, whose job is to get into the newspapers what the newspapers do not desire to print. All of which rounds out the prelude to Rajah.

There wasn't anything marvelous about him. He was only an elephant which belonged to the Lemon Brothers Circus, which, at that time, maintained its winter quarters in Argentine, Kansas, about seven miles from Kansas City, Missouri, and its several large newspapers. One day the press agent of the circus looked long and seriously at Rajah. However, once his idea had come into being, he didn't seek the newspapers. In fact, he kept as far away as possible. Instead, he went to the menagerie superintendent and with him held a long and confidential conversation. That night, a riot call rang in from Argentine. Rajah had escaped!

What really had happened was the mere fact that the menagerie superintendent had loosened Rajah's chain and kicked him out the door of the menagerie house, leaving him to wander at will. Which Rajah did. The unexpected always causes excitement, with the result that when Rajah poked an inquisitive trunk into the front door of a grocery store that was keeping late hours, it formed the beginning of a young panic.

The word spread. Persons sought the tops of their porches, barricaded their doors and telephoned for the police. Those who happened to be on the sidewalk at the time the big pachyderm wobbled up the middle of the street, took to trees and telephone poles. The police arrived, looked at Rajah, held a consultation, decided that an elephant was too large to be arrested, and put in a hurry call for the fire department. The fire department arrived, looked for a fire, couldn't find any, and turned the hose on Rajah. Which Rajah didn't relish. So he leaned against a barn or two, smashed them, walked through a few fences, and the panic was on again with renewed excitement.

Rajah had become a "story" now. He had interested the multitude and stampeded his way into print. A riot call is news. The next day, Rajah and the fact that he belonged to the Lemon Brothers Circus was on the front page of every paper—with pictures of the scene of the rampage. Which meant just this to the press agent: without cost, the press agent, simply by kicking poor old Rajah out of the menagerie house, had obtained the usually unattainable.

Back in his stall, Rajah existed in peace until another inspiration came. It was during flood times, when the Kaw and Missouri rivers were far out of their banks and overflowing the "bottoms" regions of Kansas City, Armourdale, Argentine and other suburbs. Naturally, the newspapers were printing every line that hard-working reporters could obtain. And on the first page was Rajah!

He had become news again. A train had been stalled in the danger zone; the locomotive was dead, and there was no switch engine available. It was then that Rajah had come to the rescue, to act as a switch engine and save human lives. After that, Rajah became an influential elephant.

Every few weeks his trainer would be dangerously injured and taken to his home. Just why he wasn't taken to a hospital wasn't explained. Then, at intervals of a month or so, Rajah would break loose again, until at last Argentine became somewhat accustomed to see a lost elephant loping up the street, and the news value departed. But there still remained hope, even in a shopworn performance.

Early one morning—just when Argentine was doing its best sleeping—mysterious telephone calls began to shoot about the little town. Rajah was loose again, and this time he was dangerous! He had mangled an assistant keeper, broken down the door of the menagerie house and was out for blood!

Things seem worse at two o'clock in the morning than they do at two o'clock in the afternoon. Again the riot calls went in, and when the police arrived, it was to find a number of circus men patrolling the streets, all armed with rifles.

"We've got our orders to kill him!" they announced grimly, and went on searching for Rajah.

But Rajah was lost. Parties of police, determined circus men, all looked for Rajah in vain. The menagerie house was empty; the doors were broken. Rajah was gone, and Argentine perspired with excitement. Every barn was suspected, every vacant lot. Houses were locked and barred, lest Rajah, coming suddenly out of hiding, should move in that direction.

Two days went by, in which Argentine forgot everything else and looked for Rajah, in which the newspapers of Kansas City sent special representatives to write the story of a lost elephant and a terror-ridden town, and in which hurrying circus owners went about from one detachment of searchers to another, sorrowfully but grimly repeating the order:

"This is the end. If you see that elephant, shoot, and shoot to kill! We'd rather see him dead than endangering lives and property this way. Kill him!"

But there was no Rajah to kill!

Another day slid by and into gloaming. Then the word went forth. Rajah had been found! He had waded out through the Kaw River to a small island, and there he had established his little empire. Again was shouted the order:

"Shoot and shoot to kill!"

Round after round banged forth from the rifles. But two things prohibited Rajah being killed. One was the fact that it was dark now, and that Rajah couldn't be seen. Another was a matter which wasn't mentioned at the time: the cartridges which were being fired contained no bullets!

It was all very exciting and melodramatic: the shouts of the hunters, the blaze of the rifles as they spat forth their yellow flare into the night, the sorrow of the circus owners over the loss of their prized elephant, the fear of the townspeople; it was news of a different and thrilling sort, and the melodrama lasted until the morning papers had passed their press time. Then the firing ceased, in the hope that Rajah was dead. Dawn revealed the fact that he wasn't, and with the knowledge, the last card was played.

"Men," it was the menagerie superintendent speaking, "I hate to give up like this. Rajah's always liked me, and I've—I've always thought a lot of him. I think just enough of him to—to risk my life to bring him back again."

"I won't permit it!" A terribly frightened circus owner had interrupted. "I'm not going to have you killed just to—"

"I'll sign an agreement, if you want me to, that you won't be responsible if I'm killed." The menagerie superintendent was bent glumly on suicide. "But, whether you want me to or not, I'm going after Rajah! And I'm going alone!"

Whereupon, midst the gasps of the multitude, in the gray and cheerless dawn, he rowed out into the Kaw, straight toward the terrible beast which awaited him there on the island. Two or three thousand hearts halted in their beating. Two or three thousand pairs of lungs labored in their breathing while the trainer cut down the distance with slow, steady strokes of the oars, passed out of earshot of those who waited, hoping that he wouldn't be killed, yet reflecting upon the fact that they'd never seen a man murdered by an elephant. On he went, fearless, intrepid. The boat grated on the sand of the island, the trainer leaped forth, grasped his bull-hook a bit tighter, and headed straight toward the elephant.

"Hello, Rajah," he announced.

Rajah, not being gifted with conversational powers, couldn't answer. So he did the next best thing, the kneeling salaam which he had learned in the ring. The trainer sunk the bull-hook gently behind one ear.

"Come on home, Old Kid," was his command. "Guess we've pulled enough excitement to last 'em awhile."

Far across the river, on the bank, it all looked very stagey and thrilling. It appeared even worse when the trainer, with shouts and dramatics, forced the poor old elephant to wade the river. Then the crowd scattered as Rajah ran up the bank, back to that dear old menagerie house and the hay he knew would be awaiting him.

A few weeks later, someone told the true story of Rajah's horrible escape, and grumbling newspaper men put the elephant's name on the office blacklist.

"No more fakes about that elephant!" Such was the word that went forth.

It was night a few months later. The telegraph editor of the *Kansas City Star* looked up from his desk, toward the night editor. Scorn was implanted heavily upon his features.

"They're still faking Rajah," he announced. "Here's a query from Texas."

"What's it say?"

"Plenty." Then the telegraph editor read: "Frank Fisher, trainer of Rajah, killed while trying to subdue the beast while on rampage. How much?"

Then both of them grinned. The query was crumpled into a
ball. A swerving arc, it traveled under the lights, half across the room,
into the wastebasket.

While down in Texas a bit of canvas covered the torn, broken
form of what once had been a man. Far in a corner of the menagerie
tent sulked a huge beast, Rajah, gone bad at last,—Rajah, the elephant
who had simulated viciousness until at last he had become vicious;
Rajah, who finally had become the basic force of a real news story.

That never was printed! But it wasn't the newspaper's fault.
The two editors merely were trying to guard the public from what
seemed to be another Rajah hoax. The guard had been raised at the
wrong time; that was all.

And indeed it is a good guard which can stand against the
every assault of him who desires to "make" the columns of a newspaper
with something that will advertise his wares. Out in Denver one summer night a few years ago, a black-garbed woman sauntered slowly
down Seventeenth Street. Suddenly she staggered and fell. When the
police ambulance arrived, she was, to all appearances, unconscious. An
hour later, in the county hospital, she awoke, to stare about her in non-
understanding manner, to look dazedly at the attendants, then to ask:

"Who am I?"

It was a plain case of amnesia. The doctors applied every test
known to produce the symptoms of true amnesia—non-response to
tickling the soles of the feet; no evidence of pain by being pricked with
a needle at certain points of the anatomy. Test after test—every evidence of amnesia, or forgetfulness of self—was present. Question after
question was asked, finally to bring a slight flicker of memory:

"Yes, that was it. I was going somewhere. Where was I going?"
The face became blank. "Where—where was I going?"

Hours passed. There came no answer to supply the destination
of the woman. It was on her mind, that question, even in greater
strength than curiosity as to her own identity. Where was she going?

It was a strange case. The woman was well, even richly dressed.
She had every appearance of having come from a good home and being
of aristocratic stock. In the parlance of the newspaper office it was a
"good talk yarn." The newspapers, doing their level best to aid someone

in distress, printed pictures of the woman, with descriptions of height, weight, color of eyes and hair, and did everything possible to obtain some clue to her identity. Persons by the hundreds hurried to the hospital to see her, in an effort to furnish some clue that might lead to her identity. It was impossible. For three days it continued, and then—

"I know where I was going!"

The woman had raised herself in bed, weirdly, excitedly, just at the moment when all the newspaper reporters were there. Hurriedly they clustered about the bed.

"Yes—where were you going? Do you remember?"

"Perfectly." Still the excited voice went on. "I was going to the downtown box office to buy a ticket to the show that starts tomorrow at Elitch's Gardens. I was—"

Most of the reporters began taking notes. But out of the number was a man who himself had been a press agent.

"Junk!" he snorted and started in search of the press agent of the summer resort. He found him. That night, after much sweating, the agent confessed. Later he became the city editor of the biggest newspaper in Denver, but it was after he had "reformed." For the newspaper had its revenge. It didn't even mention the fact that the woman had regained consciousness. The public, seeing nothing, naturally supposed that she still was in a state of amnesia. Another day went by, with still no mention, and a part of the public forgot. By the fourth day, there were even no inquiries over the telephone. The public's mind had turned to the latest murder, a press agent was swearing under his breath—just as city editors were swearing at him—a fair amount of expense money was gone to naught, and the mystery of "The Woman in Black" remained a mystery.

But more often the rewards lie on the other side. More, when you think of the ingenuity, the scheming, the knowledge of psychological values and the mass mind-reading which has been his, you're just a bit glad that the press agent has won and "slipped over his story." To wit, one Jimmy Fitzpatrick, and an adroit little move which accomplished many things.

Jimmy was in Detroit, and he wasn't especially fortunate. The Detroit newspapers seemed to care nothing for the fact that he was appearing in the interests of the Young Buffalo Wild West Show. There were other shows of the same type that were vastly better, which charged no more and which gave a much superior performance. So, coolly and candidly, the Detroit editors announced to Jimmy the fact that, so far as they were concerned, there was too much real news awaiting publication. Young Buffalo must struggle along without their aid.

Jimmy bowed his way tearfully out of the offices. He went to his hotel. He thought, long and hard. He figured the population of Detroit, then divided it by five in an effort to gain some hazy idea as to the number of small boys the town contained. The result evidently was satisfactory. Jimmy returned to the newspaper offices.

But this time he went no farther than the want-ad counter. There he wrote an advertisement, paid for it and departed. It read simply:

WANTED—Five dogs for Indian Feast. Must be fat, clean and healthy. Will pay five dollars apiece for right dogs. Apply Thursday morning at 9 o'clock.

JAMES FITZPATRICK, *Agent*,
Young Buffalo Wild West Show,
Blank Hotel.

Into every newspaper went the advertisement. The next morning Jimmy purposely slept late, only to be awakened. There were dogs in the lobby of the hotel, dogs in the elevators, dogs in the halls, dogs in the office, in the lounges—everywhere. There were dogs in the street, in the alleys and on the car tracks. When the number reached five hundred, the police were called. When the aggregate went to two thousand, out came the reserves. Every mongrel pup in Detroit, it seemed, had been collared by someone who needed five dollars, and hurried to Jimmy's hotel. The street became blocked with small boys, dog catchers, hobos with prospective five-dollar bills whining at the end of a string, women, girls, fox-terriers, Skye terriers, Newfoundlands, collies and just plain dogs. Every few feet a fight was in progress, with boys yelling, dogs snapping and snarling, and policemen vaguely attempting to stop the unstoppable. Two thousand kinds of barking echoed through the business district. Downtown Detroit simply stopped work and watched a conglomerate dog fight. No longer was Jimmy Fitzpatrick an outcast of the news columns. He had become the creator of the funniest story of months. That night he glowed with happiness and pride; the account of his two thousand dogs, the police and a canine-blocked street was on the first page of every paper. More—

He hadn't even been forced to part with the twenty-five dollars. For the Humane Society, aroused by the thought of a dog feast, had threatened to put him under arrest if he even attempted it. Certainly James Fitzpatrick did not care for arrest. He only wanted the name of his show in the paper, the glowing title of Young Buffalo where he desired to see it.

Incidentally, the name of "Buffalo" brings memories,—and perhaps a confession. I once was a press agent myself.

Colonel William Frederick Cody (Buffalo Bill) was the man in whom my sun of work and endeavor rose and set. More, Buffalo Bill, big, bluff, good-hearted, roaring Buffalo Bill, realized that had it not been for the first press stories which appeared in the guise of fiction and through which Buffalo Bill rode, shot, scalped Indians, saved fair maidens in distress and did everything else that a godlike hero should have done, his life might have been in vain as regarded public recognition.

Not, understand, that Buffalo Bill was not every inch the man that Young America believed him to be. For he was, and as the years go by his place in the history of western civilization, will grow constantly bigger, constantly more important. Far out upon the Sioux reservations I have seen Indian squaws who have come a hundred miles overland, carrying their papooses, that these Indian babies might look upon the great Pahaska, the man who had fought their fathers and grandfathers, and who was brave enough to be honored, even by the children of an enemy! To such Indians as Short Bull, to Woman Dress, who saved the life of General Sheridan, to No Neck and Horn Cloud and others who really knew an Indian fighter when they saw one, Buffalo Bill was little less than a god. But of what use is all the traditional glory in the world from a monetary standpoint, if the public doesn't know it, and the public isn't constantly reminded of the fact? Buffalo Bill was a showman, and I was his press agent, for a time, at least.

Which perhaps may explain several things. A certain mayor of Chicago, for instance, may remember a telegram from Colonel William Frederick Cody (Buffalo Bill) congratulating him upon being the executive of the second largest city in the United States and asking permission to salute him, with his assembled cowboys, vaqueros and rough riders of the world, from the saddle on the steps of the city hall. If the mayor does remember it, and if the mayor has prized that as a tribute, I'm sorry, but I'm in the confessional now. A bald, long-nosed press agent was behind it. There was a reason.

Buffalo Bill was to exhibit at White City. There is an ordinance in Chicago which prohibits circus parades in the loop section. But could I but have arranged that salute from the saddle on the steps of the city hall, it would have ceased to have been a circus parade, but a compliment to the mayor of a great city. Through the loop district the entire cavalcade would have gone, while the Chicago's downtown section would have seen the first circus parade in years without police interference,—in fact, one actually sanctioned by the city! But the mayor was out of town, darn it!

Or perhaps the King of England may remember the fact that he received a cablegram in the early days of the war with Germany. I know it was an enthusiastic thing, because I wrote it myself. It offered the services of Buffalo Bill and his Congress of Rough Riders of the World to go through the German lines like rain water through a gutter. If I'm not mistaken, His Majesty replied. I guess my apologies are due the King. Buffalo Bill didn't O. K. that cablegram until after it was sent. But let this be known: the "Old Man," as he was known to the ones who worked for him, fought for him, quarreled with him and loved him, was just enough of a fighter, just enough of a youth in spite of his white hairs and three-score-and-more years, to have gone!

Toby Tyler

BY JAMES OTIS

Circus people tend to see or divide the world into us and them. This is natural enough given that a circus is largely a closed community, the members dependent on one another, and having a difficult way to make it in the world. Seen from this point of view, James Otis is one of them. If "Toby Tyler—Or Ten Weeks with the Circus" is anything, it's a warning against a life under and around the big-top. This is a little odd in that Otis is said to have worked as a press agent of a circus. Or maybe it is because of this.

I hadn't read the book for forty years and I'd allowed a kind of rosy glow to surround the tale in my imagination. I'd allowed myself to regard it as a celebration of circus life. After all, hadn't it been a Disney movie? I remembered it as the story of a boy who does the quintessential American-boy thing, he runs away and joins the circus, befriends a chimp named Mr. Stubbs, and together animal and boy have many adventures. I'd forgotten just how scared and miserable and hungry poor Toby was for his ten weeks.

James Otis (Kailer) was born in Frankfort, Maine, in 1848. He tried his hand at many different kinds of work, eventually ending up as a Superintendent of Schools for South Portland, Maine. "Toby Tyler—Or Ten Weeks with the Circus" became an instant American classic when first published in 1880, and Otis went on to pen many works for young people, including a series of sermons for a press syndicate.

It's said, he loved writing sermons.

○ ○ ○

4 1

"COULDNT you give more'n six peanuts for a cent?" was a question asked by a very small boy, with big, staring eyes, of a candy vendor at a circus booth. And as he spoke, he looked wistfully at the quantity of nuts piled high up on the basket, and then at the six, each of which now looked so small as he held them in his hand.

"Couldn't do it," was the reply of the proprietor of the booth, as he put the boy's penny carefully away in the drawer.

The little fellow looked for another moment at his purchase, and then carefully cracked the largest one.

A shade—and a very deep shade it was—of disappointment passed over his face, and then, looking up anxiously, he asked, "Don't you swap 'em when they're bad?"

The man's face looked as if a smile had been a stranger to it for a long time; but one did pay it a visit just then, and he tossed the boy two nuts and asked him a question at the same time. "What is your name?"

The big, brown eyes looked up for an instant, as if to learn whether the question was asked in good faith, and then their owner said, as he carefully picked apart another nut, "Toby Tyler."

"Well, that's a queer name."

"Yes, I s'pose so, myself; but, you see, I don't expect that's the name that belongs to me. But the fellers call me so, an' so does Uncle Dan'l."

"Who is Uncle Daniel?" was the next question. In the absence of other customers the man seemed disposed to get as much amusement out of the boy as possible.

"He hain't my uncle at all; I only call him so because all the boys do, an' I live with him."

"Where's your father and mother?"

"I don't know," said Toby, rather carelessly. "I don't know much about 'em, an' Uncle Dan'l says they don't know much about me. Here's another bad nut; goin' to give me two more?" The two nuts were given him, and he said, as he put them in his pocket and turned over and over again those which he held in his hand, "I shouldn't wonder if all of these was bad. S'posen you give me two for each one of 'em before I crack 'em, an' then they won't be spoiled so you can't sell 'em again."

As this offer of barter was made, the man looked amused, and he asked, as he counted out the number which Toby desired, "If I give you these, I suppose you'll want me to give you two more for each one, and you'll keep that kind of trade going until you get my whole stock?"

"I won't open my head if every one of 'em's bad."

"All right; you can keep what you've got, and I'll give you these besides; but I don't want you to buy any more, for I don't want to do that kind of business."

Toby took the nuts offered, not in the least abashed, and seated himself on a convenient stone to eat them and at the same time to see all that was going on around him. The coming of a circus to the little town of Guilford was an event, and Toby had hardly thought of anything else since the highly colored posters had first been put up. It was yet quite early in the morning, and the tents were just being erected by the men. Toby had followed, with eager eyes, everything that looked as if it belonged to the circus, from the time the first wagon had entered the town until the street parade had been made and everything was being prepared for the afternoon's performance.

The man who had made the losing trade in peanuts seemed disposed to question the boy still further, probably owing to the fact that he had nothing better to do.

"Who is this Uncle Daniel you say you live with? Is he a farmer?"

"No; he's a deacon, an' he raps me over the head with the hymn book whenever I go to sleep in meetin', an' he says I eat four times as much as I earn. I blame him for hittin' so hard when I go to sleep, but I s'pose he's right about my eatin'. You see," and here his tone grew both confidential and mournful, "I am an awful eater, an' I can't seem to help it. Somehow I'm hungry all the time. I don't seem ever to get enough till carrot time comes, an' then I can get all I want without troublin' anybody."

"Didn't you ever have enough to eat?" "

"I s'pose I did; but you see Uncle Dan'l he found me one mornin' on his hay, an' he says I was cryin' for something to eat then, an' I've kept it up ever since. I tried to get him to give me money enough to go into the circus with; but he said a cent was all he could spare these hard times, an' I'd better take that an' buy something to eat with it, for the show wasn't very good, anyway. I wish peanuts wasn't but a cent a bushel."

"Then you would make yourself sick eating them."

"Yes, I s'pose I should; Uncle Dan'l says I'd eat till I was sick, if I got the chance; but I'd like to try it once."

He was a very small boy, with a round head covered with short red hair, a face as speckled as any turkey's egg, but thoroughly good-natured looking. As he sat there on the rather sharp point of the rock, swaying his body to and fro as he hugged his knees with his hands and kept his eyes fastened on the tempting display of good things before him, it would have been a very hard-hearted man who would not have given him something. But Mr. Job Lord, the proprietor of the booth, was a hard-hearted man, and he did not make the slightest advance toward offering the little fellow anything.

Toby rocked himself silently for a moment, and then he said, hesitatingly, "I don't suppose you'd like to sell me some things, an' let me pay you when I get older, would you?"

Mr. Lord shook his head decidedly at this proposition.

"I didn't s'pose you would," said Toby, quickly, "but you didn't seem to be selling anything, an' I thought I'd just see what you'd say about it." And then he appeared suddenly to see something wonderfully interesting behind him, which served as an excuse to turn his reddening face away.

"I suppose your Uncle Daniel makes you work for your living, don't he?" asked Mr. Lord, after he had rearranged his stock of candy and had added a couple of slices of lemon peel to what was popularly supposed to be lemonade.

"That's what I think; but he says that all the work I do wouldn't pay for the meal that one chicken would eat, an' I s'pose it's so, for I don't like to work as well as a feller without any father and mother ought to. I don't know why it is, but I guess it's because I take up so much time eatin' that it kinder tires me out. I s'pose you go into the circus whenever you want to, don't you?"

"Oh, yes; I'm there at every performance, for I keep the stand under the big canvas as well as this one out here."

There was a great big sigh from out Toby's little round stomach, as he thought what bliss it must be to own all those good things and to see the circus wherever it went. "It must be nice," he said, as he faced the booth and its hard-visaged proprietor once more.

"How would you like it?" asked Mr. Lord, patronizingly, as he looked Toby over in a business way, very much as if he contemplated purchasing him.

"Like it!" echoed Toby. "Why, I'd grow fat on it."

"I don't know as that would be any advantage," continued Mr. Lord, reflectively, "for it strikes me that you're about as fat now as a boy of your age ought to be. But I've a great mind to give you a chance."

"What!" cried Toby, in amazement, and his eyes opened to their widest extent, as this possible opportunity of leading a delight-ful life presented itself.

"Yes, I've a great mind to give you the chance. You see," and now it was Mr. Lord's turn to grow confidential, "I've had a boy with me this season, but he cleared out at the last town, and I'm running the business alone now."

Toby's face expressed all the contempt he felt for the boy who would run away from such a glorious life as Mr. Lord's assistant must lead, but he said not a word, waiting in breathless expectation for the offer which he now felt certain would be made him.

"Now I ain't hard on a boy," continued Mr. Lord, still confi-dentially, "and yet that one seemed to think that he was treated worse and made to work harder than any boy in the world."

"He ought to live with Uncle Dan'l a week," said Toby, eagerly.

"Here I was just like a father to him," said Mr. Lord, paying no attention to the interruption, "and I gave him his board and lodging and a dollar a week besides."

"Could he do what he wanted to with the dollar?"

"Of course he could. I never checked him, no matter how ex-travagant he was, an' yet I've seen him spend his whole week's wages at this very stand in one afternoon. And even after his money had all gone that way, I've paid for peppermint and ginger out of my own pocket just to cure his stomachache."

Toby shook his head mournfully, as if deploring that depravity which could cause a boy to run away from such a tender-hearted employer and from such a desirable position. But even as he shook his head so sadly, he looked wistfully at the peanuts, and Mr. Lord observed the look.

It may have been that Mr. Job Lord was the tender-hearted man he prided himself upon being, or it may have been that he wished to purchase Toby's sympathy; but, at all events, he gave him a large handful of nuts, and Toby never bothered his little round head as to what motive prompted the gift. Now he could listen to the story of the boy's treachery and eat at the same time; therefore he was an attentive listener.

"All in the world that boy had to do," continued Mr. Lord, in the same injured tone he had previously used, "was to help me set things to rights when we struck a town in the morning, and then tend to the counter till we left the town at night, and all the rest of the time he had to himself. Yet that boy was ungrateful enough to run away."

Mr. Lord paused, as if expecting some expression of sympathy from his listener; but Toby was so busily engaged with his unexpected feast, and his mouth was so full that it did not seem even possible for him to shake his head.

"Now what should you say if I told you that you looked to me like a boy that was made especially to help run a candy counter at a circus, and if I offered the place to you?"

Toby made one frantic effort to swallow the very large mouthful, and in a choking voice he answered, quickly, "I should say I'd go with you, an' be mighty glad of the chance."

"Then it's a bargain, my boy, and you shall leave town with me tonight."

○ ○ ○

Toby Runs Away from Home

Toby could scarcely restrain himself at the prospect of this golden future that had so suddenly opened before him. He tried to express his gratitude, but could only do so by evincing his willingness to commence work at once.

"No, no, that won't do," said Mr. Lord, cautiously. "If your Uncle Daniel should see you working here, he might mistrust something, and then you couldn't get away."

"I don't believe he'd try to stop me," said Toby, confidently, "for he's told me lots of times that it was a sorry day for him when he found me."

"We won't take any chances, my son," was the reply, in a very benevolent tone, as he patted Toby on the head and at the same time handed him a piece of pasteboard. "There's a ticket for the circus, and you come around to see me about ten o'clock tonight. I'll put you on one of the wagons, and by tomorrow morning your Uncle Daniel will have hard work to find you."

If Toby had followed his inclinations, the chances are that he would have fallen on his knees and kissed Mr. Lord's hands in the excess of his gratitude. But not knowing exactly how such a show of thankfulness might be received, he contented himself by repeatedly promising that he would be punctual to the time and place appointed.

He would have loitered in the vicinity of the candy stand in order that he might gain some insight into the business, but Mr. Lord advised that he remain away, lest his Uncle Daniel should see him and suspect where he had gone when he was missed in the morning.

As Toby walked around the circus grounds, whereon was so much to attract his attention, he could not prevent himself from assuming an air of proprietorship. His interest in all that was going on was redoubled, and in his anxiety that everything should be done correctly and in the proper order he actually, and perhaps for the first time in his life, forgot that he was hungry. He was really to travel with a circus, to become a part, as it were, of the whole, and to be able to see its many wonderful and beautiful attractions every day.

Even the very tent ropes had acquired a new interest for him, and the faces of the men at work seemed suddenly to have become those of friends. How hard it was for him to walk around unconcernedly; and how especially hard to prevent his feet from straying toward that tempting display of dainties which he was to sell to those who came to see and enjoy, and who would look at him with wonder and curiosity! It was very hard not to be allowed to tell his playmates of his wonderfully good fortune; but silence meant success, and he locked his secret in his bosom, not even daring to talk with anyone he knew, lest he should betray himself by some incautious word.

He did not go home to dinner that day, and once or twice he felt impelled to walk past the candy stand, giving a mysterious shake of the head at the proprietor as he did so. The afternoon performance passed off as usual to all of the spectators save Toby. He imagined that each one of the performers knew that he was about to join them; and even as he passed the cage containing the monkeys, he fancied that one particularly old one knew all about his intention of running away.

Of course it was necessary for him to go home at the close of the afternoon's performance, in order to get one or two valuable articles of his own, such as a boat, a kite, and a pair of skates, and in order that his actions might not seem suspicious. Before he left the grounds, however, he stole slyly around to the candy stand and informed Mr. Job Lord in a very hoarse whisper that he would be on hand at the time appointed.

Mr. Lord patted him on the head, gave him two large sticks of candy, and, what was more kind and surprising, considering the fact that he wore glasses and was cross-eyed, he winked at Toby. A wink from Mr. Lord must have been intended to convey a great deal, because, owing to the defect in his eyes, it required no little exertion, and even then could not be considered as a really first-class wink.

That wink, distorted as it was, gladdened Toby's heart immensely and took away nearly all the sting of the scolding with which Uncle Daniel greeted him when he reached home.

That night, despite the fact that he was going to travel with the circus, despite the fact that his home was not a happy or cheerful one, Toby was not in a pleasant frame of mind. He began to feel for the first time that he was doing wrong. And as he gazed at Uncle Daniel's stern, forbidding-looking face, it seemed to have changed somewhat from its severity, and caused a great lump of something to come up in his throat as he thought that perhaps he should never see it again. Just then one or two kind words would have prevented him from running away, bright as the prospect of circus life appeared.

It was almost impossible for him to eat anything, and this very surprising state of affairs attracted the attention of Uncle Daniel.

"Bless my heart! What ails the boy?" asked the old man, as he peered over his glasses at Toby's well-filled plate, which was usually emptied so quickly. "Are ye sick, Toby, or what is the matter with ye?"

"No, I hain't sick," said Toby, with a sigh, "but I've been to the circus, an' I got a good deal to eat."

"Oho! You spent that cent I give ye, eh, an' got so much that it made ye sick?"

Toby thought of the six peanuts which he had bought with the penny Uncle Daniel had given him; and, amid all his homesickness, he could not help wondering if Uncle Daniel ever made himself sick with only six peanuts when he was a boy.

As no one paid any further attention to Toby, he pushed back his plate, arose from the table, and went with a heavy heart to attend to his regular evening chores. The cow, the hens, and even the pigs came in for a share of his unusually kind attention; and as he fed them all, the big tears rolled down his cheeks as he thought that perhaps never again would he see any of them. These dumb animals had all been Toby's confidants; he had poured out his griefs in their ears and fancied, when the world or Uncle Daniel had used him unusually hard, that they sympathized with him. Now he was leaving them forever, and as he locked the stable door, he could hear the sounds of music coming from the direction of the circus grounds, and he was angry at it, because it represented that which was taking him away from his home, even though it was not as pleasant as it might have been.

Still, he had no thought of breaking the engagement which he had made. He went to his room, made a bundle of his worldly possessions, and crept out of the back door, down the road to the circus.

Mr. Lord saw him as soon as he arrived on the grounds, and as he passed another ticket to Toby, he took his bundle from him, saying, as he did so, "I'll pack up your bundle with my things, and then you'll be sure not to lose it. Don't you want some candy?"

Toby shook his head; he had just discovered that there was possibly some connection between his heart and his stomach, for his grief at leaving home had taken from him all desire for good things. It is also more than possible that Mr. Lord had had experience enough with boys to know that they might be homesick on the eve of starting to travel with a circus; and in order to make sure that Toby would keep to his engagement, he was unusually kind.

That evening was the longest that Toby ever knew. He wandered from one cage of animals to another, then to see the performance in the ring, and back again to the animals, in the vain hope of passing the time pleasantly. But it was of no use; that lump in his throat would remain there, and the thoughts of what he was about to do would trouble him severely. The performance failed to interest him, and the animals did not attract until he had visited the monkey cage for the third or fourth time. Then he fancied that the same venerable monkey who had looked so knowing in the afternoon was gazing at him with a sadness which could only have come from a thorough knowledge of all the grief and doubt that was in his heart.

There was no one around the cages, and Toby got just as near to the iron bars as possible. No sooner had he flattened his little pug nose against the iron than the aged monkey came down from the ring in which he had been swinging, and, seating himself directly in front of Toby's face, looked at him most compassionately.

It would not have surprised the boy just then if the animal had spoken; but as he did not, Toby did the next best thing and spoke to him.

"I s'pose you remember that you saw me this afternoon, an' somebody told you that I was goin' to join the circus, didn't they?"

The monkey made no reply, though Toby fancied that he winked an affirmative answer; and he looked so sympathetic that he continued, confidentially:

"Well, I'm the same feller, an' I don't mind telling you that I'm awfully sorry I promised that candy man I'd go with him. Do you know that I came near crying at the supper table tonight; an' Uncle Dan'l looked real good an' nice, though I never thought so before. I wish I wasn't goin', after all, 'cause it don't seem a bit like a good time now. But I s'pose I must, 'cause I promised to, an' 'cause the candy man has got all my things."

The big tears had begun to roll down Toby's cheeks, and as he ceased speaking, the monkey reached out one little paw, which Toby took as earnestly as if it had been done purposely to console him.

"You're real good, you are," continued Toby, "an' I hope I shall see you real often, for it seems to me now, when there hain't any folks around, as if you was the only friend I've got in this great, big world. It's awful when a feller feels the way I do, an' when he don't seem to want anything to eat. Now if you'll stick to me, I'll stick to you, an' then it won't be half so bad when we feel this way."

During this speech Toby had still clung to the little brown paw, which the monkey now withdrew and continued to gaze into the boy's face.

"The fellers all say I don't amount to anything," sobbed Toby, "an' Uncle Dan'l says I don't, an' I s'pose they know; but I tell you I feel just as bad, now that I'm goin' away from them all, as if I was as good as any of them."

At this moment Toby saw Mr. Lord enter the tent, and he knew that the summons to start was about to be given.

"Good-by," he said to the monkey, as he vainly tried to take him by the hand again, "remember what I've told you, an' don't forget that Toby Tyler is feelin' worse tonight than if he was twice as big an' twice as good."

Mr. Lord had come to summon him away, and he now told Toby that he would show him with which man he was to ride that night.

Toby looked another good-by at the venerable monkey, who was watching him closely, and then followed his employer out of the tent, among the ropes and poles and general confusion attendant upon the removal of a circus from one place to another.

The Night Ride

The wagon on which Mr. Lord was to send his new found employee was, by the most singular chance, the one containing the monkeys, and Toby accepted this as a good omen. He would be near his venerable friend all night, and there was some consolation in that. The driver instructed the boy to watch his movements, and when he saw him leading his horses around, "To look lively, and be on hand," for he never waited for anyone.

Toby not only promised to do as ordered, but he followed the driver around so closely that, had he desired, he could not have rid himself of his little companion.

The scene which presented itself to Toby's view was strange and weird in the extreme. Shortly after he had attached himself to the man with whom he was to ride, the performance was over, and the work of putting the show and its belongings into such a shape as could be conveyed from one town to another was soon in active operation. Toby forgot his grief, forgot that he was running away from the only home he had ever known, in fact, forgot everything concerning himself, so interested was he in that which was going on about him.

As soon as the audience had got out of the tent—and almost before—the work of taking down the canvas was begun.

Torches were stuck in the earth at regular intervals, the lights that had shone so brilliantly in and around the ring had been extinguished, the canvas sides had been taken off, and the boards that had formed the seats were being packed into one of the carts with a rattling sound that seemed as if a regular fusillade of musketry was being indulged in. Men were shouting, horses were being driven hither and thither, harnessed to the wagons, or drawing the huge carts away as soon as they were loaded. Everything seemed in the greatest state of confusion, while really the work was being done in the most systematic manner possible.

Toby had not long to wait before the driver informed him that the time for starting had arrived and assisted him to climb up to the narrow seat whereon he was to ride that night.

The scene was so exciting, and his efforts to stick to the narrow seat so great, that he really had no time to attend to the homesick feeling that had crept over him during the first part of the evening.

The long procession of carts and wagons drove slowly out of the town, and when the last familiar house had been passed, the driver spoke to Toby for the first time since they started.

"Pretty hard work to keep on—eh, sonny?"

"Yes," replied the boy, as the wagon jolted over a rock, bouncing him high in air, and he, by strenuous efforts, barely succeeded in alighting on the seat again, "it is pretty hard work; an' my name's Toby Tyler."

Toby heard a queer sound that seemed to come from the man's throat, and for a few moments he feared that his companion was choking. But he soon understood that this was simply an attempt to laugh, and he at once decided that it was a very poor style of laughing.

"So you object to being called sonny, do you?"

"Well, I'd rather be called Toby, for, you see, that's my name."

"All right, my boy, we'll call you Toby. I suppose you thought it was a mighty fine thing to run away an' jine a circus, didn't you?"

Toby started in affright, looked around cautiously, and then tried to peer down through the small, square aperture, guarded by iron rods, that opened into the cage just back of the seat they were sitting on. Then he turned slowly around to the driver and asked in a voice sunk to a whisper, "How did you know that I was runnin' away? Did he tell you?" and Toby motioned with his thumb as if he were pointing out someone behind him.

It was the driver's turn now to look around in search of the "he" referred to by Toby.

"Who do you mean?" asked the man, impatiently.

"Why, the old feller; the one in the cart there. I think he knew I was runnin' away, though he didn't say anything about it; but he looked just as if he did."

The driver looked at Toby in perfect amazement for a moment, and then, as if suddenly understanding the boy, relapsed into one of those convulsive efforts that caused the blood to rush up into his face and gave him every appearance of having a fit.

"You must mean one of the monkeys," said the driver, after he had recovered his breath, which had been almost shaken out of his body by the silent laughter. "So you thought a monkey had told me what any fool could have seen if he had watched you for five minutes."

"Well," said Toby, slowly, as if he feared he might provoke one of those terrible laughing spells again, "I saw him tonight, an' he looked as if he knew what I was doin'; so I up an' told him, an' I didn't know but he'd told you, though he didn't look to me like a feller that would be mean."

There was another internal shaking on the part of the driver, which Toby did not fear so much, since he was getting accustomed to it, and then the man said, "Well, you are the queerest little cove I ever saw."

"I s'pose I am," was the reply, accompanied by a long-drawn sigh. "I don't seem to amount to so much as the other fellers do, an' I guess it's because I'm always hungry. You see, I eat awful, Uncle Dan'l says."

The only reply which the driver made to this plaintive confession was to put his hand down into the deepest recesses of one of his deep pockets and to draw therefrom a huge doughnut, which he handed to his companion.

Toby was so much at his ease by this time that the appetite which had failed him at supper had now returned in full force, and he devoured the doughnut in a most ravenous manner.

"You're too small to eat so fast," said the man, in a warning tone, as the last morsel of the greasy sweetness disappeared, and he fished up another for the boy. "Some time you'll get hold of one of the India-rubber doughnuts that they feed to circus people, an' choke yourself to death."

Toby shook his head and devoured this second cake as quickly as he had the first, craning his neck and uttering a funny little squeak as the last bit went down, just as a chicken does when he gets too large a mouthful of dough.

"I'll never choke," he said, confidently, "I'm used to it. And Uncle Dan'l says I could eat a pair of boots an' never wink at 'em; but I don't just believe that."

As the driver made no reply to this remark, Toby curled himself up on one corner of the seat and watched with no little interest all that was passing on around him. Each of the wagons had a lantern fastened to the hind axle, and these lights could be seen far ahead on the road, as if a party of fireflies had started in single file on an excursion. The trees by the side of the road stood out weird and ghostly looking in the darkness, and the rumble of the carts ahead and behind formed a musical accompaniment to the picture that sounded strangely doleful.

Mile after mile was passed over in perfect silence, save now and then when the driver would whistle a few bars of some very dismal tune that would fairly make Toby shiver with its mournfulness. Eighteen miles was the distance from Guilford to the town where the next performance of the circus was to be given, and as Toby thought of the ride before them, it seemed as if the time would be almost interminable. He curled himself up on one corner of the seat and tried very hard to go to sleep; but just as his eyes began to grow heavy, the wagon would jolt over some rock or sink deep in some rut, till Toby, the breath very nearly shaken out of his body and his neck almost dislocated, would sit bolt upright, clinging to the seat with both hands, as if he expected each moment to be pitched out into the mud.

The driver watched him closely and each time that he saw him shaken up and awakened so thoroughly, he would indulge in one of his silent laughing spells, until Toby would wonder whether he would ever recover from it. Several times had Toby been awakened, and each time he had seen the amusement his sufferings caused, until he finally resolved to put an end to the sport by keeping awake.

"What is your name?" he asked the driver, thinking a conversation would be the best way to rouse himself into wakefulness.

"Waal," said the driver, as he gathered the reins carefully in one hand and seemed to be debating in his mind how he should answer the question, "I don't know as I know myself, it's been so long since I've heard it."

Toby was wide enough awake now, as this rather singular problem was forced upon his mind. He revolved the matter silently for some moments, and at last he asked, "What do folks call you when they want to speak to you?"

"They always call me Old Ben an' I've got so used to the name that I don't need any other."

Toby wanted very much to ask more questions, but he wisely concluded that it would not be agreeable to his companion.

"I'll ask the old man about it," said Toby to himself, referring to the aged monkey, whom he seemed to feel acquainted with. "He most likely knows, if he'll say anything." After this the conversation ceased, until Toby again ventured to suggest, "It's a pretty long drive, hain't it?"

"You want to wait till you've been in this business a year or two," said Ben, sagely, "an then you won't think much of it. Why, I've known the show towns to be thirty miles apart, an' them was the times when we had lively work of it, riding all night and working all day kind of wears on a fellow."

"Yes, I s'pose so," said Toby, with a sigh, as he wondered whether he had got to work as hard as that, "but I s'pose you get all you want to eat, don't you?"

"Now you've struck it!" said Ben, with the air of one about to impart a world of wisdom, as he crossed one leg over the other, that his position might be as comfortable as possible while he was initiating his young companion into the mysteries of the life. "I've had all the boys ride with me since I've been with this show, an' I've tried to start them right; but they didn't seem to profit by it, an' always got sick of the show an' run away, just because they didn't look out for themselves as they ought to. Now listen to me, Toby, an' remember what I say. You see, they put us all in a hotel together, an' some of these places where we go don't have any too much stuff on the table. Whenever we strike a new town, you find out at the hotel what time they have the grub ready, an' you be on hand, so's to get in with the first. Eat all you can, an' fill your pockets."

"If that's all a feller has to do to travel with a circus," said Toby, "I'm just the one, 'cause I always used to do just that when I hadn't any idea of bein' a circus man."

"Then you'll get along all right," said Ben, as he checked the speed of his horses and, looking carefully ahead, said, as he guided his team to one side of the road, "This is as far as we're going tonight."

Toby learned that they were within a couple of miles of the town and that the entire procession would remain by the roadside until time to make the grand entrée into the village, when every wagon, horse, and man would be decked out in the most gorgeous array, as they had been when they entered Guilford.

Under Ben's direction he wrapped himself in an old horse blanket and lay down on the top of the wagon. And he was so tired from the excitement of the day and night, that he had hardly stretched out at full length before he was fast asleep.

○ ○ ○

The First Day with the Circus

When Toby awakened and looked around, he could hardly realize where he was or how he came there. As far ahead and behind on the road as he could see, the carts were drawn up on one side; men were hurrying to and fro, orders were being shouted, and everything showed that the entry into the town was about to be made. Directly opposite the wagon on which he had been sleeping were the four elephants and two camels, and close behind, contentedly munching their breakfasts, were a number of tiny ponies. Troops of horses were being groomed and attended to; the road was littered with saddles, flags, and general decorations, until it seemed to Toby that there must have been a smash-up, and that he now beheld ruins rather than systematic disorder.

How different everything looked now, compared to the time when the cavalcade marched into Guilford, dazzling everyone with the gorgeous display! Then the horses pranced gayly under their gaudy decorations, the wagons were bright with glass, gilt, and flags, the lumbering elephants and awkward camels were covered with fanci-fully embroidered velvets, and even the drivers of the wagons were resplendent in their uniforms of scarlet and gold. Now, in the gray light of the early morning, everything was changed. The horses were tired and muddy and wore old and dirty harness. The gilded chariots were covered with mud-bespattered canvas, which caused them to look like the most ordinary of market wagons. The elephants and camels looked dingy, dirty, almost repulsive. And the drivers were only a sleepy-looking set of men, who, in their shirtsleeves, were getting ready for the change which would dazzle the eyes of the inhabitants of the town.

Toby descended from his lofty bed, rubbed his eyes to awaken himself thoroughly, and under the guidance of Ben went to a little brook nearby and washed his face. He had been with the circus not quite ten hours, but now he could not realize that it had ever seemed bright and beautiful. He missed his comfortable bed, the quiet and cleanliness, and the well-spread table. Although he had felt the lack of a parent's care, Uncle Daniel's home seemed the very abode of love and friendly feeling compared to this condition, where no one

appeared to care even enough for him to scold at him. He was thoroughly homesick and heartily wished that he was back in his old native town.

While he was washing his face in the brook, he saw some of
the boys who had come out from the town to catch the first glimpse of
the circus, and he saw at once that he was the object of their admiring
gaze. He heard one of the boys say when they first discovered him:

"There's one of them, an' he's only a little feller; so I'm going
to talk to him."

The evident admiration which the boys had for Toby pleased
him, and this pleasure was the only drop of comfort he had had since
he started. He hoped that they would come and talk with him; and,
that they might have the opportunity, he was purposely slow in making his toilet.

The boys approached him shyly, as if they had their doubts
whether he was made of the same material as themselves, and when they
got quite near to him and satisfied themselves that he was only washing
his face in much the same way that any well-regulated boy would do,
the one who had called attention to him said, half timidly, "Hello!"

"Hello!" responded Toby, in a tone that was meant to invite
confidence.

"Do you belong to the circus?"

"Yes," said Toby, a little doubtfully.

Then the boys stared at him again as if he were one of the
strange-looking animals, and the one who had been the spokesman
drew a long breath of envy as he said, longingly, "My! What a nice time
you must have!"

Toby remembered that only yesterday he himself had thought
that boys must have a nice time with a circus, and he now felt what a
mistake that thought was; but he concluded that he would not unde-
ceive his new acquaintance.

"And do they give you frogs to eat, so's to make you limber?"

This was the first time Toby had thought of breakfast, and the
very mention of eating made him hungry. He was just at that moment so
very hungry that he did not think he was replying to the question when
he said, quickly, "Eat frogs! I could eat anything if I only had the chance."

The boys took this as an answer to their question, and felt perfectly convinced that the agility of circus riders and tumblers depended upon the quantity of frogs eaten, and they looked upon Toby with no little degree of awe.

Toby might have undeceived them as to the kind of food he ate, but just at that moment the harsh voice of Mr. Job Lord was heard calling him, and he hurried away to commence his first day's work.

Toby's employer was not the same pleasant, kindly spoken man that he had been during the time they were in Guilford and before the boy was absolutely under his control. He looked cross, he acted cross, and it did not take the boy very long to find out that he was very cross.

He scolded Toby roundly and launched more oaths at his defenseless head than Toby had ever heard in his life. He was angry that the boy had not been on hand to help him and also that he had been obliged to hunt for him.

Toby tried to explain that he had no idea of what he was expected to do, and that he had been on the wagon to which he had been sent, only leaving it to wash his face; but the angry man grew still more furious.

"Went to wash your face, did yer? Want to set yourself up for a dandy, I suppose, and think that you must souse that speckled face of yours into every brook you come to? I'll soon break you of that; and the sooner you understand that I can't afford to have you wasting your time in washing, the better it will be for you."

Toby now grew angry, and not realizing how wholly he was in the man's power, he retorted, "If you think I'm going round with a dirty face, even if it is speckled, for a dollar a week, you're mistaken, that's all. How many folks would eat your candy if they knew you handled it over before you washed your hands?"

"Oho! I've picked up a preacher, have I? Now I want you to understand, my bantam, that I do all the preaching as well as the practicing myself, and this is about as quick a way as I know of to make you understand it."

As the man spoke, he grasped the boy by the coat collar with one hand and with the other plied a thin rubber cane with no gentle force to every portion of Toby's body that he could reach.

Every blow caused the poor boy the most intense pain, but he determined that his tormentor should not have the satisfaction of forcing an outcry from him, and he closed his lips so tightly that not a single sound could escape from them.

This very silence enraged the man so much that he redoubled the force and rapidity of his blows, and it is impossible to say what might have been the consequences had not Ben come that way just then and changed the aspect of affairs.

"Up to your old tricks of whipping the boys, are you, Job?" he said, as he wrested the cane from the man's hand and held him off at arm's length, to prevent him from doing Toby more mischief.

Mr. Lord struggled to release himself and insisted that, since the boy was in his employ, he should do with him just as he saw fit.

"Now look here, Mr. Lord," said Ben, as gravely as if he was delivering some profound piece of wisdom, "I've never interfered with you before, but now I'm going to stop your game of thrashing your boy every morning before breakfast. You just tell this youngster what you want him to do, and if he don't do it, you can discharge him. If I hear of your flogging him, I shall attend to your case at once. You hear me?"

Ben shook the now terrified candy vendor much as if he had been a child, and then released him, saying to Toby as he did so, "Now, my boy, you attend to your business as you ought to, and I'll settle his account if he tries the flogging game again."

"You see, I don't know what there is for me to do," sobbed Toby, for the kindly interference of Ben had made him show more feeling than Mr. Lord's blows had done.

"Tell him what he must do," said Ben, sternly.

"I want him to go to work and wash the tumblers and fix up the things in that green box, so we can commence to sell as soon as we get into town," snarled Mr. Lord, as he motioned toward a large green chest that had been taken out of one of the carts, and which Toby saw was filled with dirty glasses, spoons, knives, and other utensils such as were necessary to carry on the business.

Toby got a pail of water from the brook, hunted around and found towels and soap, and devoted himself to his work with such industry that Mr. Lord could not repress a grunt of satisfaction as he passed him, however angry he felt because he could not administer the whipping which would have smoothed his ruffled temper.

By the time the procession was ready to start for the town, Toby had as much of his work done as he could find that it was necessary to do, and his master, in his surly way, half acknowledged that this last boy of his was better than any he had had before.

Although Toby had done his work so well, he was far from feeling happy. He was both angry and sad as he thought of the cruel blows that had been inflicted, and he had plenty of leisure to repent of the rash step he had taken, although he could not see very clearly how he was to get away from it. He thought that he could not go back to Guilford, for Uncle Daniel would not allow him to come to his house again, and the hot, scalding tears ran down his cheeks as he realized that he was homeless and friendless in this great, big world.

It was while he was in this frame of mind that the procession, all gaudy with flags, streamers, and banners, entered the town. Under different circumstances this would have been a most delightful day for him, for the entrance of a circus into Guilford had always been a source of one day's solid enjoyment; but now he was the most disconsolate and unhappy boy in all that crowd.

He did not ride throughout the entire route of the procession, for Mr. Lord was anxious to begin business, and the moment the tenting ground was reached, the wagon containing Mr. Lord's goods was driven into the enclosure, and Toby's day's work began.

He was obliged to bring water, to cup up the lemons, fetch and carry fruit from the booth in the big tent to the booth on the outside, until he was ready to drop with fatigue, and having had no time for breakfast, was nearly famished.

It was quite noon before he was permitted to go to the hotel for something to eat, and then Ben's advice to be one of the first to get to the tables was not needed.

In the eating line that day he astonished the servants, the members of the company, and even himself, and by the time he arose from the table, with both pockets and his stomach full to bursting, the tables had been set and cleared away twice while he was making one meal.

"Well, I guess you didn't hurry yourself much," said Mr. Lord, when Toby returned to the circus ground.

"Oh, yes, I did," was Toby's innocent reply, "I ate just as fast as I could," and a satisfied smile stole over the boy's face as he thought of the amount of solid food which he had consumed.

The answer was not one which was calculated to make Mr. Lord feel any more agreeably disposed toward his new clerk, and he showed his ill-temper very plainly as he said, "It must take a good deal to satisfy you."

"I s'pose it does," calmly replied Toby. "Sam Merrill used to say that I took after Aunt Olive and Uncle Dan'l. One ate a good while, an' the other ate awful fast."

Toby could not understand what it was that Mr. Lord said in reply, but he could understand that his employer was angry at somebody or something, and he tried unusually hard to please him. He talked to the boys who had gathered around, to induce them to buy, washed the glasses as fast as they were used, tried to keep off the flies, and in every way he could think of endeavored to please his master.

O O O

The Counterfeit Ten-Cent Piece

When the doors of the big tent were opened and the people began to crowd in, just as Toby had seen them do at Guilford, Mr. Lord announced to his young clerk that it was time for him to go into the tent to work. Then it was that Toby learned for the first time that he had two masters instead of one, and this knowledge caused him no little uneasiness. If the other one was anything like Mr. Lord, his lot would be just twice as bad, and he began to wonder whether he could even stand it one day longer.

As the boy passed through the tent on his way to the candy stand, where he was really to enter upon the duties for which he had run away from home, he wanted to stop for a moment and speak with the old monkey who he thought had taken such an interest in him. But when he reached the cage in which his friend was confined, there was such a crowd around it that it was impossible for him to get near enough to speak without being overheard.

This was such a disappointment to the little fellow that the big tears came into his eyes, and in another instant would have gone rolling down his cheeks if his aged friend had not chanced to look toward him. Toby fancied that the monkey looked at him in the most friendly way, and then he was certain that he winked one eye. Toby felt that there was no mistake about that wink, and it seemed as if it was intended to convey comfort to him in his troubles. He winked back at the monkey in the most emphatic and grave manner possible and then went on his way, feeling wonderfully comforted.

The work inside the tent was far different and much harder than it was outside. He was obliged to carry around among the audience trays of candy, nuts, and lemonade for sale, and he was also expected to cry aloud the description of that which he offered. The partner of Mr. Lord, who had charge of the stand inside the tent, showed himself to be neither better nor worse than Mr. Lord himself. When Toby first presented himself for work, he handed him a tray filled with glasses of lemonade and told him to go among the audience, crying, "Here's your nice, cold lemonade, only five cents a glass!"

Toby started to do as he was bidden; but when he tried to repeat the words in anything like a loud tone of voice, they stuck in his throat, and he found it next to impossible to utter a sound above a whisper. It seemed to him that everyone in the audience was looking only at him, and the very sound of his own voice made him afraid.

He went entirely around the tent once without making a sale, and when he returned to the stand, he was at once convinced that one of his masters was quite as bad as the other. This one—and he knew that his name was Jacobs, for he heard someone call him so— very kindly told him that he would break every bone in his body if he didn't sell something, and Toby confidently believed that he would carry out his threat.

It was with a heavy heart that he started around again in obedience to Mr. Jacob's angry command; but this time he did manage to cry out, in a very thin and very squeaky voice, the words which he had been told to repeat.

This time, perhaps owing to his pitiful and imploring look, certainly not because of the noise he made, he met with very good luck, and sold every glass of the mixture which Messrs. Lord and Jacobs called lemonade and went back to the stand for more.

He certainly thought he had earned a word of praise and fully expected it as he put the empty glasses and money on the stand in front of Mr. Jacobs. But, instead of the kind words, he was greeted with a volley of curses; and the reason for it was that he had taken in payment for two of the glasses a lead ten-cent piece. Mr. Jacobs, after scolding poor little Toby to his heart's content, vowed that the amount should be kept from his first week's wages, and then handed back the coin, with orders to give it to the first man who gave him money to change, under the penalty of a severe flogging if he failed to do so.

Poor Toby tried to explain matters by saying, "You see, I don't know anything about money; I never had more'n a cent at a time, an' you mustn't expect me to get posted all at once."

"I'll post you with a stick if you do it again; an' it won't be well for you if you bring that ten-cent piece back here!"

Now Toby was very well aware that to pass the coin, knowing it to be bad, would be a crime, and he resolved to take the consequences of which Mr. Jacobs had intimated, if he could not find the one who had given him the counterfeit and persuade him to give him good money in its stead. He remembered very plainly where he had sold each glass of lemonade, and he retraced his steps, glancing at each face carefully as he passed. At last he was confident that he saw the man who had gotten him into such trouble, and he climbed up the board seats, saying, as he stood in front of him and held out the coin, "Mister, this money that you gave me is bad. Won't you give me another one for it?"

The man was a rough-looking party who had taken his girl to the circus, and who did not seem at all disposed to pay any heed to Toby's request. Therefore he repeated it, and this time more loudly.

"Get out of the way!" said the man, angrily. "How can you expect me to see the show if you stand right in front of me?"

"You'll like it better," said Toby, earnestly, "if you give me another ten-cent piece."

"Get out, an' don't bother me!" was the angry rejoinder, and the little fellow began to think that perhaps he would be obliged to "get out" without getting his money.

It was becoming a desperate case, for the man was growing angry very fast, and if Toby did not succeed in getting good money for the bad, he would have to take the consequences of which Mr. Jacobs had spoken.

"Please, mister," he said, imploringly, for his heart began to grow very heavy, and he was fearing that he should not succeed, "won't you please give me the money back? You know you gave it to me, an' I'll have to pay it if you don't."

The boy's lip was quivering, and those around began to be interested in the affair, while several in the immediate vicinity gave vent to their indignation that a man should try to cheat a boy out of ten cents by giving him counterfeit money.

The man whom Toby was speaking to was about to dismiss him with an angry reply, when he saw that those about him were not only interested in the matter but were evidently taking sides with the boy against him. And knowing well that he had given the counterfeit money, he took another coin from his pocket and, handing it to Toby, said, "I didn't give you the lead piece; but you're making such a fuss about it, that here's ten cents to make you keep quiet."

"I'm sure you did give me the money," said Toby, as he took the extended coin, "an' I'm much obliged to you for takin' it back. I didn't want to tell you before, 'cause you'd thought I was beggin'; but if you hadn't given me this, I 'xpect I'd have got an awful whippin', for Mr. Jacobs said he'd fix me if I didn't get the money for it."

The man looked sheepish enough as he put the bad money in his pocket, and Toby's innocently told story caused such a feeling in his behalf among those who sat near that he not only disposed of his entire stock then and there, but received from one gentleman twenty-five cents for himself. He was both proud and happy as he returned to Mr. Jacobs with empty glasses, and with the money to refund the amount of loss which would have been caused by the counterfeit.

But the worthy partner of Mr. Lord's candy business had no words of encouragement for the boy who was trying so hard to please.

"Let that make you keep your eyes open," he growled out sulkily, "an' if you get caught in that trap again, you won't be let off so easy."

Poor little Toby! His heart seemed ready to break, but his few hours' previous experience had taught him that there was but one thing to do and that was to work just as hard as possible, trusting to some good fortune to enable him to get out of the very disagreeable position in which he had voluntarily placed himself.

He took the basket of candy that Mr. Jacobs handed him and trudged around the circle of seats, selling far more because of the pitifulness of his face than because of the excellence of his goods; and even this worked to his disadvantage. Mr. Jacobs was keen enough to see why his little clerk sold so many goods, and each time that he returned to the stand he said something to him in an angry tone, which had the effect of deepening the shadow on the boy's face and at the same time increasing trade.

By the time the performance was over, Toby had in his pocket a dollar and twenty-five cents which had been given him for himself by some of the kind-hearted in the audience, and he kept his hand almost constantly upon it, for the money seemed to him like some kind friend who would help him out of his present difficulties.

After the audience had dispersed, Mr. Jacobs set Toby at work washing the glasses and clearing up generally, and then the boy started toward the other portion of the store—that watched over by Mr. Lord. Not a' person save the watchmen was in the tent, and as Toby went toward the door, he saw his friend, the monkey, sitting in one corner of the cage and apparently watching his every movement.

It was as if he had suddenly seen one of the boys from home, and Toby, uttering an exclamation of delight, ran up to the cage and put his hand through the wires.

The monkey, in the gravest possible manner, took one of the fingers in his paw, and Toby shook hands with him very earnestly.

"I was sorry that I couldn't speak to you when I went in this noon," said Toby, as if making an apology, "but, you see, there were so many around here to see you that I couldn't get the chance. Did you see me wink at you?"

The monkey made no reply, but he twisted his face into such a funny little grimace that Toby was quite as well satisfied as if he had spoken.

"I wonder if you hain't some relation to Steve Stubbs?" Toby continued, earnestly, "for you look just like him, only he didn't have quite so many whiskers. What I want to say was, that I'm awful sorry I run away. I used to think that Uncle Dan'l was bad enough, but he was just a perfect good Samarathon to what Mr. Lord an' Mr. Jacobs are. An' when Mr. Lord looks at me with that crooked eye of his, I feel it 'way down in my boots. Do you know"—and here Toby put his mouth nearer to the monkey's head and whispered—"I'd run away from this circus if I could get the chance; wouldn't you?"

Just at this point, as if in answer to the question, the monkey stood up on his hind feet and reached out his paw to the boy, who seemed to think this was his way of being more emphatic in saying, "Yes."

Toby took the paw in his hand, shook it again earnestly, and said as he released it, "I was pretty sure you felt just about the same way I did, Mr. Stubbs, when I passed you this noon. Look here"—and Toby took the money from his pocket which had been given him—"I got all that this afternoon, an' I'll try an' stick it out somehow till I get as much as ten dollars, an' then we'll run away some night, an' go 'way off as far as—as—as out West, an' we'll stay there too."

The monkey, probably tired with remaining in one position so long, started toward the top of the cage, chattering and screaming, joining the other monkeys, who had gathered in a little group in one of the swings.

"Now see here, Mr. Stubbs," said Toby, in alarm, "you mustn't go to telling everybody about it, or Mr. Lord will know, an' then we'll be dished, sure."

The monkey sat quietly in the swing, as if he felt reproved by what the boy had said; and Toby, considerably relieved by his silence, said, as he started toward the door, "That's right—mum's the word; you keep quiet, an' so will I, an' pretty soon we'll get away from the whole crowd."

All the monkeys chattered, and Toby, believing that everything which he had said had been understood by the animals, went out of the door to meet his other taskmaster.

○ ○ ○

A Tender-Hearted Skeleton

"Now, then, lazy bones," was Mr. Lord's warning cry as Toby came out of the tent, "if you've fooled away enough of your time, you can come here an' tend shop for me while I go to supper. You crammed yourself this noon, an' it'll teach you a good lesson to make you go without anything to eat tonight. It'll make you move round more lively in future."

Instead of becoming accustomed to such treatment as he was receiving from his employers, Toby's heart grew more tender with each brutal word, and this last punishment—that of losing his supper— caused the poor boy more sorrow than blows would. Mr. Lord started for the hotel as he concluded his cruel speech, and poor little Toby, going behind the counter, leaned his head upon the rough boards and cried as if his heart would break.

All the fancied brightness and pleasure of a circus life had vanished, and in its place was the bitterness of remorse that he had repaid Uncle Daniel's kindness by the ingratitude of running away. Toby thought that if he could only nestle his little red head on the pillows of his little bed in that rough room at Uncle Daniel's, he would be the happiest and best boy in the future, in all the great, wide world.

While he was still sobbing away at a most furious rate, he heard a voice close at his elbow and, looking up, saw the thinnest man he had ever seen in all his life. The man had flesh-colored tights on, and a spangled red velvet garment that was neither pants, because there were no legs to it, nor a coat, because it did not come above his waist, made up the remainder of his costume. Because he was so wonderfully thin, because of the costume which he wore, and because of a highly colored painting which was hanging in front of one of the small tents, Toby knew that the Living Skeleton was before him, and his big, brown eyes opened all the wider as he gazed at him.

"What is the matter, little fellow?" asked the man in a kindly tone. "What makes you cry so? Has Job been up to his old tricks again?"

"I don't know what his old tricks are," and Toby sobbed, the tears coming again because of the sympathy which this man's voice expressed for him, "but I know that he's a mean, ugly thing—that's what I know. An' if I could only get back to Uncle Dan'l, there hain't elephants enough in all the circuses in the world to pull me away again."

"Oh, you run away from home, did you?"

"Yes, I did," sobbed Toby, "an' there hain't any boy in any Sunday-school book that ever I read that was half so sorry he'd been bad as I am. It's awful, an' now I can't have any supper, 'cause I stopped to talk with Mr. Stubbs."

"Is Mr. Stubbs one of your friends?" asked the skeleton as he seated himself in Mr. Lord's own private chair.

"Yes, he is, an' he's the only one in this whole circus who 'pears to be sorry for me. You'd better not let Mr. Lord see you sittin' in that chair or he'll raise a row."

"Job won't raise any row with me," said the skeleton. "But who is this Mr. Stubbs? I don't seem to know anybody by that name."

"I don't think that is his name. I only call him so, 'cause he looks so much like a feller I know who is named Stubbs."

This satisfied the skeleton that this Mr. Stubbs must be someone attached to the show, and he asked:

"Has Job been whipping you?"

"No; Ben, the driver on the wagon where I ride, told him not to do that again; but he hain't going to let me have any supper, 'cause I was so slow about my work—though I wasn't slow. I only talked to Mr. Stubbs when there wasn't anybody round his cage."

"Sam! Sam! Sam-u-el!"

This name, which was shouted twice in a quick, loud voice and the third time in a slow manner, ending almost in a screech, did not come from either Toby or the skeleton, but from an enormously large woman, dressed in a gaudy red-and-black dress, cut very short and with low neck and an apology for sleeves, who had just come out from the tent whereon the picture of the Living Skeleton hung.

"Samuel," she screamed again, "come inside this minute, or you'll catch your death o' cold, an' I shall have you wheezin' around with the phthisic all night. Come in, Sam-u-el."

"That's her," said the skeleton to Toby, as he pointed his thumb in the direction of the fat woman, but paying no attention to the outcry she was making, "that's my wife, Lilly, an' she's the Fat Woman of the show. She's always yellin' after me that way the minute I get out for a little fresh air, an' she's always sayin' just the same thing. Bless you, I never have the phthisic, but she does awful. An' I s'pose 'cause she's so large she can't feel all over her, an' thinks it's me that has it."

"Is—is all that—is that your wife?" stammered Toby, in astonishment, as he looked at the enormously fat woman who stood in the tent door and then at the wonderfully thin man who sat beside him.

"Yes, that's her," said the skeleton. "She weighs pretty nigh four hundred, though of course the show card says it's over six hundred, an' she earns almost as much money as I do. Of course she can't get so much, for skeletons is much scarcer than fat folks; but we make a pretty good thing travelin' together."

"Sam-u-el!" again came the cry from the fat woman, "are you never coming in?"

"Not yet, my angel," said the skeleton, placidly, as he crossed one thin leg over the other and looked calmly at her. "Come here an' see Job's new boy."

"Your imprudence is wearin' me away so that I sha'n't be worth five dollars a week to any circus," she said, impatiently, at the same time coming toward the candy stand quite as rapidly as her very great size would admit.

"This is my wife Lilly—Mrs. Treat," said the skeleton, with a proud wave of his hand, as he rose from his seat and gazed admiringly at her. "This is my flower—my queen, Mr.—Mr.—"

"Tyler," said Toby, supplying the name which the skeleton—or Mr. Treat, as Toby now learned his name was—did not know, "Tyler is my name—Toby Tyler."

"Why, what a little chap you are!" said Mrs. Treat, paying no attention to the awkward little bend of the head which Toby intended for a bow. "How small he is, Samuel!"

"Yes," said the skeleton, reflectively, as he looked Toby over from head to foot, as if he were mentally trying to calculate exactly how many inches high he was, "he is small; but he's got all the world before him to grow in, an' if he only eats enough— There, that reminds me. Job isn't going to give him any supper, because he didn't work hard enough."

"He won't, won't he?" exclaimed the large lady, savagely. "Oh, he's a precious one, he is. An' some day I shall just give him a good shakin'-up, that's what I'll do. I get all out of patience with that man's ugliness."

"An' she'll do just what she says," said the skeleton to Toby, with an admiring shake of the head. "That woman hain't afraid of anybody, an' I wouldn't be a bit surprised if she did give Job a pretty rough time."

Toby thought, as he looked at her, that she was large enough to give 'most anyone a pretty rough time, but he did not venture to say so. While he was looking first at her and then at her very thin husband, the skeleton told his wife the little that he had learned regarding the boy's history; and when he had concluded, she waddled away toward her tent.

"Great woman that," said the skeleton, as he saw her disappear within the tent.

"Yes," said Toby, "she's the greatest I ever saw."

"I mean that she's got a great head. Now you'll see about how much she cares for what Job says."

"If I was as big as her," said Toby, with just a shade of envy in his voice, "I wouldn't be afraid of anybody."

"It hain't so much the size," said the skeleton, sagely, "it hain't so much the size, my boy; for I can scare that woman almost to death when I feel like it."

Toby looked for a moment at Mr. Treat's thin legs and arms and then he said, warningly, "I wouldn't feel like it very often if I was you, Mr. Treat, 'cause she might break some of your bones if you didn't happen to scare her enough."

"Don't fear for me, my boy—don't fear for me. You'll see how I manage her if you stay with the circus long enough. Now, I often—"

If Mr. Treat was about to confide a family secret to Toby, it was fated that he should not hear it then, for Mrs. Treat had just come out of her tent, carrying in her hands a large tin plate piled high with a miscellaneous assortment of pie, cake, bread, and meat.

She placed this in front of Toby, and as she did so, she handed him two pictures.

"There, little Toby Tyler," she said, "there's something for you to eat, if Mr. Job Lord and his precious partner Jacobs did say you shouldn't have any supper; an' I've brought you a picture of Samuel an' me. We sell 'em for ten cents apiece, but I'm going to give them to you, because I like the looks of you."

Toby was quite overcome with the presents and seemed at a loss how to thank her for them. He attempted to speak but could not get the words out at first. Then he said, as he put the two photographs in the same pocket with his money, "You're awful good to me, an' when I get to be a man, I'll give you lots of things. I wasn't so very hungry, if I am such a big eater, but I did want something."

"Bless your dear little heart, and you *shall* have something to eat," said the Fat Woman, as she seized Toby, squeezed him close up to her, and kissed his freckled face as kindly as if it had been as fair and white as possible. "You shall eat all you want to; an' if you get the stomachache, as Samuel does sometimes when he's been eatin' too much, I'll give you some catnip tea out of the same dipper that I give him his. He's a great eater, Samuel is," she added, in a burst of confidence, "an' it's a wonder to me what he does with it all sometimes."

"Is he?" exclaimed Toby, quickly. "How funny that is, for I'm an awful eater. Why, Uncle Dan'l used to say that I ate twice as much as I ought to, an' it never made me any bigger. I wonder what's the reason?"

"I declare I don't know," said the Fat Woman, thoughtfully, "an' I've wondered at it time an' time again. Some folks is made that way, an' some folks is made different. Now, I don't eat enough to keep a chicken alive, an' yet I grow fatter an' fatter every day. Don't I, Samuel?"

"Indeed you do, my love," said the skeleton, with a world of pride in his voice, "but you mustn't feel bad about it, for every pound you gain, makes you worth just so much more to the show."

"Oh, I wasn't worryin', I was only wonderin'. But we must go, Samuel, for the poor child won't eat a bit while we are here. After you've eaten what there is there, bring the plate in to me," she said to Toby, as she took her lean husband by the arm and walked him off toward their own tent.

Toby gazed after them a moment, and then he commenced a vigorous attack upon the eatables which had been so kindly given him.

Of the food which he had taken from the dinner table he had eaten some while he was in the tent, and after that he had entirely forgotten that he had any in his pocket; therefore, at the time that Mrs. Treat had brought him such a liberal supply he was really very hungry.

He succeeded in eating nearly all the food which had been brought to him, and the very small quantity which remained he readily found room for in his pockets. Then he washed the plate nicely, and seeing no one in sight, he thought he could leave the booth long enough to return the plate.

He ran with it quickly into the tent occupied by the thin man and fat woman and handed it to her, with a profusion of thanks for her kindness.

"Did you eat it all?" she asked.

"Well," hesitated Toby, "there was three doughnuts an' a piece of pie left over, an' I put them in my pocket. If you don't care, I'll eat them some time tonight."

"You shall eat it whenever you want to, an' any time that you get hungry again, you come right to me."

"Thank you, ma'am. I must go now, for I left the store all alone."

"Run, then; an' if Job Lord abuses you, just let me know it, an' I'll keep him from cuttin' up any monkey shines."

Toby hardly heard the end of her sentence, so great was his haste to get back to the booth. And just as he emerged from the tent on a quick run, he received a blow on the ear which sent him sprawling in the dust, and he heard Mr. Job Lord's angry voice as it said, "So, just the moment my back is turned, you leave the stand to take care of itself, do you, an' run around tryin' to plot some mischief against me, eh?" And the brute kicked the prostrate boy twice with his heavy boot.

"Please don't kick me again!" pleaded Toby. "I wasn't gone but a minute, an' I wasn't doing anything bad."

"You're lying now, an' you know it, you young cub!" exclaimed the angry man as he advanced to kick the boy again. "I'll let you know who you've got to deal with when you get hold of me!"

"And I'll let you know who you've got to deal with when you get hold of me!" said a woman's voice, and, just as Mr. Lord raised his foot to kick the boy again, the Fat Woman seized him by the collar, jerked him back over one of the tent ropes, and left him quite as prostrate as he had left Toby. "Now, Job Lord," said the angry woman, as she towered above the thoroughly enraged but thoroughly frightened man, "I want you to understand that you can't knock and beat this boy while I'm around. I've seen enough of your capers, an' I'm going to put a stop to them. That boy wasn't in this tent more than two minutes, an' he attends to his work better than anyone you have ever had, so see that you treat him decent. Get up," she said to Toby, who had not dared to rise from the ground, "and if he offers to strike you again, come to me."

Toby scrambled to his feet and ran to the booth in time to attend to one or two customers who had just come up. He could see from out the corner of his eye that Mr. Lord had arisen to his feet also and was engaged in an angry conversation with Mrs. Treat, the result of which he very much feared would be another and a worse whipping for him.

But in this he was mistaken, for Mr. Lord, after the conversation was ended, came toward the booth and began to attend to his business without speaking one word to Toby. When Mr. Jacobs returned from his supper, Mr. Lord took him by the arm and walked him out toward the rear of the tents; and Toby was very positive that he was to be the subject of their conversation, which made him not a little uneasy.

It was not until nearly time for the performance to begin that Mr. Lord returned and he had nothing to say to Toby, save to tell him to go into the tent and begin his work there. The boy was only too glad to escape so easily, and he went to his work with as much alacrity as if he were about entering upon some pleasure.

When he met Mr. Jacobs, that gentleman spoke to him very sharply about being late and seemed to think it no excuse at all that he had just been relieved from the outside work by Mr. Lord.

○ ○ ○

An Accident and Its Consequences

Toby's experience in the evening was very similar to that of the afternoon, save that he was so fortunate as not to take any more bad

money in payment for his goods. Mr. Jacobs scolded and swore alter-
nately, and the boy really surprised him by his way of selling goods,
though he was very careful not to say anything about it, but made
Toby believe that he was doing only about half as much work as he
ought to do. Toby's private hoard of money was increased that
evening, by presents, ninety cents, and he began to look upon himself
as almost a rich man.

When the performance was nearly over, Mr. Jacobs called to
him to help in packing up; and by the time the last spectator had left
the tent, the worldly possessions of Messrs. Lord and Jacobs were ready
for removal, and Toby allowed to do as he had a mind to, as long as he
was careful to be on hand when Old Ben was ready to start.

Toby thought that he would have time to pay a visit to his
friends, the skeleton and the Fat Woman, and to that end started toward
the place where their tent had been standing. But to his sorrow he
found that it was already being taken down, and he had only time to
thank Mrs. Treat and to press the fleshless hand of her shadowy husband
as they entered their wagon to drive away.

He was disappointed, for he had hoped to be able to speak
with his new-made friends a few moments before the weary night's
ride commenced; but, failing in that, he went hastily back to the monkey's cage. Old Ben was there, getting things ready for a start, but the
wooden sides of the cage had not been put up and Toby had no difficulty in calling the aged monkey up to the bars. He held one of the
Fat Woman's doughnuts in his hand and said, as he passed it through to
the animal:

"I thought perhaps you might be hungry, Mr. Stubbs, and this
is some of what the skeleton's wife give me. I hain't got very much time
to talk with you now, but the first chance I can get away tomorrow, an'
when there hain't anybody 'round, I want to tell you something."

The monkey had taken the doughnut in his hand-like paws
and was tearing it to pieces, eating small portions of it very rapidly.

"Don't hurry yourself," said Toby, warningly, "for Uncle Dan'l
always told me the worst thing a feller could do was to eat fast. If you
want any more before we start, just put your hand through the little
hole up there near the seat, an' I'll give you all you want."

From the look on his face Toby confidently believed the monkey was about to make some reply, but just then Ben shut up the sides, separating Toby and Mr. Stubbs, and the order was given to start.

Toby clambered up on to the high seat, Ben followed him, and in another instant the team was moving along slowly down the dusty road, preceded and followed by the many wagons, with their tiny, swinging lights.

"Well," said Ben, when he had got his team well under way and felt that he could indulge in a little conversation, "how did you get along today?"

Toby related all of his movements and gave the driver a faithful account of all that had happened to him, concluding his story by saying, "That was one of Mrs. Treat's doughnuts that I just gave to Mr. Stubbs."

"To whom?" asked Ben, in surprise.

"To Mr. Stubbs—the old fellow here in the cart, you know, that's been so good to me."

Toby heard a sort of gurgling sound, saw the driver's body sway back and forth in a trembling way, and was just becoming thoroughly alarmed, when he thought of the previous night and understood that Ben was only laughing in his own peculiar way.

"How did you know his name was Stubbs?" asked Ben, after he had recovered his breath.

"Oh, I don't know that that is his real name," was the quick reply, "I only call him that because he looks so much like a feller with that name that I knew at home. He don't seem to mind because I call him Stubbs."

Ben looked at Toby earnestly for a moment, acting all the time as if he wanted to laugh again, but didn't dare to, for fear he might burst a blood vessel; and then he said, as he patted him on the shoulder, "Well, you are the queerest little fish that I ever saw in all my travels. You seem to think that that monkey knows all you say to him."

"I'm sure he does," said Toby, positively. "He don't say anything right out to me, but he knows everything I tell him. Do you suppose he could talk if he tried to?"

"Look here, Mr. Toby Tyler," and Ben turned half around in his seat and looked Toby full in the face, so as to give more emphasis to his words, "are you heathen enough to think that that monkey could talk if he wanted to?"

"I know I hain't a heathen," said Toby, thoughtfully, "for if I had been some of the missionaries would have found me out a good while ago; but I never saw anybody like this old Mr. Stubbs before, an' I thought he could talk if he wanted to, just as the Living Skeleton does, or his wife. Anyhow, Mr. Stubbs winks at me; an' how could he do that if he didn't know what I've been sayin' to him?"

"Look here, my son," said Ben, in a most fatherly fashion, "monkey's hain't anything but beasts, an' they don't know how to talk any more than they know what you say to 'em."

"Didn't you ever hear any of them speak a word?"

"Never. I've been in a circus, man an' boy, nigh on to forty years, an' I never seen nothin' in a monkey more'n any other beast, except their awful mischiefness."

"Well," said Toby, still unconvinced, "I believe Mr. Stubbs knows what I say to him, anyway."

"Now don't be foolish, Toby," pleaded Ben. "You can't show me one thing that a monkey ever did because you told him to."

Just at that moment, Toby felt someone pulling at the back of his coat and, looking round, he saw that it was a little brown hand reaching through the bars of the air hole of the cage, that was tugging away at his coat.

"There!" he said, triumphantly, to Ben. "Look there! I told Mr. Stubbs if he wanted anything more to eat, to tell me, an' I would give it to him. Now you can see for yourself that he's come for it." And Toby took a doughnut from his pocket and put it into the tiny hand, which was immediately withdrawn. "Now what do you think of Mr. Stubbs knowing what I say to him?"

"They often stick their paws up through there," said Ben, in a matter-of-fact tone. "I've had 'em pull my coat in the night till they made me as nervous as ever any old woman was. You see, Toby, my boy, monkeys is monkeys; an' you mustn't go to gettin' the idea that they're anything else, for it's a mistake. You think this old monkey in here knows what you say? Why, that's just the cuteness of the old fellow. He watches you to see if he can't do just as you do, an' that's all there is about it."

Toby was more than half convinced that Ben was putting the matter in its proper light, and he would have believed all that had been said if, just at that moment, he had not seen that brown hand reaching through the hole to clutch him again by the coat.

The action seemed so natural, so like a hungry boy who gropes in the dark pantry for something to eat, that it would have taken more arguments than Ben had at his disposal to persuade Toby that his Mr. Stubbs could not understand all that was said to him. Toby put another doughnut in the outstretched hand and then sat silently, as if in a brown study over some difficult problem.

For some time the ride was continued in silence. Ben was going through all the motions of whistling without uttering a sound—a favorite amusement of his—and Toby's thoughts were far away in the humble home he had scorned, with Uncle Daniel, whose virtues had increased in his esteem with every mile of distance which had been put between them, and whose faults had decreased in a corresponding ratio.

Toby's thoughtfulness had made him sleepy, and his eyes were almost closed in slumber, when he was startled by a crashing sound, was conscious of a feeling of being hurled from his seat by some great force, and then he lay senseless by the side of the road, while the wagon became a perfect wreck, from out of which a small army of monkeys was escaping. Ben's experienced ear had told him at the first crash that his wagon was breaking down, and, without having time to warn Toby of his peril, he had leaped clear of the wreck, keeping his horses under perfect control, and thus averting more trouble. It was the breaking of one of the axles which Toby had heard just before he was thrown from his seat and when the body of the wagon came down upon the hard road.

The monkeys, thus suddenly released from confinement, had scampered off in every direction, and by a singular chance, Toby's aged friend started for the woods in such a direction as to bring him directly before the boy's insensible form. The monkey, on coming up to Toby, stopped, urged by the well-known curiosity of its race, and began to examine the boy's person carefully, prying into pockets and trying to open the boy's half-closed eyelids. Fortunately for Toby, he had fallen upon a mud bank and was only stunned for the moment, having received no serious bruises. The attentions bestowed upon him by the monkey served the purpose of bringing him to his senses; and, after he had looked around him in the gray light of the coming morning, it would have taken far more of a philosopher than Old Ben was to persuade the boy that monkeys did not possess reasoning faculties.

The monkey was busy at Toby's ears, nose, and mouth, as monkeys will do when they get an opportunity, and the expression of its face was as grave as possible. Toby firmly believed that the monkey's face showed sorrow at his fall, and he imagined that the attentions which were bestowed upon him were for the purpose of learning whether he had been injured or not.

"Don't worry, Mr. Stubbs," said Toby, anxious to reassure his friend, as he sat upright and looked about him. "I didn't get hurt any; but I would like to know how I got 'way over here."

It really seemed as if the monkey was pleased to know that his little friend was not hurt, for he seated himself on his haunches, and his face expressed the liveliest pleasure that Toby was well again—or at least that was how the boy interpreted the look.

By this time the news of the accident had been shouted ahead from one team to the other, and all hands were hurrying to the scene for the purpose of rendering aid. As Toby saw them coming, he also saw a number of small forms, looking something like diminutive men, hurrying past him, and for the first time he understood how it was that the aged monkey was at liberty, and knew that those little dusky forms were the other occupants of the cage escaping to the woods.

"See there, Mr. Stubbs! See there!" he exclaimed, pointing toward the fugitives, "they're all going off into the woods! What shall we do?"

The sight of the runaways seemed to excite the old monkey quite as much as it did the boy. He sprang to his feet, chattering in the most excited way, screamed two or three times, as if he were calling them back, and then started off in vigorous pursuit.

"Now he's gone, too!" said Toby, disconsolately, believing that the old fellow had run away from him. "I didn't think Mr. Stubbs would treat me this way!"

Peck's Bad Boy with the Circus

BY HON. GEORGE W. PECK

The first time I was ever in Milwaukee was thirty years ago and I was with the circus, and it rained. We fairly drowned in the mud. The next time I was to visit, I was also with the circus, and it rained also. The mud, even under the big top was heroic, epic, biblical. I'm sorry, but for me, Milwaukee means mud. And I haven't been back. It's odd how personally I still take it.

Now, George W. Peck is well known as a son of Milwaukee, though he was born in New York, in 1840. Three years later his family moved west to Wisconsin. George took early to newspapering, working for various rags in Whitewater, Jefferson, La Crosse, and Milwaukee. In 1874 he put together a small paper in La Crosse and named it "The Sun." In a short time he moved the paper to Milwaukee, and renamed it "Peck's Sun." (I suppose to distinguish it from somebody else's Sun.) It was then his rise truly began. He became a very popular mayor of his city, and later Governor of Wisconsin. His writings made him famous throughout the country, especially popular were the dozens and dozens of Bad Boy tales; eventually collected in books like "Peck's Bad Boy with the Cowboys" "Peck's Compendium of Fun," "Peck's Sunshine," and "Peck's Bad Boy with the Circus."

Though we think of them as boy's books, these sketches and stories are really, like the circus, for children of all ages; and "Peck's Bad Boy with the Circus," here excerpted, is about the most fun you can have reading.

I find it amusing that when the Bad Boy and his Pa join up with the circus, it is already mid-April and the show has yet to go out.

By my lights, this is a little late in the season to still linger in winter quarters. But then I suppose the roads would need to be dry, or paved, in order for the show to travel, and perhaps in Milwaukee . . .

○ ○ ○

April 10, 19. .—I never thought it would come to this, that I should keep a diary, because I am not a good little boy. Nobody ever keeps a diary except a boy that wants to be an angel, and with the angels stand, or a girl that is in love, or an old maid that can't catch a man unless she writes down her emotions and leaves them around so some man will read them, and swallow the bait and not feel the hook in his gills, or a truly good bank cashier who teaches Sunday school, and skips out for Canada some Saturday night, after the bank closes, and on Monday morning they find the combination of the lock on the safe changed, and when they hire a reformed burglar to open the lock the money is all gone with the cashier. Those are the only people that ever kept a successful diary.

But I had to promise ma that I would keep a diary, so she could read it, or I never could have got her consent for me to go with pa on the road with a circus. All ma asks of me is to tell the truth about everything that happens to me and to pa during the whole summer, and I have consented, and I can see my finish, and pa's finish and ma's finish, and the finish of the circus that is going to take us along.

Gee, but we have had a hot time at our house since pa and I got back from our trip abroad. I brought pa back in better health than he was when he went away, but he has got so accustomed to excitement that I knew something would be doing pretty soon, so I was not surprised when he told us at the breakfast table that he supposed he should have to go and travel with a circus this summer.

Ma looked at pa as though she wanted to call the police and an ambulance to take him to the emergency hospital. He looked at ma and at me, speared another waffle, and said: "I know you will think I am nutty, but for almost ten years I have had a block of stock in a circus and menagerie. I went into it to help some young circus fellows, and put up quite a bunch of money, because they were honest and poor, and for a few years things went wrong, and I thought my money was gone, but for the last six years the circus has paid dividends bigger than Standard Oil, and today it stands away up among the financial successes, and the dividends on my circus stock is better than any bank stock I have got, and it comes just like finding money. The company decided at its annual meeting to invite me to take the position of one of the managers, and I shall soon go to the winter quarters of the show, to arrange to put it on the road about the 1st of May. Now any remarks may be made, pro or con, in regard to my sanity, see?"

Well, ma swallowed something crosswise down her Sunday throat, and choked, and pa swatted her on the back so she would cough it up, and when she could speak she said: "Pa, do you have to wear tights, and jump through hoops on the back of a horse, and cut up didoes, at your time of life? For if you do I can never live to witness any such performances."

Pa was calm, and did not fly off the handle, but he just said, kindly: "Mother, you have vague ideas of the duties of the owners of a circus. The owners hire performers to do stunts, and break their necks, while we manage them and take in the shekels from the Reubens who come into town on circus day. We proprietors touch the button, and the actors and animals do the rest. I shall be a director who directs, a man who sets a dignified and pious example to the men and women who adorn the profession, coming as they do from all climes, and your pa will be the guide, philosopher and friend of all who belong to the grandest aggregation of talent ever gathered under one canvas, at one price of admission, and do not fail to witness the concert which will be given under this canvas after the main performance is over."

Ma looked at pa pretty savage, and said: "O, I see, you are going to be ringmaster, but what is to become of Hennery and me while you are cracking your whip around the hind legs of the fat woman, and ogling the Circassian beauty?"

Pa put his hand on my head and said: "Mother, Hennery will go with me, to see that I do not get into any trouble as a circus financier and general manager of the menagerie and Wild West aggregation, and hippodrome, in the great three-ring circus, and you can stay home and give us absent treatment for what ails us, and pack the money I shall send you in bales with a hay press, and put it in cold storage till we come back in the fall. It is settled, we go to conquer, and the world will lay at our feet before the middle of August, and you will be a proud woman to own a husband who will be pointed at as the most successful amusement purveyor the world has ever witnessed, and a son who will start in at the bottom round of the circus ladder and rise, step by step, until he will stand beside the great Barnum."

Ma thought seriously for a few minutes, and then she said: "O, pa, if it was anything but the circus business you and Hennery went into, like selling soap or being a bank defaulter, or something re-spectable, I could look the neighbors in the face, but of course if there is money in it, and you feel that the good Lord has called you to the circus field, and you will see that Hennery does not stay out nights, and Hennery will promise to see that you put on a clean collar occasionally, and you will promise me that you will not let any of those circus women in spangles make eyes at you, I will consent to your going with the circus, just this once, as the doctor has advised that you lead an ac-tive life, and I guess you will get it traveling with a circus, for it nearly killed me that time I took Hennery to see the animals, and the tent blew down, and we got separated and the sacred cow chased ma up the church steps, and Hennery and a monkey were brought home by a po-liceman about daylight the next morning, that time you were off fish-ing, and I never told you about going to the circus when you were away. So we are circus proprietors, are we? Well, it ain't so bad," and ma went upstairs to cry at our success, and pa and I went out to walk off the effects of the breaking the news to ma.

I had a long talk with pa about our changed circumstances, and asked him what I would be expected to do in the show, and he says I will fit in anywhere. He says that a boy who knows as much about everything as I think I know, but don't know a blamed thing about, will be invaluable about a show, and that going into a new business is like going to college as a freshman, as all the old circus men will haze us, and we must not expect an easy life, but one full of ex-citement, sleepless nights, ginger, the glare of the torchlights, the races, the flying trapeze, the smell of the sawdust and tanbark, the howling of the wild beasts, and the plaudits of the multitude of jays and jayesses, and it will be like one grand circus day spread all over the summer and fall. He says he wants me to learn the circus business from the ground up, from the currying of the hyenas with a curry-comb and brush, to going up into the roof of the tent on the trapeze and falling into the net, while the audience faints with excitement. I asked pa if he wanted me to keep on playing tricks on him while we were on the road, and he said he had got so used to my tricks that he couldn't live without them, and he didn't want me to let a chance escape to make him have a good time.

April 11.—Ma and pa have had several discussions about what kind of a position it is going to leave her in, among the neighbors, for pa and I to go off with a circus, and ma wanted to withdraw from the church, and board up the windows of the house, and make folks think we had gone to the seashore, but pa convinced her that we would have preaching in the main tent every Sunday, and he says there is no more pious lot of people on earth than those who travel with a circus, and then ma wanted to go along. She said she could do the mending of the long socks that the women wear when they ride barebacked, but we had to shut down on ma's going with the show, cause we never could have any fun with a woman to look after. Pa says nowadays the men and women who ride on bareback horses in the ring dress in regular evening costume, the women with low-necked dresses and long trains, and the men with swallow-tail coats and patent leather shoes, and they are as polite as dancing masters.

We have compromised with ma, and she is to meet the show at Kalamazoo and go with us to Kankakee and Keokuk until she is over-come by nervous prostration, when we shall have her go home. Pa thinks ma would last about two days with the show, but I guess if she took a course of treatment with peanuts and red lemonade one after-noon and evening, she would want to throw up her job, and go back home in charge of a stomach specialist.

Well, pa showed up at the house in his circus clothes this after-noon, and he certainly is a peach. Pa has been letting his chin whiskers grow for about six weeks, and today he had them colored black, and he looks as though he had swallowed the blacking brush, and left the bunch of bristles outside, on his chin. He looks fierce. Then, he has got a new brand of silk hat, with a wide, curling brim, and he has had a vest made of black and blue check goods, the checks as big as the checks on a checker board, and a pair of pants that look like a diamond-back rattlesnake, and he has got an imitation diamond stud in his white shirt that looks like a paper weight.

Ma wanted to know if there was any law to compel pa to dress like that, 'cause he looked as though he was a gambler or a train robber. Pa says that a circus proprietor has got to look different from anybody else, in order to inspire fear and respect on the part of the hands around the show, as well as the audiences that flock to the arena, and he asked ma if she didn't remember old Dan Rice, and old John Robinson. Ma didn't remember them, but she remembered Barnum, because Barnum lectured on temperance, and she said she hoped pa would emulate Barnum's example, and pa said he would, and then he took a watch chain with links as big as a trace chain and spread it across his checkered vest, from one pocket to the other, with a life-size gold elk hanging down the middle, and ma almost had a convulsion.

Gee, but if pa wears that rig in the menagerie tent the animals will paw and bellow like a drove of cattle that smell blood. Pa is going to wear a sack coat with his outfit, so as to look tough, and he wouldn't hear to ma when she tried to get him to wear a frock coat. He said a frock coat was all right in society or among the crowned heads, but when you have to mingle with lions and elephants one minute that would snatch the tail off a coat and chew it and the next minute you are mixed up with a bunch of freaks or a lot of bareback riders or trapeze performers, you have got to compromise on a coat that will fit any climate, and not cause invidious remarks, whatever that is.

I will have to stand up beside the giant once in a while to show the difference in the size of men, and at other times I will have to stand beside the midgets and look like a giant myself. We are all packed up, and in two days we start for the winter quarters of the show, to pound it into shape for the road. By ginger, I can't hardly wait to get there and see pa boss things.

April 15.—We are now at the winter quarters of the show, in a little town, on a farm just outside, where the tent is put up and the animals are being cared for in barns, and the performers are limbering up their joints, wearing overcoats to turn flip-flaps, and everybody has a cold, and looks blue, and all are anxious for warm weather.

Pa created a sensation when we arrived by his stunning clothes, his jet black chin whiskers and his watch chain over his checkered vest, and when the proprietors introduced pa to the performers and hands, as an old stockholder in the show, who would act as assistant manager during the season and pa smiled on them with a frown on his forehead, and said he hoped his relations with them would be pleasant, one of the old canvasmen remarked to a girl who rides two horses at once with the horses strapped together, so they can't get too far apart and cause her to break in two, said that old goat with the silk hat would last just about four weeks, and that he reminded the canvasman of a big dog which barked at people as though he would eat them, and at the same time wagged his tail, so people would not think he was so confounded dangerous.

The principal proprietor of the circus told pa to make himself at home around the tent, and not be offended at any pleasantry on the part of the attaches of the show, for they were full of fun, and he went off to attend to some business and left pa with the gang. They were practicing riding barebacked horses around the ring with a rope hitched in a belt around the waist of the rider and an arm swinging around from the center pole, so if they fell off the horse the rope would prevent the rider from falling to the ground, a practice that the best riders adopt early in the season, the same as new beginners, 'cause they are all stiffened up by being out of practice. One man rode around a few times, and pa got up close to the ring and was making some comments such as: "Why, any condemned fool could ride a horse that way," when the circus gang as quick as you could say scat, fastened a belt around pa's stomach, that had a ring in it, and before he knew it they had hitched a snap in the ring, and pa was hauled up as high as the horse, and his feet rested on the horse's back, and the horse started on a gallop.

Well, say, pa was never so surprised in his life, but he dug his heels into the horse's back, and tried to look pleasant, and the horse went halfway around the ring, and just as pa was getting confidence someone hit the horse on the ham with a piece of board, and the horse went out from under pa and he began to fall over backwards, and I thought his circus career would end right there, when the man who had hold of the rope pulled up, and pa was suspended in the air by the ring in the belt, back up, and stomach hanging down like a pillow, his watch dangling about a foot down toward the ring, and the horse came around the ring again and as he went under pa, pa tried to get his feet on the horse's back, but he couldn't make it work, and pa said, as cross as could be: "Lookahere, you fellers, you let me down, or I will discharge every mother's son of you."

But they didn't seem to be scared, for one man caught the horse and let it out of the ring, and the man who handled the rope tied it to the center pole by a half hitch, and the fellows all went into the dressing room to play cinch on the trunks, leaving pa hanging there. Just then the boss canvasman came along and he said: "Hello, old man, what you doing up there?" And pa said some of the pirates in the show had kidnaped him, and seemed to be holding him up for a ransom, and he said he would give ten dollars if someone would let him down.

The boss canvasman said he could fix it for ten, all right, and he blew a whistle, and the gang came back, and the boss said: "Bring a blanket and help this gentleman down"; so they brought a big piece of canvas, with handles all around it, and about a dozen fellows held it, and the rope man let pa down on the canvas, and unhitched the ring, and when pa was in the canvas he laughed and said: "Thanks, gentlemen, I guess I am not much of a horseback rider," and then the fellows pulled on the handles of the canvas, and by gosh, pa shot up into the air halfway to the top of the tent, and when he came down they caught him in the canvas and tossed him up a whole lot of times until pa said: "O, let up, and make it $20." Just then the proprietor who had introduced pa to the men came in and saw what was going on, and he said: "Here, you heathen, you quit this hazing right here," and they let pa down on the floor of the ring, and he got up and pulled his pants down, that had got up above his knees, and shook himself and took out his roll, and peeled off a $20 bill and gave it to the canvasman, and he shook hands with them all, and said he liked a joke as well as anybody, and for them to spend the money to have a good time, and they all laughed and patted pa on the back, and said he was a dead game sport, and would be an honor to the profession, and that now that he has taken the first degree as a circus man he could call on them for any sacrifice, or any work, and he would find that they would be Johnny on the spot.

Then he went out to the dining tent and took dinner with the crowd and had a jolly time. There was a woman trapeze performer on one side of pa at dinner, and she began to kick at once about the meals, and when the waiter brought a piece of meat to us all—a great big piece, that looked like corned beef, she said: "For heaven's sake, ain't that elephant that died all been eaten up yet?" and then she told pa that they had been fed on that deceased elephant, until they all felt like they had trunks growing out of their heads, and pa poked the meat with his fork, and thought it was elephant, and he lost his appetite, and everybody laughed. I eat some of it and if it was elephant it was all right.

Well, when dinner was about over, all filled their glasses to drink to the health of pa, the old stockholder and new manager, and pa got up and bowed, and made a little speech, and when he sat down one of the circus girls was in his chair, and he sat in her lap, and the crowd all yelled, except a Spanish bull-fighter, who seemed to be the husband of the woman pa sat on, and he wanted pa's blood, but the old circus manager took him away to save pa from trouble, and he glared back at pa, and I think he will stab pa with a dirk knife.

We got out of the dining tent, and went to the barn, where the animals are kept all winter, and pa wanted me to become familiar with the habits of the beasts, 'cause they were to be in pa's charge, with the keepers of the different kinds of animals to report to pa. Nobody need tell me that animals have no human instincts, and do not know how to take a joke. We are apt to think that wild animals in captivity are worrying over being confined in cages, and gazed at and commented on by curious visitors, and that they dream of the free life they lived in the jungles, and sigh to go back where they were captured, and prowl around for food, but you can't fool me. Animals that formerly had to go around in the woods, hungry half the time and occasionally gorging themselves on a dead animal and sleeping out in the rain in all kinds of weather, know when they have struck a good thing in a menagerie, with clean straw to sleep in, and when they are hungry all they have to do is to sound their bugle and they have pre-digested beefsteak and breakfast food brought to them on a silver platter, and if the food is not to their liking they set up a kick like a star boarder at a boarding house. Their condition in the show, in its changed condition from that of their native haunts, is like taking a hobo off the trucks of a freight train and taking him to the dining car of the limited, and letting him eat to a finish. People talk about animals escaping from captivity, and going back to the jungles and humane societies shed tears over the poor, sad-eyed captives, sighing for their homes, but you turn them loose at South Bend, and run your circus train to New Albany without them and they would follow the train and overtake it before the evening performance the next day, and you would find them trying to break into their cages again, and they would have to be fed.

When pa and I went into the barn where the cages were, to take an account of stock, and get acquainted with our animals, they acted just like the circus men did when they saw pa's clothes. The animals were about half asleep when we went in, but a big lion bent one eye on pa, and then he rose up and shook himself and gave a roar and a cough that sounded like he had the worst case of pneumonia, and he snorted a couple of times, as though he was saying to the other animals: "Here's something that will kill you dead, and I want you all to have a piece of it, raw," and he brayed some more, and all the animals joined in the chorus, the big tiger lying down on his stomach and waving his tail, and snarling and showing his teeth like a cat that has located a mouse hole, and the tiger seemed to say: "O, I saw it first, and it's mine."

The hyena set up a laugh like a man who is not tickled, but feels that it is up to him to laugh at a funny story that he can't see the point of at a banquet where Chauncey Depew tells one of his crippled jokes, and pa was getting nervous. A big grizzly bear was walking delegate in his cage, and he looked at pa as much as to say: "Hello, Teddy, I was not at home when you called in Colorado, but you get in this cage, and I will make you think the Spanish war was a Sunday school picnic beside what you will get from your uncle Ephraim," and a bobcat jumped up into the top of his cage and snarled and showed his teeth, and seemed to say: "Bring on your whole pack of dogs and I will eat them alive."

Pa threw out his chest in front of a monkey cage, and a monkey snatched his watch, and then all the animals began to laugh at pa just like a lot of bad boys in school when visitors make a call. Pa went around to visit all the animals, officially, while I got interested in a female kangaroo, with a couple of babies, not more than three weeks old, and I noticed the mother kangaroo made the old man kangaroo, her husband, stand around and he acted just like some men I have seen who were afraid to say their souls were their own in the presence of their wives.

The female kangaroo is surely a wonder, and seems to be built on plans and specifications different from any other animal, cause she has got a fur-lined pouch on her stomach, just like a vest, that she carries her young in. When the babies are frightened they make a hurry-up move toward ma, the pouch opens, and they jump in out of sight, like a gopher going into its hole, and the mother looks around as innocent as can be, as much as to say: "You can search me. I don't know, honestly, where those kids have gone, but they were around here not more than a minute ago." And when the fright is over the two heads peep out of the top of the pouch, and the old man grunts, as much as to say: "O, come on out, there is no danger, and let your ma have a little rest, 'cause she is nervous," and then the babies come out and run around the cage, and sit up on their hind feet and look wise. That kangaroo pouch is a success, and I wonder why nature did not provide pouches for all animals to carry their young in. I think Pullman must have got his ideas for the upper and lower berths of a sleeping car by seeing a kangaroo pouch. I am going to study the kangaroo and make friends with the old man kangaroo, 'cause he looks as though he had troubles of his own.

Pa showed up without any coat, while I was kangarooing, and there was a rip in his pants, and I asked him what was the trouble, and he said he got too near the cage of a leopard that seemed to be asleep, and the traitor reached out his paw and gathered in the tail of pa's coat, and just snatched it off his back as though it was made of paper.

Pa is a little discouraged about his experience in the circus the first day, but he says it will be great when we get the run of the business. He says every day will have its excitement. Tomorrow they are going to extract a tooth from the boa constrictor, and pa and I are going to help hold him, while the animal dentist pulls the tooth, and then we scrub the rhinoceros, and oil the hippopotamus, and get everything ready to start out on the road, and I can't write any more in my diary until after we fix the snake. Gee, but he is as long as a clothesline.

Winter Quarters of the Only Circus, April 20.—Pa has had a hard job today. The boss complained to pa that the fat woman had been taking anti-fat, or dieting, or something, 'cause she was losing flesh, and the living skeleton was beginning to fat up. He wanted pa to call them into the office and have a diplomatic talk with them about their condition, 'cause if this thing continued they would ruin the show.

So pa went to the office and sent for them, and I was there as a witness, in case of trouble. The fat woman came in first, and there was no chair big enough for her, so she sat down on a leather lounge, which broke and let her down on the floor, and pa tried to help her up, but it was like lifting a load of hay. So he leaned her against the wall and said:

"Madame, the management has detailed me to censure you for losing flesh, and I am instructed to say if you do not manage to take on about fifty pounds more flesh before the show starts on the road, you don't go along. What you want to do is to eat more starchy food and sleep more at night. They tell me you go out nights to dances and drink high balls, and this has got to stop. Drink beer and eat cheese sandwiches at night, or it is all off. This show can't afford to take along no 400-pound fairy for a fat woman when the contract calls for a 500-pound mountain of flesh, see?" and pa looked just as stern as could be.

The fat woman began to cry and sob, so it sounded like an engine blowing off steam, and she told pa that the cause of her losing flesh was that she was in love with the living skeleton, and that he had been paying attention to the bearded woman, and she would scratch her eyes out if she could catch her. Just then the living skeleton came in, and when he saw the fat woman sitting on the floor crying, and pa talking soothing to her and telling her he could appreciate her condition, 'cause he had been in love some hisself, the skeleton pushed pa away and tried to lift it, and said: "What is the matter with my itty tootsy-wootsy, and what has the bad old man with spinach on his chin been doing to you?"

Then he turned on pa and his legs began to shake and rattle like a pair of bones in a minstrel show, and he said: "I will hold you responsible for this." Pa said he was not going to interfere in the love affairs of any of the freaks, and just then the bearded woman came in, and when she saw the living skeleton holding the hand of the fat woman, who sat on the floor like a balloon blowed up, the bearded woman gave a kick at the living skeleton which sounded like clothes bars falling down in the laundry, and she grabbed the fat woman's blonde wig and pulled it off, and then the bearded woman began to cry and she threw herself into pa's arms and began to sob on his bosom and mingle her whiskers with his.

Pa yelled for help, and I thought it was time for me to be doing something, so I went outside the office—to the fire alarm box and touched a button, and then I run like thunder for the police, and the firemen came with the extinguishers and began to throw chemically charged water into the room, and the police dragged out the fat woman, who had fainted, and the living skeleton, whom she had pulled down into her lap, and laid them out in the ring, and then they got hold of pa and pulled him out, and the bearded woman had fainted in pa's arms and the stove was tipped over and was setting fire to the furniture and they brought the bearded woman and the fat woman to their senses by pouring water on them from a hose. Finally they were sent to their quarters, and the other owner of the show came to pa and said he hoped this would be the last of that kind of business, as long as pa remained with the show, that one of the rules was that no man in an executive capacity must under any circumstances take any liberties with any of the females connected with the show.

Pa was hot, and said when women got crazy in love no man was safe, and the other owner of the show said that was all right this time, but not to let it occur again, and pa tried to explain how the bearded woman came to jump on to him and faint in his arms, but the owner said: "That is all right, but you can't hold 'em in your arms before folks," and then pa offered to whip any man who said he was in love with any bearded woman, and he pulled off his coat. Just then I came along and told the whole story, and then the crowd all had a good laugh, and pa took them all out and treated.

I guess it is all settled now, 'cause the living skeleton and the fat woman have got permission to get married, the bearded lady is sweet on pa, and a girl has just joined the show, who walks a wire, and she says I am about the sweetest thing that ever came down the pike, and I guess this show business is all right, all right.

April 21.—We are getting acquainted with the animals, and it is just like going into society.

There is the aristocracy, which consists of the high born animals, the middle class and the low down, common herd, and when you go among the animals as strangers you are received just as you would be in society. If you are properly introduced to the elephants by the elephant keeper, who vouches for your standing and honor, the elephants take to you all right and extend to you certain courtesies, same as society people would invite you to dinner, but if you wander around and sort of butt in, the elephants are on to you in a minute and roll their eyes at you and look upon you as a common "person," and if you attempt any familiarity they look at you as much as to say: "Sir, I am not allowed to associate with any except the 400." Then they turn their backs and act so much like shoddy aristocracy that you would swear they were human.

I remember when pa was first in the elephant corral, the keeper forgot to tell the big elephant who pa was, and when the keeper raised up one foot of the elephant and examined a corn, pa went up and pinched a bunch on the elephant's leg and said to the keeper: "That looks to me like a spavin," and he nebbed it hard. Well, the elephant groaned like a boy with a stone bruise on his heel, and before pa knew what was coming the elephant wound his trunk under pa and raised pa upon his tusks and was going to toss him in the air and catch him as he came down and walk on him, when pa yelled murder and the keeper took an iron hook and hooked it into the elephant's skin, and said: "Let that man down," and he let pa down easy, and the keeper some way showed the elephant that pa was one of the owners of the show, and that elephant acted just as human as could be, for he fairly toadied to pa, like a society leader that has given the cold shoulder to someone that is as good or better than they, or like an impudent employee who has insulted his employer and is afraid of losing his job. After that whenever pa and I go around the elephants they bow down to us, and I think I could take an iron hook and drive an elephant anywhere.

There are all classes among the animals in a menagerie the same as human society. The lions are like the leaders of society who are well born and proud but poor. They are always invited everywhere, but never entertain, though they kick and find fault and ogle everybody and look wise and distinguished.

The sacred cattle are too good to live and pose as the pious animals who do not want to associate with the bad animals and are constantly wearing an air of "I am holier than any of you," but they will reach through the bars of their cage and steal alfalfa from the Yak and the mule deer, and if they kick about it the sacred cattle look hurt and act like it was part of their duty to take up a collection, and they bellow a sort of hymn to drown the kicking.

The different kind of goats in a menagerie are the butters-in, or the new rich, who get in the way of the society leaders and try to outdo them in society stunts, but they smell so that the other animals are made sick and the goats are only tolerated because animal society is afraid to offend them, for fear the leaders may some time go into bankruptcy and the goats will take their places and never let them get a smell of the good things of life.

The bears are the working people of the show, and the big grizzlies are the walking delegates who control the amalgamated association of working bears, and the occupants of the other cages have got to cater to Uncle Ephraim, the walking delegate, or be placed on the unfair list and slugged.

The hyenas and the jackals and the wolves represent the anarchists who are down on everybody in the show, who won't do a thing to help along and won't allow any other animal to do anything, and who seem to want to burn and slay, to carry a torch by night and poison by day, and want everything in the show to be chaos. Those animals are never so happy as when the wind and lightning strike the tent, and blow it down and kill people and create a panic, and then these anarchists sing and laugh and enjoy their peculiar kind of animal religion.

The zebras and giraffes are the dudes of the show, and you can imagine, if they were human, they would play tennis and golf, drive four in hands and pose to be admired, while the Royal Bengal tigers, if they were half human, would drive automobiles at the rate of a mile a minute on crowded streets, run over people and never stop to help the wounded, but skip away with a sneer, as much as to say: "What are you going to do about it?"

The hippopotamus is like the lazy fat man that groans from force of habit, sits down as though it was the last act of his like and only gets up when the bell rings for meals, and he sweats blood for fear he will lose his meal ticket and starve to death.

The seals are the clean-cut Baptists of the show, who believe in immersion, and they have more brain than any animals in the show, because they live on a fish diet, though they have a pneumonia cough that makes you feel like sending for a doctor.

Gee, but last night when we thought spring had come and we could start on the road pretty soon, the snow fell about a foot deep, and it was so cold that all the animals howled all night, and shivered, and went on a regular strike. We had to put blankets on them, and no one of them seemed to be comfortable except the polar bears, the arctic foxes and the fat woman. The other owners of the show thought it was a good time to take the boa constrictor and pull an ulcerated tooth, 'cause he was sort of dumpish, so pa and I helped hold the snake, which is about twenty feet long.

Pa was up near the snake's head, and when the man with the forceps got hold of the tooth and gave it a yank, the confounded snake come to and began to stand on his head and thrash around, and pa dropped his hold and started to climb the center pole, but he got caught in a gasoline torch, and they had to turn a hose on pa, and he was awful scared, 'cause he always did hate snakes, but they gave the snake chloroform and got him quiet, and pa came down, and they gave him a pair of baggy trousers belonging to the clown, to go to dinner in, and pa was a sight.

May I.—We had the darndest time getting packed up and started on the road. How in the name of heaven we ever got half the things on the cars is more than I know, but it seems as though the circus company had a man to look after everything, and he had men under him to look after his regular share of things, so when the cars were loaded, and the boss clapped his hands, and the engineer tooted his whistle, there wasn't a tent stake or a rope, or a board seat, or anything left behind. Every man knew exactly where the things were that he was responsible for, so he could lay his hands on them in the dark, and he knew just what wagon his stuff was to go in.

Gee, but you talk about system, there is no business in the world that has a system like a show on the road. Every performer was in his or her section in the sleeper, and pa and I got an end section with the freaks, the fat woman across the aisle from us. That fat woman is going to make life a burden for pa, I can see that plain enough. She is engaged to the living skeleton, and he sleeps in the upper berth, over her, and he is jealous of pa, while the fat woman has got to depending on pa to do little things for her.

Of course, the first night out is always the worst on a sleeper, and the poor woman is nervous, and when the animal train, in the second section, ran on a side track beside our train of sleepers, and Rajah, the boss lion, got woke up and exploded one of his roars, within six feet of the fat woman's berth, she just gave one yell, and reared up, and came down hard in the berth. Something broke, and she went right through the bottom of the berth to the floor, doubled up like a jackknife.

Pa got up and went to her berth, though I told him to keep away, 'cause he would get into trouble. First he stumbled over one of her shoes, and said he thought he had told everybody to keep their telescope valises in the baggage car, and that made her mad. Then he reached in the berth and got hold of one of her feet, and pa got the men to help and they got her out, but she seemed all squished together. She sat up all night and wanted to lean on pa, but the skeleton kept his head over the rail of the upper berth and his snake-like eye never left pa all night.

The bearded woman got up out of her berth about daylight, to go to the toilet room for a shave, or a hair cut, or something, and when she saw pa trying to soothe the fat woman and hold her from breaking in two, she screamed and slapped pa's face, and had a mess of hysterics. The fat woman grabbed a couple of handfuls of female whiskers, and was going to pull them out by the roots, when the bearded woman begged her not to pull them out, as to lose her whiskers would destroy her means of livelihood.

Then the bugle blew for everybody to get up and go to the show lot, and put up the tents for the first show of the season. When we got out of the sleeper we asked where we were, and a man told pa we were at Peoria, Ill., and he wanted pa to give him a complimentary ticket for telling what town we were in, but pa looked fierce at the man and asked what kind of an easy mark he took him for, and the man slunk away. You wouldn't think they could unload those two trains of cars, about 80 in all, in a week, but when we got out the horses were hitched on the wagons, and in 15 minutes they were loaded and on the way to the lot, and pa and I got on the first wagon.

Talk about system. The surveyors were there ahead of us, and had measured off the lot and pushed wire stakes in the ground where the grub tent was to be, and when the first wagon of the grub outfit arrived, which contained a big range, big enough to cook for a thousand men, stove pipes were put on, which telescoped up into the air, and in two minutes a fire was built and bacon and potatoes and coffee were cooking, local bread wagons were unloading bread on the grass, 50 men put up poles and spread the tent on, and others set up tables in the tent, and in half an hour breakfast was served to the first 500 men. Pa and I drew up to the first table, but there was a yell to "put 'em out," and we found we had sat down to the table of the negro canvasmen, and they struck because they would not associate on an equality with white trash.

Gee, but pa was mad. He said he was as good as any nigger, and that made them mad and they threw boiled potatoes and scrambled eggs at pa, and we had to retire, but when pa complained to the boss canvasman, he told pa to go and eat with the freaks and try and keep in his place.

We got breakfast at another table, and then we went out on the lot to superintend the putting up of the big tents. The greatest thing was a wagon containing a miniature pile driver, run by steam, which was driven around outside of where the big tents were to be, and it drove down the big stakes so quick it would make your head swim, and the grounds were covered with Peoria people who wanted to see how it was done.

Pa imitated the boss canvasman by walking around the lot with his coat over his arm, and a dirty shirt on, trying to look tough, and he bossed the sightseers about, and acted cross, and told a man and woman with a baby wagon to get off the lot, but pa was called down by the principal owner of the show good and plenty.

Said the owner to pa: "Remember, the success of our show depends on the friendship and good will of the people who think enough of us to come out to see us set up keeping house, and that they are all our guests, and if they get in our way we should go around them, and look pleasant. We must not get the big head and show that our hair pulls, and that we are tired and cross. This is a place of amusement, and all connected with the show are expected to heal up sores, instead of causing bruises, and if you ever see an employee of this show treating a visitor unkindly, send him to the ticket wagon to get his wages, and tell him to go away quick, and stay away long."

You could have lit a match to pa's face, it was so red hot, but he learned a lesson, for I saw him holding a tired mother's baby up on his shoulders, so it could see the drove of camels come up to the lot from the train, soon after. It was great to see all the tents go up as if raised by machinery, and after all were erected, and the rings were graded, and the animals in the menagerie tent all fed and watered, and the performers in the dressing-room ready for the afternoon performance, pa was the proudest man ever was. He walked all around, inspecting everything, and kicking occasionally at something that got balled up, and when the crowd came to buy tickets, he stood around the grand entrance, looking wise, and he was so good-natured that he bet ten dollars he could guess which walnut shell a bean was under, which a three-card monte man was losing money at, and pa lost his ten with a smile. He said he wanted to be kind to the patrons of the show.

This was my first appearance in the show business. I had to stand up beside the giant, to show how little I was, and then I had to stand up beside the midget to show how big I was compared with him. It went all right with the giant, because he was so big I was afraid of him, but I thought the midget was about my age, and needed protection, and when the crowd surged around us I said: "Don't be afraid, little fellow, I will see that no one harms you." The look he gave me was enough to freeze water.

When the crowd had gone into the big show tent, what do you think, that confounded midget began to ask me how I stood on the tariff question, and he argued for free trade, whatever that is, for half an hour, and made me think of Bryan during a campaign, and then he branched off on to the Monroe doctrine, which I suppose is something connected with a rival show, and I guess he would be talking yet, only a big husky fellow came along, a fellow about 25 years old, and he stooped over and put his hand on the midget's shoulder and said: "Hello, dad," and by gosh, the midget introduced me to the big galoot as his youngest son. Wouldn't that skin you.

The first day of the season was great, only all the performers had not got limbered up. One of the girls on the flying trapeze fell off into the net from the roof of the tent and broke her suspenders, so when they got her down in the ring it seemed as though everything she had on was going to shuck loose, and leave her with nothing but a string of beads, and pa went up to wrap his coat around her, and she kicked his hat off and ran into the dressing-room. The audience just yelled, and pa blushed scarlet, 'cause he saw it was a put-up job to make him ridiculous.

During the chariot races pa had to jump like a box car to keep from being run over by a four-horse chariot driven by a one-horse girl, and the attendants dragged pa out from under a bunch of horses being ridden barebacked, like fury. Then two horses hitched together with a strap were being ridden by a woman, the strap broke and the horses spread apart, and someone yelled that she had split clear in two. Pa rushed in to help carry one half of her into the dressing-room, but she wasn't hurt at all, 'cause the peanut boy told me she was a rubber woman, and you could stretch her halfway across the ring, and she would come together all right, and eat a hearty meal. Gee, but a circus is a great place to study human nature.

In the evening performance at Peoria there came up a wind-storm which blew down part of the menagerie tent, where the freaks were, and when the storm was over, and the tent top was pulled up again, they found pa all right. He started to crawl under the canvas, and skip out for fear of the animals, but the fat lady caught him and sat down on him.

May 6.—We had the worst time at Akron last week and pa proved himself a hero, though he was swatted good by the rogue elephant before he got his second wind and went for the animal.

We have a male elephant that is almost human, 'cause he gets on a tear about once a month, like a regular ugly husband. You can't tell when his mind is in condition for running amuck, but suddenly he will whoop like a drunken man, strike his poor patient wife over the back with his trunk and grab her tail and try to pull it out by the roots, and jump up and crack his heels together like a drunken shoemaker, and bellow as though he was saying he was a bad man from Bitter Creek.

Well, at Akron, the keeper of this elephant, Bolivar, had to go and see a girl that he met when the show was here last year, and settle a case of breach of promise before a justice of the peace, and the boss told pa to look after the elephant for an hour or so. So pa took a pole with a hook in it and sat down on a bale of hay to watch Bolivar. It was one of those hot days, and Bolivar stood drooping and perspiring, and wishing the show was in Alaska, and pa was kind of sleepy, like everybody in the show, when suddenly that elephant whooped, and swatted Jeanette, his wife, a couple of times, and she cried pitiful, and pa put the hook in Bolivar's hide and gave a jerk, and told him to hush up that noise, but Bolivar just reared and pitched and walked right through the side of the menagerie tent, and seemed to say to the other animals: "Come on, boys; there is going to be something doing," and the animals all set up a howl in their own language, as though they were saying: "Whooper up, old man, and don't let them monkey with you."

Bolivar went out in the street and mowed a wide swath, with pa after him, hooking him all the time, but he paid no attention to pa. He put his head under the side of a street car loaded with negroes that had come to see the show, dressed in their Sunday clothes, and tipped the car over on the side, and the negroes crawled through the windows and went uptown yelling murder, while Boliver went in front of a grocery store where there was a pile of watermelons, and began to throw them at the people in the street, and the negroes thought an elephant was not so bad, so they came back and had a feast.

Pa tried to head off Bolivar at the grocery, but Bolivar took half a watermelon and put the red side on top of pa's head, and squashed it down so the seeds and juice and pulp ran down pa's shirt and neck, and he looked as though murder had been committed, but pa wiped his face on his shirtsleeve and showed game, because he kept mauling Bolivar with the hook. Bolivar broke up a millinery store by throwing tomatoes at the women in the windows, and he went into a yard where a woman was washing and squirted the bluing water all over the woman, and all over pa, and then he chewed the clothes on the line, and drove the family over the fence.

You'd a died to see those milliners climb over a high board fence head first, and Bolivar actually seemed to laugh. Bolivar run one of his tusks through a barrel of gasoline, and it run out on the street car track, and an electric spark set it on fire, and the fire department turned out, but the engines had to all go around Bolivar, 'cause he wouldn't budge an inch, but seemed to say: "Let 'er rip, boys; this is the Fourth of July."

The circus men began to come with ropes and clubs, to tie Bolivar and throw him, but he escaped into a side street and watched the engines put out the fire, and he swung around with his trunk and tusks and wouldn't let anyone come near him but pa with the hook, and he seemed to enjoy the prodding, but I guess that gave him courage to keep on doing things.

The principal proprietor of the show came along, and when he saw pa with watermelon and bluing water all over him, and perspiration rolling down his face, he said to pa: "Why don't you take your elephant back to the lot, 'cause the afternoon performance is about to begin," and that made pa mad, and he said: "You go on with your afternoon performance, and I will have Bolivar there all right," and then everybody laughed, but pa knew what he was about.

Pa dropped his hook and went to a hose cart and took a Babcock extinguisher and strapped it on his back and went up to Bolivar, who was tipping over some dummies in front of a clothing store, and pa said: "Bolivar, you lay down," but Bolivar threw a seven-dollar suit of clothes at pa, and bellowed, as much as to defy pa. Pa turned the cock of the extinguisher, and pointed the nozzle at Bolivar's head, and began to squirt the medicated water all over him. For a moment Bolivar acted as though he couldn't take a joke, and was going to start off again, but pa kept squirting, and when the chemical water began to eat into Bolivar's hide, the big animal weakened, and trumpeted in token of surrender, and kneeled down in front of pa, and finally got down so pa could get on his back, and pa took the hook and hooked it in the flap of Bolivar's ear, where is a tender spot, and he told Boliver to get up and go back to the tent, and Bolivar was as meek as a lamb, and he got up, with pa on his back, and the fire extinguisher on pa's back, and marched back to the tent, through the hole he had made coming out. Thousands of people followed, and cheered pa, and when they got in the tent pa said to the principal owner of the show, who had made fun of him: "Here's your elephant, and whenever any of your old animals get on the warpath, and you want 'em rounded up, don't forget my number, 'cause I can knock the spots out of any animal except a giraffe." The crowd cheered pa again and he got down off the elephant, took off his fire extinguisher, and handed Bolivar a piece of rag carpet, and said: "Eat it, you old catamaran, or I'll kill you," and Bolivar was so scared of pa he eat the carpet, which shows the power of brain over avoirdupois, pa says.

The regular keeper of Bolivar heard he was on the rampage, and he came back on the run to conquer him, after pa had got him back in the tent, but Bolivar looked at him with a faraway look in his eyes, as much as to say: "Seems to me I have met you somewhere before, but a new king has been crowned," and he took his old keeper by the back of his coat and threw him toward the monkey cage. The monkeys gave the keeper the laugh, and Bolivar put his trunk lovingly on pa's shoulder, and seemed to say: "Old man, you are it, from this time out." Pa looked proud, and the old keeper looked sick. The people in the show are going to present pa with a loving cup, and I guess he can run the menagerie part of the show.

When the freaks heard of pa's bravery, the fat woman and the bearded lady wanted to hug pa, but pa waved them away, and said he liked the elephant business best.

May 7.—I used to think that if I could belong to a circus, and go away with it when it left the town I lived in, that it would be pretty near going to heaven. I used to hope for the time when I would get nerve enough to run away, and go with a circus, and wear a dirty shirt, and be around a tent and wash off the legs of a spotted horse with castile soap, and when people gathered about me to watch the proceedings, to look tough and tell them in a hoarse voice way down my throat, sort of husky from sleeping in the wet straw with the spotted horse, that they must go on about their business, and not disturb the horse.

I had thought if I should run away and go with a circus, some day, when I got far enough away from ma, that I would up and swear, and be tough, and when I came home in the fall, and the neighbor boys would come around me, I would chew tobacco and tell them of the joys of circus life. Well, maybe I will some day, but at present I am sleepy all the time.

We have showed six times the last week, and traveled a thousand miles, and it seems as though there is nothing doing but putting up and taking down tents, and going to and from the cars, and you can't be tough, 'cause there is always some boss around to tell you to look pleasant if you are cross, and to tell you to change your shirt or get out of the show, and if you swear at anything you are called down.

Pa and I put in a good deal of time during the afternoon and evening performances in the dressing-room, near the door leading to the main tent. That is the nearest to being in an insane asylum of any place I was ever in. The performers get ready for their several acts in bunches or families, all in one spot, and they act serious and jaw each other, and each bunch acts as though their act was all there was to the show, and if it was cut out for any reason, the show would have to lay up for the season, when in fact each one is only a cog in the great wheel, and if one cog should slip, the wheel would turn just the same. These people never smile before they go in the ring, but just act as though too much depended on them to crack a smile. When a bunch is called to go in the ring, they all look at each other as though it was the parting of the ways, and they clasp hands and go out of the dressing-room as though walking on eggs. When they get in the ring they look around to see if all eyes are upon them, and bow to people who are looking at something going on in another ring, and who don't see them, and then they go through their performance with everybody looking somewhere else.

When the act is over the audience seems glad, and clap their hands because they are polite, and it don't cost anything to clap hands, and the performers turn some more flip flaps, and go running out to

the dressing-room, and take a peek back into the big tent as though expecting an encore, but the audience has forgotten them and is looking for
the next mess of performers, and the ones who have just been in go and
lie down on straw and wonder if they can hit the treasurer for an advance
on their salaries, so they can go to a beer garden and forget it all.

An average audience never gets its money's worth unless someone is hurt doing some daring act. Pa suggested that they have someone
pretend to be hurt in every act, and have them picked up and carried
out on stretchers with doctors wearing red crosses on their arms in at-
tendance, giving medicine and restoratives. The show tried it at Bucyrus,
O., and had seven men and two women injured so they had to be carried out, and the audience went wild, and almost mobbed the dressing-
room, to see the doctor operate on the injured. It was such a great
success that next week we are going to put in an automobile ambulance
and have an operating table in the dressing-room with a gauze screen so
the audiences can see us cut off legs like they do in a hospital. Maybe we
shall put in a dissecting room if the people seem to demand it.

The Circus Lady

BY JOSEPHINE DEMOTT ROBINSON

In my time with the circus there were only few lone (I won't say single) women working our show. Even today, most women travel in family units or as members of an act. This allows for a support structure and some measure of protection against the various dangers one might encounter in a life on the road. One exception to this norm on our show was the side-show Snake Lady, but she was a formidable old bird and kept pretty much to herself, if you don't count the snakes. Another worked the refreshment stand, also on the midway. We called her, aptly, Candy. She lived in a small truck she had fitted out for one. She was cheerful, fifty-ish and at the time—unmarried, with a daughter gone off to college somewhere. We got to be pals and one day I asked her: was it hard traveling with the circus and being on her own? Wasn't she lonesome? Didn't she get hassled all the time? I'll never forget what she said. "If the girl ain't pretty, it doesn't matter. And if she is pretty, it doesn't matter either." Sibylan, perhaps, but by this I took her to mean that every woman is always alone and on her own, no matter what, or who, or where.

This excerpt from Josephine DeMott Robinson's "Circus Lady" has lots to offer. First it's a coming of age story, though a memoir written late in her life, it's still touched with the kind of early teenage anxiety you might expect from a child of the Victorian age (and indeed, still recognizable today). It is also ripe with the flavor of the performer's life on a big-time circus in that golden age before the turn of the last century. Her 19th Century stalker (she calls him a Grifter) is a real villain. And the whole telling is melodramatic, slightly hysterical, fast-paced, and thrilling, easy as a beach read.

○ ○ ○

On our return to the United States we opened at Madison Square Garden, with the Barnum show. I rode a black pony in what is called a "high-school act," and later a white pony in a hurdle act. Immediately we found ourselves in trouble, and were called to account by the authorities for allowing a child under sixteen to perform, but when they found I was nearly sixteen, they let me go on. This age-dodging is a most interesting thing anyway: all our younger life we try to dodge ahead of our real age, and all our later life we spend trying to dodge backward. It is a nice game when well played.

It was years before I knew my real age anyway. Circus people never know how old they are, for their ages are usually shifted ahead, so that the authorities will let them alone. In fact, unless there is a birth certificate to prove the thing, some circus people never do know just how old they are.

I was a real star now, however, and treated as such by everyone except my family—and I had the treasured center place in the dressing room. The one thing that established your importance in the early circus days was your place in the woman's dressing room. Here more than anywhere was shown the layers of society of which a circus is composed, and no senator's wife who is seated ahead of a representative's was any more jealous of her position than was the bareback rider. The tent proper was round with a center pole, on which hung the chandelier for lighting at night—a crude affair made of iron. And it was the bareback rider who had the choice place in the dressing room—the one right up next the center pole. Also, though later all trunks had to be a standard size, in early days she was allowed a larger trunk than the others, partly because her tarleton skirts required more room. All the other trunks were placed after hers was in place. First came hers, then in a very definite order of precedence, came the trapeze performer's, the dancing rope artist's, the gymnast's, divided on either side of the star's trunk. If it had not been correctly placed, it would have been considered very sufficient reason for quitting a show.

Only on rainy days when the edges dripped and the water poured on the edge trunks were the others allowed to pull their trunks in close to the bareback rider's. No doubt this is how it came about that the bareback rider, as the star of the show, got the center pole location: it was always dry there and there was no one to bump you.

The trunk open, the back of it served as a resting place for a mirror, although the people along the edge of the tent usually pinned theirs up on the canvas near their trunks. Also each carried a little piece of carpet in his or her trunk, to put down in front while he or she dressed,—all, that is, but the bareback rider. She had a groom who put hers in the trapping-box at the end of a performance, and brought it out for her at the next one. It was pleasant, after years of hard work, to have won my position at the top.

When Mr. Bailey, of the Barnum and Bailey show, heard that I was a somersault rider, but was without a horse, since I had been riding one of Mr. Orrin's horses in Mexico, he presented me with a mare named Jeanette, one who had served for many years under his management, who was too old to be ridden by men somersault riders, and was too young to be retired. These horses are very difficult to break in; only one out of many here and there measures up satisfactorily. I used this somersault horse then and for a later engagement with the Robinson show. She had the best of everything—a padded stall, and every comfort, and when we retired her to live the rest of her life on a farm near Philadelphia, the farmer who boarded her told us that he needed no timepiece since Jeanette had come, for every afternoon at two o'clock she started up and galloped around the field in a circle, keeping remarkably even gaits all the time. This even gait had been one of her chief virtues, for we could depend on her to make exactly twenty-two steps to a forty-two-foot ring. And the ring that she made for herself in her field was exactly twenty-two feet! Every time we visited her, we hated to leave her again, and if we had been in a permanent place we would have had her with us for years longer. But she was too old to stand the wear-and-tear of travel.

The Wallace show had an interesting retired horse, too—an old black horse that Mr. Wallace had planned to leave for the summer on the farm at Peru, Indiana, which was the show's winter quarters. Now the breaking up of winter quarters and starting on tour is always a sentimental occasion for a circus. All the wagons with their teams line up ready to pull out, and when the last one is out the gate is sprung, and with that the whole line starts at once. That sound of a closing gate means farewell to the old and on to the new. The black horse was left at the farm, the men calling good-bye back to her as she watched them over the wall, sad to see her left behind, but knowing it was much better for her. The overseer rode from the first to the last wagon to make sure all was well, so that when they reached their first stand everything would be ready, and when he came to the last wagon, trotting quietly along behind was the black horse, following the show. When he heard the sound of the slamming gate, he had jumped the wall at a low place, and followed along with the show as he knew he should. The overseer hadn't the heart to turn him back, but let him spend the day on the lot. When they took him back to the farm they had to lock him in the barn for a long time, for he jumped the fence every time they let him out in the field.

Circus horses lead the best life I know of. The ring or bareback horse could not be happier, for his training is done in such a way that he is afraid of nothing. A horse that fears even an uplifted arm would be unsafe to ride, for when the rider is up in the air turning a somersault or some trick where the rider must face the horse's tail, the horse must be reliable and dependable, or death for the rider may be the result. And there is so much going on all the time in the circus—nets being thrown, carpets and ropes and poles and all sorts of things being carted around for the next act, perhaps fifty men arranging things for the next performance, that if the horse had any fear to remember he would naturally shy and jump from all this and be of no use—in fact, dangerous.

Carrots and sugar and much patting enter largely into their training. They are led about the tent and allowed to sniff at everything so they may know it is harmless. As soon as the horse can be taught that nothing will harm him, he is ready for use. But every little thing he is asked to do in the way of training must have its reward, until he grows to feel the world is made just for him, whether he is going up a narrow runway on shipboard, or through a crowded street, or through a moving train. But nothing must frighten him. He must never be jerked or pulled around. He must just be taught to go steadily on and on at the word of command, and when the day's work is done a pat and a lump of sugar must always reward him.

If a horse passes these tests, he is sure of being in clover for the rest of his life. Even if he shies and the somersault rider is thrown and hurt, the horse is never lashed. He is merely given a reassuring pat to calm him, and the baby carriage or the program waved suddenly too near him is put farther away.

We riders of the circus can never understand how the ordinary saddle-horse ever endures his lot, as we see him ridden on country roads or along bridle paths, pulled and jerked by the unskillful, the foolish, the mean, who happen to own or ride him. And we cannot understand how it is that people can bear to sell off their family saddle-horses, because they get old or go lame or have some other accident. You have seen these poor animals, so petted and well-treated in their prime, standing in front of some peddler's cart, in all weathers, thin, ill-fed, or perhaps whipped up to some speed by the casual owner who bought him from his former owner for a few dollars. It would have cost so little to have had him killed, and it would not cost very much to pension him on some friendly farm.

No circus animal suffers thus. They are members of our family. Even a snakecharmer, asked if it is really possible to love snakes, grows indignant at the question. When a pet horse dies, he is mourned like the good friend that he was. I think I should rather be a circus horse than a gillie horse, for with them the end is as good as the middle and the beginning.

Most traveling circuses carried at one time what were called professionally "grafters." These people traveled under various arrangements, sometimes renting the privilege of traveling with the show, conducting their games of chance in and about it.

Sometimes without permission or paying for it, they traveled through a section of the country with the show people and these were powerless to prevent them. They went ahead and fixed the town, and if they could not fix a town they did not work it. Alas, however, for the honesty of the town officials: as a rule they fixed the town without difficulty.

Each body of grafters carried a man "fixer," whose business it was to settle all differences between the gillie who lost and the show. He was usually a man of very suave manner, a good judge of human nature, and with a very convincing line of argument. It was his business to know just how far a man could be bluffed into or out of an argument. He usually dressed well and was a good handshaker. Also he had to have a fair amount of courage. It took nerve to face a furious crowd of town people who had lost at the game where they had hoped to do the besting. With a lot of money lost, they of course were furious, and it took courage for a fixer to stand alone and argue with them while the men actually controlling the game were making their way to safe quarters.

These games always included the "three shell" game. Of course not one hick went up against these games intending to do anything but put it over the game owner and win a lot of money. But naturally these grafters did not carry an expensive outfit through the country in order to distribute largess to deserving rustics. They were there to win. And win they did—always.

Managers throughout the country were getting stronger and stronger against this grafter system. Sometimes the towns were objecting, though many liked the graft because of the little extra revenue it brought them. Sometimes the loser in the game would make such a fuss, backing up his objections by gun-play, that the grafters could not even depend on the fixed officials helping them through, but scattered in all directions, hastily changing their clothing, pulling off their hayseed disguises, or jumping hurriedly into animal men's coats and assuming that job. Anything to get away was their motto at these times. I have heard the story of a well-known, present-day vaudeville man, who once was a grafter—and a good one. One day an acrobat coming into the dressing room of the circus found his trunk top open, and was annoyed, for he hated his things misplaced. Hearing the men laughing, he decided the dark object he saw in the bottom of his trunk was some joke they were playing on him, and said nothing. A minute later someone pushed him aside, pulled down the top of the trunk, just as the sheriff of the town came tearing in, looking for a grafter. After he had looked around and departed, the lid of the trunk went up slowly and the grafter's alarmed face appeared. He got away safely, and, as I said, is now reformed and has acquired a large income by honest vaudeville methods. But once he was a king of grafters.

After a few big squeals, the managements grew more and more anxious to do without these traveling fakirs, and as a consequence, the shows they could travel with were getting scarce.

The summer that I was seventeen a body of these men were traveling with the Robinson show, of which I was the featured bare-back rider. As I grew older my mother grew more and more watchful of me. She could not tolerate my hobnobbing with the married women, and as girls are scarce around circuses I was permitted little companionship.

I had a beau, however—a distant beau. We smiled shyly at each other, glanced up and down as we met, and passed notes. He was a very little older than I, and was a relative of the heads of the show. Now and then, not often, we had a chance to say a word or two to each other. It is not easy to talk to the opposite sex in a circus. As soon as a man and woman or boy and girl sit down to talk to each other alone, someone comes along and stops it. If he persists, there is a fine or perhaps dismissal. And besides these powers there was my mother's eagle eye.

My mother would not allow me in the dressing room except-ing when it was time for me to dress for my act, but as a special favor I was allowed to sit with an elderly woman ticket-taker at the edge of a row of reserved seats. It was in full view of everyone, and everything I did was visible to all.

Now in towns where the grafters found it hard work or where there was too much whiskey in evidence, the grafters were usually made into ticket-sellers. In this case, the fixer himself was allotted to the re-served seats near me. He spoke to me several times as he passed, but my attention was all taken up with the boy who was trying to pass me a note while he was strolling back and forth. It was not until some days later that I realized that the fixer had smiled at me several times. Had I not been so engrossed with my beau in the distance, I should surely have noticed this, for the circus people are not friends of the grafters, and having them try to be nice to you was rather more of an insult than a pleasure.

Now one of the fakirs had a wife who came to this show at this particular town—Selma, North Carolina, it was,—an unforgettable name to me. She was quite an invalid, supposedly suffering from some serious ailment, and my mother and I felt very sorry for her. Our stands were quite small through here—the hotels were too small to hold all the performers. The fakir's wife had a room in a private house near our hotel.

After breakfast on Sunday morning she asked my mother to let me come over to her room to see some crochet patterns she had. Now I was a crochet hound, being deprived of most other methods of amusement, and even a private view of crochet patterns was better than nothing on a Sunday. So my mother let me go.

We had been talking for a few minutes when the fixer and the husband of this woman came in together. It was apparent by their faces that something was very wrong. The fixer looked terribly downcast and the woman's husband looked upset. Not knowing any of them, I tried not to look their way much, thinking they were in some trouble about their business. The arguing kept up. Then, though I tried not to see it, I realized the fixer was crying, that his hands were hanging helplessly at his side, and that the woman's husband—I think his name was Lane—was supporting him. Later Mrs. Lane went over to them. Suddenly I heard Mr. Lane say, "I can't do a thing with him, I have talked and talked, and he is still bent on it."

Then Mrs. Lane began pleading with the fixer to reconsider, to pull himself together, which advice brought only moans from the unhappy man. Now suddenly I realized that they were staring at me. The fixer was looking at me helplessly, moaning, "The poor little thing—so innocent, so innocent."

Finally the woman said, "Well, ask her," but this brought only fresh moans from the fixer.

"No, no," he begged, "she won't understand."

But Mrs. Lane came over to me, where I sat ill at ease. "Perhaps, my dear, you can do something to help him, to prevent a terrible thing which might bring everlasting sorrow to you. Won't you help us to prevent it?"

In alarm I nodded my head. Of course I would.

Now Mrs. Lane explained to me that her husband had spent the entire morning keeping the other man, the fixer, from killing himself, that the fixer had fallen in love with me, and realizing his love was in vain, for I wouldn't even look at him, had tried to take his life. That if he were left to himself he would surely try it again, unless I could help prevent it. This responsibility alarmed me, and I hesitated. At that, a commotion took place in the corner, and the fixer tried to break away from his friend again.

Mrs. Lane urged me again. "My dear, save the man's life. It will save your soul from eternal unrest if you prevent this deed."

"Of course I will. Tell me what I can do—but how can I do anything to help?"

"Just go over to him, and tell him not to do what he intended to do—that he is not entirely distasteful to you—use just those words, my dear."

I hesitated, but he began to break loose again, so I conquered my fear, went over to him, and said, "Please, don't do anything like that for me," whereupon he broke into fresh moans.

He stopped sobbing long enough to say, "She's such a good girl—so innocent," but he would say nothing more.

Mrs. Lane whispered to me to tell him I did not think unkindly of him and that I would do what I could to prevent his hurting himself. So I did. And he seemed to feel better.

My mother called me just here and I went back, all shaken and fearful lest something happen and it be my fault, and trying to find some way to prevent this crime I knew nothing about. By morning I was ready to believe it a terrible nightmare. I had mentioned it to no one. My mother had always been so strict with me that I made no unnecessary confidences, and in this case, too, I kept silent.

Mrs. Lane came in during the morning and told me that the fixer was feeling better and wanted to thank me because I had saved his life. I went with her, much relieved to know everything had been settled so simply, but still puzzled as to my presence in the story. We went into her room and waited till the fixer came. Down in the streets I could hear the band playing as the parade went marching through the town. Suddenly I felt cold and fearful and wished with all my heart I were down there marching with them behind the band wagon. It was only a moment, however, before the door opened and Mr. Lane, the fixer, and three other men came in. I thought they were there on Mr. Lane's business, and expected the fixer to thank me and bow me out.

Instead I heard one of the strangers, with a badge showing one of its points from under his coat, say, "Hurry this up, boys."

Mrs. Lane came over to me smiling, "Now, my dear, you have really saved his life with your promise to marry him. That was the one thing that kept him from carrying out his death threat last night."

I listened to her in horror, and when I understood what she was saying, I tried to protest.

"Now, my dear," she said firmly, "my husband is worn out watching him, and if you go back on your promise he'll do it sure. You'll be responsible for sending a soul to hell if you go back on that promise."

"But," I wailed, thoroughly frightened now, "I didn't promise it. I said I would help him, that's all. I don't want to marry him. I don't want to marry anybody. I don't even know this man's name."

"Sh," she warned me, "don't let anybody hear you," and she pushed me gently toward the men.

"I can't do it. I won't," I managed to cry out, but they either did not hear me or ignored me. The fierce-looking stranger with the badge looked threateningly at me. I felt the woman's arms around me as she moved me, almost paralyzed with fear, to the group of waiting men.

I felt myself falling. From far away I heard the woman saying, "She's going to faint," and someone held a glass of water to my lips. A long, long moment went by. Then I heard two voices at once. Mrs. Lane's saying in a satisfied voice, "Well, you're married, my dear," and down in the street my mother calling me to come to the hotel for dinner.

I broke from them and fled and ran into the street crying to my sister, whom I met first, that something terrible had happened to me, that I was married.

"To whom?" she asked, and I said I didn't know what his name was, but I told her he was the fixer and what he looked like. By this time we had come up to my mother and father, on their way to dinner. My sister told them the story.

"But I'm not!" I sobbed distractedly, "they said I was, but I know I'm not."

Naturally my father and mother heard the news as if they had suddenly heard a bomb from the clouds explode before them. My father was dazed and looked at me helplessly, but my mother went straight to Mrs. Lane's room for an explanation.

When she had gone, father turned to me and said very gently that he wanted me to tell him what it was all about, but I could only go on crying and tell him that I didn't know what had happened, I didn't know whether I was married or not, but I didn't really think I was. He asked me if I had been drugged—had I taken anything from Mrs. Lane? Yes, I had had a glass of water—at least they had put it to my lips. I didn't even know if I had swallowed it.

"Father," I said earnestly, "I don't think I said a word—then how could I be married?"

And I went on crying back there near the hotel till outsiders began looking at me, thinking in all probability that I was being made to do some act in the show of which I was afraid. That was always the first gillie thought when he saw a child or a girl crying.

So we went to our rooms and my father again began questioning me, using the word marriage once or twice.

"Don't say that terrible word again, please," I begged him. It was a word that had never been in my thoughts at all—not even about the beau I liked, who passed me notes and smiled at me. And it was years before I stopped shivering when I heard the word.

My mother came back, and she at least had definite information. She came in with a beaten look on her face.

"Well, she's married. It's true," she said, and went on to explain that Mrs. Lane had been very defiant, had told her sharply that the time had come when my services to them—my family—should cease, that I had worked for them long enough, and that in the future I was to work for myself. That I was married and that was all there was to it, and my mother would please get out.

"Now who," she demanded, "is it you are supposed to have married?"

I explained as best I could who it was, how it had happened. I did not even know the man's name, but knew him simply as the fixer for the grafters.

Of course, by noon, which it now was, my story had reached the ears of even the boy potato-peeler in the cook tent and the chandelier man. In a minute I was transformed from the show's principal rider to a freak. No one ventured to speak to me—whether afraid or what, I don't know.

As for me, my lips were sealed too, tighter than with sealing wax from the fear that if I told the whole story of how they had lured me up there and arranged things, my father or brother might kill the fixer and be hanged for murder. Things were very dark. A short time ago I was afraid the fixer might kill himself and damn my soul: now it seemed to me that that would be far better than what had happened.

My father told me he wished to help me, to tell him everything I could, but I, with fear at my heart for his safety, was stubbornly silent, much to his sorrow and my mother's indignation. My father seemed to want to believe me, but my mother, as is often the case with good narrow women, felt it must somehow be my fault.

As for myself I felt sure I had said no word in that room that could bind me to the fixer, but I was not sure. All I knew was that I had turned faint, and as I came back I heard Mrs. Lane say, "You're married," and I flew blindly out of the room.

After dinner, or rather after dinner time, for none of us could eat, Charles Robinson, the Governor's brother, came up to me and asked my father to let him talk to me alone.

My one hope was to be let alone, to stay close to my people and be free from questioning. But Mr. Robinson had always been very nice to me, and so half unwillingly I made ready for another avalanche of questions.

He talked to me very quietly, telling me how he had watched me advance in my work, and how he had always liked it, that he knew I was a good girl, and that although he couldn't understand what had happened to give these grafters the right to say what they did, still he wanted me to know that he was my friend in any event. If what had happened was with my wish, well and good; never mind the consequences, if it was what I wanted. If it were true that I had gone through a marriage ceremony and wanted it to hold, and only feared disagreeable conditions for my family or criticism, he said he would see that everything was fixed right. The grafters could remain with the show and he would see that my people felt all right. But if they could prove that such a thing had actually happened and it was against my will, then he wanted me to know that no power on earth could force me to comply with these grafters. No one could force me to go with them, even if they said they could.

I should have protection in any event, and he would be my friend no matter what happened.

"If you are really a party to this contract, and want to stand by it," he said, "do so, and I will protect you. But if you have somehow got into this without your own will in the matter, then tell me. Tell me just that, no more. Remember, no power on earth can keep you from him or make you go with him. Just say, 'I want him,' or 'I do not want him.'"

I looked up at him, as a hurt child looks at someone who is kind to him. "Oh, Mr. Robinson," I said, "I do not want him."

He got up instantly. "All right, now, stick to that."

I stopped him for a moment. "Mr. Robinson, can anything happen to my father because of this?"

He assured me it could not and went out, for it was show time by now.

So we all went to the lot and the show took place as usual, and I smiled my mechanical smiles and waved my mechanical arms at the gillies as I went swinging around on my horse. Everything went on quite as usual. Only, though I looked around fearfully, I saw the fixer nowhere about.

And there was one different thing. Not one person in the show spoke to me, and this was hard on me, for I was a chatterbox always. My voice sounded queer in my own ears, when I spoke to my horse in my act. The show was over. I was out of the strange, unfriendly dressing room, and back to the hotel. Here things had happened. One Jerry Daly, who had been one of the witnesses to the supposed contract, but had not been wholly in on the game, when he saw things seemed very irregular, made a getaway. When he learned my stand in the matter and that all the grafters had been ordered out of the show for good, he went to the management and told about what he claimed was a frame-up. The fixer and the grafters, he said, had conceived the idea that if my act could be controlled by them, it would enable them to travel with the show more easily. From everywhere they heard rumors that the grafters were to go, and they thought by taking away the show's star—that act that was advertised far ahead along the route—they could stay with the show indefinitely, or take me away for a show of their own. So the woman was brought on, and she played sick to get my mother's and my confidence, and then they could put the deal over as easily as they fixed towns. With the help of a corrupt official or two the rest was easy.

For thus turning show evidence, Jerry was allowed to stay along, not as grafter, however, but as ticket-seller and odd-job man. All the rest were given warning that any of them found near the show on our next day's stand would get into trouble.

So that was the end of the grafting business with the Robinson show for all time. And after this the shows had not only to look out for the grafters, but had trouble with some of the towns, where the officials were waiting eagerly to be fixed. We had to carry detectives to spot fakirs off the lot and on.

But to come back to my story. After supper my father was called out to see the sheriff and the magistrate and the fixer, and his pal. The two former had come, they said, to see justice done the fixer. They said the laws of North Carolina gave a man a right to demand a woman to whom he was married, and that was exactly what the fixer should do immediately, but that they did not want any trouble, simply wanted a few minutes alone with me, away from my family, to straighten out this tangle. Only the sheriff was to be with us. My father, knowing my state of mind, was about to refuse curtly, when Mr. Robinson who had been listening, said, "It's all right. Let him see her, De Mott. Go right here in the parlor. You (to me) sit in this chair, this one by the window. Don't be afraid, for they can't hurt you."

He turned to the men and eyed them coldly. "Make it damn short. And the first guy that raises a hand towards her, I'll see he never has time to raise another. As for you, you've fixed your last job, my man."

The sheriff came forward and said, "Now see here, Mr. Robinson, we want to be decent about this. This man has married this girl good and proper, with witnesses, and I am here to see he gets fair play. Our State law gives him the right to demand her. But he don't want trouble."

Mr. Robinson interrupted him. "Go in there and talk your ten minutes and then get out. Not a damn minute more."

The fixer broke in with his best fixer manner. "Now, Mr. Robinson, look here, we're peaceful people; all we want is an understanding. I just want to talk to the girl a little, that's all."

He was relying, no doubt, on my fright and the presence of the sheriff with him backing his game. I was to be my own undoing. But Mr. Robinson had given me the assurance that things would come out all right.

I sat very still while the sheriff told me the laws of North Carolina in regard to marriage—that this man had a right to me, and that the thing for me to do was to walk over to him, take him by the hand, and walk out with him, and so avoid any trouble. If I wouldn't, he was there to see I did it anyhow. If I wouldn't go willingly it would mean lots of trouble for the Robinsons and my people and in the end I would have to go with him anyway. The State laws were not to be trifled with by traveling circus people, who thought they could walk away with anything they wanted to. I was married and nothing could undo it. Everything would be all right if only I would do as I should.

All this while the fixer was sobbing and shaking his head helplessly and saying, "She is such an angel—so good, so pure. She'll do it, Sheriff, I know she will."

However, I was rather fed up on the fixer's histrionic ability by this time, so he did not move me. But my senses were numb. I don't think I really cared any more what happened—I think an earthquake swallowing up everything would have been preferable. I sat quite still and said nothing and did nothing, till finally the sheriff said gruffly:

"Well, I guess I'll have to send you down to Smithfield."

This was a threat, no doubt, but it left me unmoved. I learned later it was the jail.

"Want to go there?" I shook my head. The two men began to argue with me. But I merely shook my head to anything they said, borne up by Mr. Robinson's promise.

There came a banging at the door. "Ten minutes up," called Mr. Robinson. The sheriff seemed disinclined to notice this, but the fixer, apparently realizing they would have to wait awhile, said, "Oh, let him in. The poor child don't know what she is doing."

So I was escorted out and back to my family. And in a little while we went to our train, for this was a small town where we gave only one show.

After this I was never left quite alone. I was very unhappy for my father could not understand why I would not come straight to him and make everything plain, and my mother felt I must have had some sort of hand in the thing, and often told me so. As for me, I hoped if I did not try to offer any solution perhaps the matter would be dropped. I knew the facts I could tell them would only enrage them, and since it seemed as if the thing could not be sifted out, perhaps in time it could be forgotten.

All I asked was to be permitted to stay with my family, to keep on riding, to have my father look at me less sorrowfully, my mother less angrily, and the people around me take me to their hearts again.

We traveled on as usual and nearly a week had gone by and I was beginning to breathe naturally again and not start at every unusual noise, when one night my brother came running to my dressing room curtain and called me just as the tournament was beginning in the Big Top for the night performance. I threw a cloak about my shoulders hastily and went with him into the pad room where we stood in the middle under the lights, while he explained to me that some men had been caught outside the dressing room, and the management feared it was a plot to kidnap me. We waited till the women came back to the dressing room and then my brother went with me to the room, saying, "You're all right now."

The Barnum and Bailey show was going to England that season. It was the first time a large American show had crossed the Atlantic, and we were engaged to go with them. We spent a great deal of time practicing our horses and trimming new costumes, of which I accumulated plenty. We were in England six weeks and played twice a day, and I never wore a costume twice. I trained my horse, and sewed new spangles, and I was beginning to think I had almost forgotten my nightmare, when something brought it all up again. We had left our show and hurried to New York, and, not being able to make the boat with the entire show on it, we were the only Barnum people on our ship. Friends had come to see us off, and we were talking together, when suddenly an officer approached me, accompanied by the man I hoped I would never see again, the amiable fixer smile still on his face. The officer gave my father a habeas corpus writ restraining me from continuing the trip.

I refused to go with him, though he began telling the officer how my family had turned me against him. My father ordered us all ashore, and began collecting our baggage. The fixer said all he wanted was a word with me. But I refused. Mr. Orrin, the owner of the circus we had traveled with in Mexico, was one of those seeing us off, and he said he would see if he couldn't do something to prevent such a person from putting us to this trouble.

The fixer looked sad. "Oh, I won't take advantage of my power. I can prevent her sailing, but I won't do it. I'll drop it right now." Mr. Orrin only laughed. "Quit playing to the gallery," he said. "How can you get her if she refuses to go? If she isn't of age, here's her father controlling her actions."

So the fixer left, and our baggage went on, and we sailed. It was wonderful to know so much space and so much water were between myself and my trouble, but sometimes it seemed as if I could never get far enough away from it. I used to lean over the back of the boat, and stare down at the water, and stare, wishing for the courage to throw myself into that friendly foaming mass. It seemed about the only place where I could find rest and happiness.

But I didn't do it, as most of us don't, and after a while we were in Southampton, and then in London.

The Barnum and Bailey show which went to England in 1889 was, at that time, the most stupendous venture known to the show world. It took both men to make it a success. Mr. Barnum was the advertiser, who loved the limelight, who rode around in the ring, and announced who he was. But Mr. Bailey was the business man, content to be invisible, demanding it in fact, and interested only in the success of the show.

He had a marvelous crop of managers and agents, tried and trained and never caught napping. Their ears were like wireless outfits— they caught any whisper about anything anywhere. And when one of them made known what he had heard, he was dispatched to go get it. "Go get it" and "go do it" were almost patented expressions with Mr. Bailey. "Can't do it," or "Can't get it," were phrases he simply didn't understand. One thing that demonstrated this very clearly was at our opening in London.

Mr. Imre Kiralfy had been engaged to put on the spectacular production of "Nero and the Fall of Rome," wherein nearly two thousand people took part. This we had never been able to give in its entirety at home, for the Garden was not large enough. But the London Olympic held it all easily. Coppini, the famous ballet master from La Scala in Milan, had charge of the ballet, and Lombardi, who has since carried out huge productions in this country, including the "Slums of Paris," was chorus master. Cocia, a very celebrated male dancer, was on the bill. As to any other celebrated dancers from Italy, men or women, down went their names when heard about, and out went the order, "Go get them." Expense and salaries were no object.

The hundreds of ballet girls were provided with silk tights of the finest quality with satin pumps, and the best of everything.

For my act Mr. Bailey had provided that my garters—the banners over which the rider jumps—were to be made of the finest silk-backed satin; and my garlands—the hoops through which I jumped—were to be covered with silk-petalled flowers.

Mr. Bailey had not yet run out of ideas. He thought the appearance of men well-trained in army tactics would add a lot to the spectacle. Someone suggested that tall men like the "Queen's Own" would be the proper persons, and Mr. Bailey thought a moment, nodded his head, and said briskly, "Go get them."

"Get who?" chorused the staff.

"The Queen's soldiers," said Mr. Bailey and turned to other things.

He was really serious. So out went one of his men, and sure enough, it was arranged to have the "Queen's Own" appear in the "Fall of Rome." Their red coats, their height and their military bearing added a great deal to the performance. As for their compensation, it was a mere tip and looked foolish beside some of the other salaries—a shilling a performance for each man, and expenses to and from their barracks was the sum agreed on. They were a good advertisement for the show, stepping through the streets so gallantly and colorfully, going from barracks to the Olympic.

The girls in our ballet were picked from among the best dancers available, and they were a charming sight in their satin garb.

The Kiralfy Brothers had a reputation for being expensive, and their productions were very elaborate. Also they had been accustomed to having their slightest wish carried out, and Mr. Bailey was willing to humor them. Rehearsal after rehearsal was the order of the day, and night too. The squares about the Olympic seemed a continuous medley of chariots and horses and girls and men. Animal men rushed here and there at the Kiralfy command. Besides, we performers had our various acts to rehearse. It was difficult to imagine how this show, so involved, so huge, would ever open as scheduled.

As the date came nearer it became more and more evident that it could not be done. Even Kiralfy began to express that opinion, and finally, only one day before the show was to open, he came to Mr. Bailey with the news that he was not ready with the "Fall of Rome." Mr. Bailey showed no temper—he never did—but he calmly told Kiralfy that the show would open tomorrow as announced, Nero or no Nero.

Mr. Kiralfy tore out most of his hair, but Mr. Bailey for once refused to humor him, and his hysterics made no impression whatever on the American showman. And sure enough, the next evening we opened, and "Nero and the Fall of Rome" also opened in fine shape.

Our show took London by storm. After the opening, it was impossible to get tickets for the Olympic unless you ordered them for weeks ahead. Mr. Bailey, who knew that the failure of this enterprise would mean not only the loss of a lot of money, but also a lot of prestige, was jubilant.

One very sad thing happened on our opening night, and in front of thousands of people who never dreamed that they had seen a tragedy and not a part of the show. One of the elephants was not moving ahead fast enough, and somebody behind him punched him to hurry him up. There was a keeper directly in front of the elephant, a man, as it happened, whom the elephant never liked. The beast made one rush forward, picked the man up, and dashed him to the floor. It happened so quickly that before anyone could interfere he had been crushed to death.

Nero, aloft with his fiddle, saw it all, but he played on undisturbed, and added a lot of quavers and runs to distract the crowd's attention. The man was taken out, and the show went on, and not any of the audience and not many of the troupe knew of the tragedy.

During our stay here we had as frequent visitors all the royal family except Queen Victoria. The then Prince of Wales, later King Edward the Seventh, liked the show so much that he said he would come all the time, if only there might be no fuss about his visits. Ferns, palms and a separate entrance had been arranged to prevent people staring at him as he came and went. But the Prince did not like it, so it was all taken down, and he came continually after that.

Mr. Bailey as usual was invisible, but Mr. Barnum rode around the track in an open barouche and smiled and bowed to the applause that greeted him. The former was perfectly willing to let the latter do the host stuff, so long as he could direct the destinies of the show.

I am reminded of the way in which Mr. Bailey was obeyed by all who worked for him. His head manager, Harvey Watkins, who was, of course, well known to everyone, rushed one day into a back entrance in a great hurry. But the doorman refused to allow him to enter. He was furious, but he had to go all the way around the Olympic and came in the back door and then go all the way back to the dressing rooms. He met Mr. Bailey, and told him what had happened, so Mr. Bailey took him back to the doorman who had refused him entrance.

"Don't you know Mr. Watkins?" he asked.

"Certainly, Mr. Bailey," was the answer, "but you said to allow no one except Mr. Barnum to come in here."

"That's right," said Mr. Bailey, "I did say that. But after this you may allow Mr. Watkins to go in, too."

His oft-repeated remark was, "I want every cog in my working wheel perfect."

There were some foggy days that seemed very funny to me, who had never seen such things. Sometimes I could not see the rider in the next ring, nor any of the audience except the people in the first rows. But they crowded the house anyway. Perhaps they had learned to see through the fog because of much experience. I could never get accustomed to it—yellow fogs or black ones, I hated them both. I would go around the ring, seeing only my horse and a few unearthly faces beyond the ring, feeling enclosed in some strange substance that was trying to choke me, while all outside noises had a queer, unreal sound filtered through the fog.

At the close of our stay, an affecting ceremony took place. High in the royal box, side by side, sat Mr. Gladstone and Mr. Barnum, watching the show together. When the band played, "Should Old Acquaintance Be Forgot," they stood up together and clasped hands and stood so till the tune was ended, while the people cheered and applauded. Then the band broke into "Home Sweet Home," and hats were thrown high into the air and the building rang with cheers and all the people stood up. It was a very impressive scene.

But enough of the public and the show. Meantime I had suffered some more at the fixer's hands.

We had secured rooms on our arrival at a private house with a most estimable woman and her fat little serving maid. The latter did our marketing and cared for our rooms and made us very comfortable. We were contented and happy, and even my mother was beginning to forget my disgrace. Things were so different here, and everything that had happened in America was so far away.

Then suddenly, one night, just as I was about to jump the broad banner, I looked up toward the audience, and in a box I saw the face of the fixer. I was so startled that I started to jump, then balked, then started again, and, as the banner holder was not prepared for this, he threw the banner at the wrong time, and I fell into it, all tangled up, and tumbled to the ground. Fortunately I was not hurt, but it made a very bad finish to my act.

I dared not look into the box again and make sure it was he. I wanted so to believe it was not. All the old distress came back again—even worse in this far-off land.

Now with our show there had been a woman rider named Annie, who, because of injuries, had been out quite a bit, and even now, though back with the show, she had to rest a bit between the acts.

She dressed near me, and on this night she had called to me to wear a flower in my hair for her to bring her luck. I told her I wore my hair always hanging and very loose, but she begged me again, so, feeling sorry for the poor thing, I said I would.

A few days afterwards my landlady, with many apologies, told my father that she wanted to tell him about a man who had come to see her, and had asked to arrange a meeting between him and me, because I was his wife and was being forcibly kept away from him; that was the reason, he said, that I was such a still little thing; and that I was rapidly pining away because I loved him and my family would not let me see him. She almost consented, but when he said he would make it worth her while if he could see me, she, being an honest old soul, lost her belief in him, and decided to tell us about it.

I had previously told my father about seeing him in the box, so he now went to Mr. Bailey, explaining our plight, and asking that the fixer be kept away from the Olympic. Then Mr. Bailey said that they knew the story from the man himself; that he had come in one night and announced to them that I was his wife, and that he would prove it, because I who never wore flowers in my hair had promised to wear one that night for his sake. And they had seen the flower. And he also said I carried a two-cent piece with his picture inside it in my bag.

In dismay my father came to me, and asked me if I had worn that man's token. Indignantly I denied it. I told him about the flower Annie had given me, but vowed it had nothing to do with the fixer. So my father went back to the office and Annie was sent for.

Yes, said Annie, she had given me the flower, but hadn't mentioned who gave it to her. She saw no harm in it, and she felt very sorry for the man who wanted his wife back—he had cried and she wanted to help him. That little act of kindness almost cost Annie her job.

My father came back to ask me about the picture in my bag. I denied it vigorously and handed him my bag. What was my horror to see him take out a two-cent piece, one of those large coins no longer made, and snap it open, like a locket, disclosing the fixer's face smiling up at us.

It seemed that I was hemmed in no matter which way I turned. I think my father believed me. I hope he did. But by this time I didn't much care if anyone did.

Meanwhile we engaged lawyers in Philadelphia to find out the truth as fast as they could, and to dissolve any contract made under duress. They advised an annulment, for fear of the people who had sworn to the validity of the contract and who could not go back on their oaths without laying themselves open to perjury. When we left England in the spring, we came home to Philadelphia to find that our grafters had put us to one more inconvenience before they departed. They had demanded a trial by jury. My lawyers wanted me to tell them more facts, but I was tongue-tied as ever. So my father gave me pencil and paper and told me that now I must write the simple facts and tell just what had happened.

I went into a room by myself and wrote everything just as it had happened, and all the old fear and pain swept over me again that I had thought gone forever.

I put in, as they asked me to, everything I was willing to swear to. Then I gave it to my father to read. And when he had read it, he came to my room, and stood looking at me, saying over and over, in a voice so raging that I hardly knew it, "That man ought to be shot! He ought to be shot!"

And then I knew I had done well to be silent—that my fears and apprehension were justified. And I felt now that the whole thing would end happily, with no penalty except memory.

The court and its surroundings, all new to me, I was glad to see only a short while. The jury was out only long enough to decide the case for me and come back again. So ended that. And so ended the grafters.

Razorbacks and Skin Games

BY ROBERT EDMOND SHERWOOD

Razorbacks are sharpies, and skin games are flim-flams. But in my time as a circus clown I never saw a real honest-to-goodness con practiced on the public. Sure, I've heard plenty of midway come-ons and side-show patter calling on the "ladies and gentlemen, boys and girls" to spend just one more dollar to "see things you will remember for the rest of you life!" But if the leopard in the menagerie is a little sleepy, or the fat man's been dieting, the people take it in stride. They are complicit. Secretly, it's what they've been expecting. Hyperbole is certainly the most all-pervasive con, and perhaps also the gentlest. Each circus claims to be the greatest show, under the biggest big top, exhibiting the best in entertainment, featuring the finest animals, the most death-defying performances, and so on. We're complicit here too, because most times we believe them.

After a long career as a clown, Robert Edmond Sherwood quit life on the huskings and settled down to write two wonderful books: "Hold yer Hosses! The Elephants are Coming!" and "Here We Are Again: Recollections of an Old Circus Clown"—from which this selection is excerpted.

These days, circuses are on their best behavior and they do whatever they can to live up to their claims to be family shows. But still, I suppose if you know where to look . . . and pick-pockets will always be with us.

○○○

Canvasmen or "razorbacks," as they are known in the slang of the circus, are rarely in funds. Their tippling habits, coupled with their receiving only half pay while on the road, keep them continuously in financial distress. Settlement in full is made only at the end of a season, or on being discharged. This method of payment was established by the Miles Orton show in 1876, in the hope that razorbacks could be kept in working condition throughout the season. Vain hope! It did not take them long to learn how to beat the game. Just as soon as the parade left the grounds, two men would leave the lot, carrying an empty gallon jug and bound for the nearest saloon. Selecting one which the parade would pass, they would step in and order the jug filled with the best whisky in the house. On being told the best whisky would cost them eight dollars per gallon, (a big price in those days) they would reply, "Oh, that's all right, the liquor is for Mr. Barnum's personal use, and he drinks only the best." A bold statement, considering Mr. Barnum's temperance principles were well known.

The jug being filled and set up on the bar, the spokesman would airily say, "Mr. Barnum sent us over here after this liquor, and he said to tell you that he would come right over after the parade and pay for it."

Then the proprietor would indignantly refuse to let them have it. Heated argument would ensue; finally, with a gesture of disgust, the head spokesman would say, "Well, then, I guess you will have to pour it back in the barrel." The liquor being poured back, they would leave the saloon with alacrity; arriving on the lot, the jug would be broken and almost a quart of liquor would be squeezed out of a big sponge in the bottom of the jug, and a general good time would be had by all.

Not only would the gin-mill keeper lose the whisky, but often a five or ten-dollar bill in addition. These were the days before cash registers came into use, and it was customary among bartenders to lay the paper money and small change on the back bar for the sake of convenience. While the bartender would be under the bar drawing the whisky, one of the men would stick a wad of warm chewing gum on the end of a cane he carried, reach over the bar and pick up any bills in sight. He stood in little danger of detection, as all the customers would be outside looking at the parade.

When money was required, canvasmen sold "tickets" to the ladies' dressing tents. The price of the tickets depended on the amount the purchaser could be cajoled into paying. There were always young farmer boys, and old ones too for that matter, walking around the horse tents during the afternoon show. Selecting one who looked particularly impressionable, the canvasman would start a dialogue somewhat like the following:

"Say, how'd you like to go through the ladies' dressing tent?"

"Wall, I wouldn't mind. How can I dew it?"

Peering cautiously about, the canvasman whispers, "I can sell you a ticket."

Having paid, the yokel asks, "Where's the ticket?"

"Oh, you don't need a ticket; all you got to do when you meet a circus man is to raise two fingers; that shows you have a ticket to the ladies' dressing-room."

The raising of two fingers marks him as a sucker for every one around the show; he gets down to the entrance of the dressing tent, is kicked out and that ends it. He doesn't dare complain to the authorities lest he advertise his credulity to his acquaintances.

Often the very razorback who sold him the ticket would be the one to eject him. This was certainly adding insult to injury. I have seen as much as fifty dollars paid for such a ticket to the ladies' dressing tent.

Circus men as a class possess good memories. Let the show unload in the same railroad yard each year, the drivers will pilot the wagons to the lot used the season before, without a single question as to direction. Also they never forget a favor, or forgive an injustice inflicted on them.

"Porky" O'Brien's show was notorious for one thing—a total failure to pay anything to performers or workmen if it was possible to avoid it. Musicians were generally paid because they were the only men who could tie up the show. Getting money out of the old man was like trying to get "blood out of a turnip." Late one season I overheard a canvasman tackle "Porky" for his overdue salary.

"Money," said the old man. "What do you want with money? Here you are eating three times a day, and getting the wrinkles out of yourself, and now you want money, huh."

"Yes, I know, Mr. O'Brien," said the razorback, "but I want to buy me a shirt."

"Shirt!" snorted the old man. "What's the matter with the one you have on? What do you want with another shirt? But if you're so keen on having two shirts, when we go over the road tonight, find a clothes line and get yourself another. And while you're down there, get me one—I wear a number seventeen."

As luck would have it, the route of the night jump led past a clothes line, stretched in the back yard of a farmer living about two miles from the last lot.

Remembering "Porky's" advice, he hopped over the fence and proceeded to help himself. Unfortunately for the razorback, the owner of the clothes line, a hard-fisted old deacon, was concealed on his back porch waiting for the return of his two young sons who had sneaked off to the circus against his orders. The culprit was caught red-handed. No amount of persuasion on his part would induce his captor to let him go. The law must be respected, and to jail he must go.

He was suddenly struck with an idea. It was the end of the circus season, and the prospect of a hard winter lay before him. He could get no worse break from the farmer if he offered to work for his board and keep than he was getting from the circus owner; besides, here was a chance of warm and comfortable sleeping quarters, a luxury he would not be able to enjoy in the city. The deal was made. In exchange for a pardon, board and keep, the razorback was to do the daily chores during the coming winter. Seemingly he was perfectly satisfied with his lot, and the deacon on his part was highly entertained with stories of the circus told by the canvasman, while the family sat around a crackling log fire in the open grate.

But the lure of the life under the billowing canvas of the white tops is ever appealing. The razorback longed for the old associations as soon as spring came and the bluebirds began to sing.

Early in the season, the O'Brien show was billed in a nearby town, and the call was overwhelming. Much to his surprise the deacon suggested that the entire family go over on circus day. As the canvasman knew all about the circus, he would be included. Bright and early, they set out, driving a pair of perfectly matched horses which the deacon hoped to sell to the circus for a good price.

Here was an opportunity to get revenge. With the plea that he knew how to beat the shell game, he persuaded the old deacon to back him in bucking it. In less than ten minutes all the cash received from the sale of the horses reposed safely in the pocket of the shell man. When it came time for the deacon to go home the razorback was missing and a careful search failed to disclose his whereabouts. Concealed within a baggage wagon, safe from the prying eyes of the law, the shell game man and the razorback divided the fruits of their labor fifty-fifty. The canvasman marked the score paid in full.

Pilfering gangs were pretty well organized in those days. If they were unable to locate the lucre, a tall ministerial-looking gentleman stood sedately on a soap box near the entrance to the tent and gave forth this admonition, "*L-a-d-i-e-s* and *g-e-n-t-l-e-m-e-n*, I appear before you on behalf of the circus management. The *gentlemanly* proprietors request me to advise you that among this large gathering there are a number of thieves and pickpockets, and I am *requested* by the management to advise you to keep your hands upon your pocketbooks." Thus warned, it was only natural that his hearers did put their hand on their pocketbooks. With the location of the money pointed out to them, nothing was easier for the pickpockets than the getting possession of it.

The "guess your weight" machines were first brought into use by these light-fingered gentlemen to assist in locating the money they later stole. These machines, made in platform style, were used for this nefarious purpose years before the ones having a swinging seat and dial appeared at beach amusement resorts.

The appeal to get weighed free, was made to men only; to locate the purse of a woman, wearing voluminous skirts such as were in style in those days was a feat that not even a professional pickpocket could accomplish. And again, was there ever a woman who would consent to being weighed in public?

Grasping the victim by the shoulders, the genial gentleman of the scales began to feel the body of the candidate carefully under the pretense of determining the solidity of his flesh. He slapped him on the thigh, hip and chest, at the same time saying, "I *think* you weigh," or "I *guess* your weight to be," or "I'll *say* you weigh," etc. The words *think*, *guess* and *say* were easily interpreted by his confederate to mean the location of the dupe's pocketbook. *Think* meant the money was in the coat pocket; *guess*, the trousers pocket; and *say*, the hip pocket. The money rarely escaped changing hands.

Farmers were not the only victims of these nimble-fingered gentry. They tackled both great and small, high and low, shrewd and simple. The sophisticated were just as easy for them as the ingenuous.

Shortly after retiring to private life, I became quite friendly with Charles E. Van Loan, the well-known writer of sport stories. Notwithstanding Van's experience acquired in his profession, he was as impressionable as a schoolgirl. As he lived on the next block to me, we were often together, and many of the incidents mentioned here were made the basis for some of his very interesting stories.

Like all grown-up boys he was much interested in the circus, and one night suggested we visit a small circus then showing in Brooklyn. Arriving at the grounds, he said: "Here, Bob, you're up on the ways of the circus, I'll give you the money to buy the tickets."

"Now," said I, "wait a minute, and I'll probably see someone I know who will give us passes."

He complained that all that would take time, and reached for the roll of bills which he always carried.

"Now," I said, "Charlie, don't pull that roll out in this crowd. There are always a lot of 'dips' around a circus and you are likely to have your pockets picked."

"Who, me?" he asked. "Why I've traveled all over the world reporting prize fights, horse races, and baseball games, mixing in all sorts of tough crowds, and I've never yet been frisked." He laughed long and loud and peeled off a bill from the roll and handed it to me to buy the tickets.

As I went past the ticket wagon, I spied a pickpocket who in years gone by had followed one of the tent shows I was with. This man had the reputation of being one of the smoothest short-change artists in the business. Here was a chance to teach Van a lesson. I got the "dip's" eye, pointed to Van Loan and wigwagged the location of his money. In a good dark place, I gave Van a prodigious shove and—the "dip" got the money.

Branding me a "clumsy old fool," we passed into the menagerie top, where Van suggested he buy reserved seats. This time I did not oppose him. He again reached for the roll—but the roll was gone. The bull of Bashan roared no longer or louder than he. It wasn't so much the loss of the money, but he was peeved by the fact that he, of all persons, had had his pocket picked. I joshed him a bit and that made him all the madder. Then I said, "Now, Van, I don't think your money was stolen; I think it came out of your pocket when I stumbled against you. You stay here, and I think I can go right back and pick it up."

He insisted on going back with me, but I prevailed upon him to let me go alone. It was a good while before I could find the man, but I finally located him in the horse top.

"Well, Tom," I said, "I guess you'll have to come across. The sucker is making an awful squawk. He is a very good friend of mine, and I was only trying to teach him a lesson."

He handed me the roll intact, and I gave him ten dollars from my own pocket which seemed to satisfy him. I found Van Loan where I had left him and handed him the money, remarking: "It was just as I said; I found it right where you dropped it. Now put it in your pocket and keep it there."

It was some months before I could get up sufficient courage to tell him the truth. He listened to me in silence while I related it to him. From his facial expression I could readily see that he did not believe me; when I had finished he said: "I've met a lot of liars in my time, but you've got them all lashed to the mast howling for mercy. They couldn't pick my pocket in a hundred years."

Like Balzac and Dickens, Van had a hard time getting publishers to believe in him. At the beginning of his career as a writer, manuscript after manuscript was returned to him with the endorsement "Many thanks, not available for our use at present," and "Good story, but not suited to our publication," etc.

So regularly did the practice continue that Van began to fear that his scripts were not being read. In order to test his suspicion, he pasted the first three sheets of a manuscript together and sent it in to the publication office of a prominent periodical.

In due course of time back came the script with the first three pages still stuck together, just as he had despatched them. Boiling with righteous wrath, he indited an excoriating epistle to the editor, in which he expressed his belief that his manuscript had been returned without being read, and cited as proof the three pages pasted together.

The editor replied promptly: "Dear Mr. Van Loan: When I open my egg at breakfast, and find it bad, I do not eat *all* of it to satisfy myself. I read the first page of your manuscript."

Best of all sure-fire losers for the player was the "Spinning Jinney." There was not a chance in the world for the customer to beat it, unless the operator saw fit to let him win.

This gambling device was very simply constructed. A large wooden arrow having a metal point was balanced perfectly on a pivot set in the center of a round piece of wood, having about the same diameter as a barrel head. Around the outer edge of the circular board were laid one, five and ten-dollar bills, interspersed with watches and a collection of cheap miscellaneous jewelry. Between the prizes were small brass buttons, each connected with the others by hidden wires centering in a metal terminal. The operator carried a small set of batteries in his pocket, wired to a metal button on his vest. The terminal on the board and the button on his vest were directly opposite.

Seated with the layout in front of him, he exhorted the crowd to spin the arrow. His spiel was always the same:

"Round and round she goes,
Where she stops nobody knows."

One dollar was the usual charge for spinning the arrow.

When it was desired the capper should win, the operator leaned back. When the sucker played, the proprietor, under the pretense of watching the arrow, leaned forward until the two metal buttons touched, which energized the circuit, and the metal point of the arrow invariably came to rest over a blank.

For two hours before the circus performance opened, the busiest men on the lot were those who sold special admission and reserved seat tickets to avoid the rush at the box office, charging an advance of ten cents per ticket. The public looked on this as a great favor on the part of the management. Had they thought to count their change from a five or ten-dollar bill, they would have changed their opinion. As much as twenty-five dollars per day was paid for this privilege.

For large profits the men who sold electric belts, supposed to restore lost vitality to the aged, had all the other fakirs backed off the boards. These men usually worked uptown between parade time and afternoon performance. They possessed just enough knowledge of medicine and anatomy to make their talk appeal. The belts had absolutely no galvanic value. They were fashioned from ordinary canvas or duck cloth, to which several small circular pieces of tin were attached. In order to simulate electricity capsicum vaseline or red pepper was rubbed on the tin disks, which, when coming in contact with the skin, produced a slight burning sensation, and this was mistaken for galvanism.

Knowing that many of his hearers would be reluctant to come forward in public and thus disclose their disabilities to their neighbors, the fakir gave glowing descriptions of a special belt, which he sold only at his hotel. This belt he urged all to inspect without the assumption of any obligation on their part. The article he sold at his hotel differed from the one sold on the street in only one particular. The price was five dollars instead of one.

Jewelry or silverware was usually the merchandise sold by street fakirs with the circus for the reason that there were few experts in these lines among his audience.

His "pitch" set, and an audience collected, he would begin:

"Ladies and gentlemen, I appear before you this afternoon for the purpose of promulgating publicity for the Syracuse Silverware Company, the l-a-r-g-e-s-t manufacturers of this product on this mundane sphere.

"I choose to address you on circus day for the reason that I can reach a greater number of astute people on that day. The firm which I represent pays *all* the cost of advertising. I have here a genuine sterling silver spoon plated over white metal. I will now demonstrate and prove that assertion."

Taking the spoon in his left hand and a large pair of tinner's shears in his right, he would cut the spoon in half at the shank, the rough shears pulling the cheap plating over the cut ends and giving the erroneous impression of white metal.

"You see, ladies and gentlemen, just as I told you, 'quadruple' plating on white metal, guaranteed to last a lifetime. Now who will give me the advertising price of one dime for this dollar article?"

Several confederates would promptly purchase, while he as promptly would deliver the spoons and return the money with the merchandise, producing mild excitement among the audience. Note that at no time during his hectic harangue, would he agree to return the money, but he did so nevertheless.

"Now, good p-e-e-p-u-l, we will offer as a matter of advertising for my wonderful firm a half-dozen of these superb spoons for a quarter of a dollar." This time a confederate is not necessary. A dozen or two gullible persons would rush forward, receive their spoons, and have their money returned. Then a limited number of forks put up in half-dozen to the package would be sold for a half-dollar and the money returned to the purchasers. Excitement become a furor.

"And now, l-a-d-i-e-s and gentlemen, I will proceed to present to you the crowning climax of this most marvelous and magnificent campaign. Before I do so, I want all the hard-shell Shylocks with shoe strings around their pocketbooks to move on. I want only *large hearted, public spirited* citizens to have the opportunity to avail themselves of this wonderful advertising proposition which I will now unfold to you in detail."

Picking out his own watch, a very good one, from among a large grip full of cheap cases, he would proceed: "Now here is a watch containing seventeen ruby jewels, adjusted to synchronism, all oscillations of the body, is heat and cold, steam and dust proof. The case is made of a rolling of pure gold swaged over a composition of white gold, and guaranteed for twenty years. As an advertisement, I will proceed to pass these watches out among you generous and genial gentlemen at the unbelievable price of one dollar each. Please remember that you are not to open them for your stingy neighbor's inspection, until I have finished the distribution of this wonderful bargain bonanza. To all those holding wrapped watches after the sale is ended, I am going to give a gorgeous present. Will the marshal of your pretty little city please come forward and receive the money while the sale is in progress?"

I have seen these men pass out as many as two hundred of these worthless watch-cases in a single pitch. Men who were careful and close dealing in their business clawed their way through the crowd of women and children in a mad scramble to get something for nothing. I have seen prominent people of the town slyly open their purchase, see they were skinned, and straightway induce their neighbor to invest in order to keep from being derided for their credulity. The cases were merely gilded metal which had been stamped out by machinery at an approximate cost of fifteen cents each.

"And now, ladies and gentlemen," he would continue, "I promised to present each and every one holding watches a gorgeous gift," says the fakir. "Well, I will now do so." Whereupon there is extreme excitement among the easy marks who expect to have their money returned as in the case of the spoons. Vain hope!

"I could give you a brick house, a toothpick, or a match. That would be a present, would it not? But I will be more generous than this. To all those holding watches, I will present one of these gold wedding rings which sell at five dollars in regular jewelry stores. In closing I wish to say that I will be on this spot tonight at seven o'clock prepared to continue this wonderful campaign. Go home, relate your good fortune to your friends, and bring them with you tonight."

Promptly at the time specified, he would again appear and proceed in a manner similar to his afternoon program. His former victims would be there to a man, each with a firm determination to give him the horse laugh when he offered his watches for sale. But he never went that far. He always stopped at the fork sale, one notch below, and got two pitches out of the same crowd in one day. He was rarely ever arrested because no purchaser was willing to draw the ridicule of his neighbor by admitting that he was a customer.

I often watched these gentlemen work, and marveled at their nerve. So sore were their victims that I expected any minute to see them roughly handled. The only thing that saved them was the customer's fear of derision.

A clever prestidigitator was necessary when a soap game was operated. The better the sleight of hand performer, the greater the success. This game consisted in wrapping five or ten twenty-dollar bills around rectangular pieces of soap, enclosing them in blue litmus paper, and apparently dropping them into a small grip suspended from the operator's neck by a strap. In the satchel were perhaps a couple of dozen rectangular packages wrapped in the same way. These were blanks. As a matter of fact, the packages containing money were either not dropped in the satchel at all, the operator cleverly palming them and dropping in blanks instead, or else were so manipulated in the satchel that the victim could not reach them. One, two or three dollars was charged for making a draw. As the customer withdrew his hand containing his selection, it would be grabbed by the operator, who offered him first one, then five, and finally ten dollars for his choice. Feeling sure he had the grand prize of twenty dollars in his hand he refused, only to find on opening the package that he had drawn a blank.

The operator expected to be, and usually was, arrested in every town in which he worked; but was generally acquitted because he was able to show he had offered the player (before he opened the package) more money than he paid for his chance.

The only person I ever knew to beat the soap game was Elbert Hubbard—Fra Elbertus. Frequently when business was dull, the proprietor, in order to create the impression that the game was on the level, would hand the real money packages to some bystander to drop in the bag. The "Fra" once happened to be the one selected to drop the grand prize in the bag.

At that particular time Mr. Hubbard was eating some juicy grapes from a bag in his hand; in the act of dropping the packages, he noticed that the grape juice on his fingers put pink spots on the paper wherever he touched it. This escaped the notice of the flim-flam man. When the offer was made to draw, Mr. Hubbard paid his money, carefully and calmly stirred the packages until he uncovered the ones with the pink spots, and walked away with the "bacon."

The star performer of the entire lot of these circus fakirs of old times was a man I shall call "Rawbone" Ferguson because it was not his name. Rawbone was positively the best manipulator of the three-card monte game I ever knew, and I have known a lot of them in my time. He never worked on circus day, but began operations the next morning.

Boarding an early train the next day dressed as a farmer boy, he took a seat in the smoking car. As the train got under way big tears would begin to trickle down his cheeks and his great frame would be shaken with sobs. In a short while a kind-hearted fellow traveler would stop to inquire the cause of his grief, dropping perhaps a word or two of condolence.

"Wall," Rawbone would say between sobs, "my dad sent me down to (naming the town where the circus had shown the day before) to sell a car load of cattle. I sold the cattle, got into a three-card monte game with some circus gamblers and lost all the money. I 'low dad will just about kill me when I get home." Whereupon his grief would burst out anew, and others would gather round.

"Oh, well," his comforters would say, "I wouldn't take it so hard. You'll get over it in time, and no doubt your experience will prove a good lesson to you."

"Anyhow," Rawbone would reply, "I learned the game well enough to skin the boys when I get home."

Partly to comfort him, and also to find out just how clever he might be at the game, they would request that he demonstrate it to them.

Acting on the suggestion, Rawbone would select three jacks from a pack of cards and awkwardly throw them face down on the cushions of the car seat.

With much laughter at his blundering efforts, his fellow travelers would pick up the winning jack every time.

"That's queer," Rawbone would remark, "I thought I'd learned her better than that. Let's try her again." The next time it would not be so easy; the wrong jack would be selected, and again it would be tried.

In less than a half-hour, the seeming farmer boy would skin them out of four or five hundred dollars, get off the train at the next stop, and leave them believing they had been trimmed by a youthful yokel.

These few anecdotes should prove to persons of average intellect that no confidence man travels round the country with a game the public can beat.

Often the simplest-looking game was the biggest skin. The red and black wheel, which all men over fifty can no doubt remember, was one of these. Who of us does not recall the operator as he sat on a high stool, his eagle eye glued on the layout in front of him as he made his spiel?

"*C-o-m-e o-n, boys*. Even money on the red or black, and five to one on the star green. There's twenty-one blacks and twenty-one reds, and five star greens. *C-o-m-e o-n, boys*, who else can guess it out now for a quarter, half or a dollar? Are you all down? All down. Let her roll. R-o-l-l! The black wins!"

When the machine stopped on the black, there was more money on the red, and vice versa. The proprietor had a secret infallible method of stopping it on the color which would win for him.

These old skin-games are a thing of the past. Not only are they no longer permitted with the big tent attractions of today, but it is to be seriously questioned whether or not a sufficient number of unsophisticated persons could be secured to play them. The telephone, radio and automobile have been great educators of the class on whom these fakirs depended to unload their wares in the years gone by.

When the Animals Escape

BY C. R. COOPER

At one afternoon show I saw the big black bear make a beeline for freedom. I said to myself "That bear is gone!" But there are escapes, and then there are escapes. Only very rarely does a circus animal make a real break for it, and even if the animal manages a bust-out, what then? Whither to? And how shall he employ himself? Circus work is all most show animals know, and it's one thing to get loose, but quite another thing to make good the getaway. Occasionally you hear of one of the smaller big-cats taking it on the lam, and by dint of stealth, native cunning and good luck, disappearing into high country to make a new life. But these are the exceptions. The toughest problem for the escapee, is to make herself scarce. She must be able to proceed unnoticed, disappear into the background, blend into the crowd. For circus animals, this is often difficult. Elephants, for example, find invisibility a challenge.

Anyway, about the bear. I was hanging around near the back door of the big top, just abaft the band. I had just come out of the ring, or was just getting ready to enter—I don't recall which. But I was only half paying attention, when suddenly I felt that something had changed. It was not that a hush had fallen, rather the frequency of the crowd's buzz had altered, or the temperature had dropped. I looked into center ring where the Bear Act was in progress, and I saw what everybody saw—everybody except the Trainer, who, intent upon putting a pair of gamboling cubs through their paces, hadn't noticed. The huge old black bear had turned her back upon the Act, departed her pedestal and was standing straight up (all seven or eight feet of her) on the ring-curb, her nose high in the air as if to smell out some rare thing. One sickening moment later she lowered her head and with a great leap, headed straight for me. Did I see headlines?

"Molloy the Clown Mauled!" or "Bear Eats Clown!" Unlikely. Was I scared? You bet. I ducked behind the bandstand, but it soon was clear that I was not her object at all, she had been aiming for the exit behind me. She blew by and out the back door. Turning right onto the main drag of backlot, she tore away down the street until she reached her truck, climbed up the stairs to her cage, opened the door, entered, then pulled the door closed behind her. She wasn't working, and that was that.

There are escapes, and there are escapes.

○ ○ ○

Perhaps at some time in your life you've stood in front of a lion's cage at a circus, watching the pacing beast within and speculating upon what is happening in the mind of the shifting, uneasy creature as he makes the rounds from one end of the den to the other, poking his heavy nose against the bars, leaping upon the partition at one end, rebounding, growling, then springing at the heavily barred, double-locked door before taking up his pacing step once more.

Presumably it is easy to read that mind. He wants to get out. There is murder in those deep eyes; you can see it. The gruff growl is one of hate and malice and enmity toward all those about him, toward the trainers with their feeding forks, toward the massing crowds flooding through from the marquee for their look at the menagerie before traveling on to the seats of the big show. You can see viciousness there, and bloody desire and determination. You know that only one thought occupies that bestial brain,—to escape those steel bars, to break forth upon the humans he hates, to destroy, to devour.

And the only discrepancy about the meditation is the fact that you are entirely wrong! If that lion is thinking at all, he's wondering whether he's going to get a bone for breakfast the next morning, or whether it will be lean meat. As for escaping,—why should he leave a good home and make a lot of trouble for himself? That pacing and leaping is merely obedience to a natural law which commands that he take a certain amount of exercise, nothing more.

Not that jungle animals often do not commit murder when they escape. But when this happens it usually is the result of long waiting for a specific object. A leopard, for instance, will take its chance at death that it may kill a trainer it hates. But ordinarily the jungle animal that you see within a cage at a circus has no idea and no desire to leave. If it does, it isn't happy until it gets back into its dear old cage once more, back home where there is safety and comfort and where the world isn't rough and uneven and decidedly unpleasant,—as it is outside the bars. Queer, but it's true; the escape of an animal about a circus is often funnier than it is serious.

There must be a reason, and there is. The usual animal that you see in the circus isn't a product of the jungle. He wouldn't recognize his "native heath" if he should be introduced to it. His world from cubhood has been a cage; he was born in one, he was reared in one, and he knows absolutely nothing about the other life. He regards his cage as his home, as his natural habitat, and is lost without it. True, give a lion or tiger or leopard even a day in the open country, and he will revert to type. The old instincts will come upon him, he will kill his food in the same manner that his ancestors killed, when they were wild, free creatures, knowing nothing else. He will become the savage beast that his instincts command him to be. He will fall as naturally into the stealth, the sagacity and the cunning of the jungle as though he had been bred to that life. But he can't do this in a few minutes. The result is that when he does escape, through innate animal curiosity which leads him to investigate why his cage door should be open instead of closed, or why a lock or bar should give beneath his weight when he leaps, he finds himself in an unkind, noisy, excited sphere full of troubles and annoyance, and wishes that he'd never wandered from the old fireside.

It's a sort of animal psychology. A beast may be mean within an arena. He may even be a killer. Yet once on the outside, he may be a poor, befuddled thing, happy to find again the open door leading to his cage, and glad to get away from the hurly-burly into which a misstep of curiosity led him. His mind leads no more naturally to thoughts of escape than it would to tatting or embroidery. If you doubt the fact, watch closely the next time you witness a wild-animal act. You will see that the arena is of steel, that the door is safely trussed and laced with heavy leather straps. But that the entire top of the great, metal enclosure is covered with nothing more than a broad expanse of woven hemp netting! And as an illustration of that little remark about the "killer":

One time, Ed Warner, general agent of a circus, and myself stood in the wings of a theater in Denver. We were making the lions and tigers of the circus pay for their winter feed by a short tour of vaudeville performances, and out upon the stage Captain Ricardo, the trainer, high-booted, gold-laced, was sending the tawny beasts through their category of tricks, meanwhile keeping a weather eye trained upon a vicious, murderous, inbred lion, whose sole desire seemed to consist of an ambition to separate "Cap" from his internal arrangements. Day after day, week after week, and month after month, through the summer season of the circus they had fought and sparred, the lion snarling and roaring on his pedestal, his claw-fringed forefeet striking out in vicious circles as the whip of the trainer curled toward him, the lips drawn back from the ugly, yellow teeth, the evil eyes narrowed and squinted, his whole being one of fierce animosity toward this one hated personage, his trainer.

The act was nearing its finish, the leaping of the hurdles by the various trained beasts and "Cap" was putting the barricades in place. One of them stuck; the trainer yanked at it in an effort to straighten it and failed. With a leap, he then rushed forward to correct the position of the hurdle, and in doing so cramped himself between the "turntable" and the steel walls of the arena, with his back half-turned toward the killer.

"Cap! *Cap!* Look out!"

Ed and I were shouting from the wings, regardless of what the audience might think. For the killer had jumped from his pedestal and was creeping forward with all the sinuosity of a snake, toward the victim for whom he had waited. The trainer turned to find the ugly, open jaws of the lion not three feet away!

An instantaneous action and he had drawn his revolver, with its heavily wadded blank cartridges, sending shot after shot straight into the eyes of the malicious beast, the powder singeing the hair of the broad, flat forehead, the wadding stinging and disconcerting him. The lion whirled dazedly and pawed with the pain of the attack. The instant was enough for the trainer to jump clear and bring his bull-whip into action, while Ed and I—it was in the days before the Eighteenth Amendment—hurried out to get something that would put the strength back into our knees.

A week later, we were in another theater. It was just before the performance, and the three of us were in the trainer's dressing room listening to a recital by the lion-man of how he inadvertently allowed one finger to rest too long near a lion's mouth,—hence the missing digit. Above us was scuffling and noise, bumping and shouts, and Warner grunted.

"They sure make plenty of noise when they set a stage at this show shop, don't they?"

"You said it."

We continued our talk, while the noise above grew greater, finally to still. There came the sound of clanging steps on the iron stairs leading from the stage. Then the door was thrown open, and a belligerent stage carpenter faced the animal trainer.

"I wish you'd keep them toothless ole lions o' yours locked up," he blurted. "I've had a helluva time with 'em!"

"You?"

"Yeh. Came on the stage just now and found three of 'em wandering around. I gave two of 'em a kick and they jumped back in their cage, but the third one tried to get funny with me. So I whaled the tar out of him with a stage prop and made a cut alongside his head. Better get up there. He's bleedin'. But I couldn't help it; we can't have them things runnin' loose when we're trying to set a stage."

We went upstairs, to find, half-sitting, half-leaning against the side of the cage, a disconsolate, amazed lion, staring dejectedly through the bars and licking the blood which ran down his nose from a cut just in front of one ear. He had the appearance of someone who had encountered a very, very rough time, and who had not yet recovered from his fright and his surprise. We simply stood and stared. It was the inbred, the killer! Nor did we tell the stage carpenter his record.

The explanation is simple. In his cage, that lion was a bully and a ruffian because that was his element, that his stamping ground, that his home. But once outside, he had lost his bearing, the attack of the stage carpenter literally had swept him from his feet, and he had turned from a killer to a coward.

Nor is this the only instance. There is in the carnival business a personage known as Bill Rice. Everyone in the circus or carnival business knows Bill. They don't know his shows, for the simple reason that he changes his mind about every season and puts out a new one. This was one of the years when he was running a circus and, of course, presenting each day a street parade.

Among his animals was a vicious lion. And one day as the den was being cleaned for the parade, the animal man forgot to put into place the bar which held tight the steel door.

The cage went out on parade. The lion began to pace its prison. A jolt, and it struck the door. A second later, while telephone poles became clustered with human fruit, while horses reared and plunged, while women reached for baby buggies and hurriedly got them out of the way, forgetting entirely the fact that the babies themselves had been placed on the curbing, while men seized wives in their arms and hustled them to safety, without looking to see whether they were their own wives or the wives of someone else, the lion plumped to the pavement and stared dizzily about him for an instant, while he tried to fathom what had happened.

Then came panic. On all sides, including that of the lion. The cage had gone on. The horses pulling the den immediately in the rear had engaged in a runaway. Everywhere, people were shouting, milling, running and climbing trees and telephone poles. The lion scrambled vaguely, made a false start or two, whirled, then dived straight for a small negro restaurant across the street.

The restaurant had been full when things started. But its windows had opened automatically, through the simple method of persons going through glass, sash and all. At the instant the lion entered the door, a negro waiter was just arriving at one of the front tables with a tray of food. He saw the lion. One wild toss and the leonine beast found himself in the midst of a shower of soup, ham bones, chitlins and whatnot, while the waiter, screaming, made for the kitchen.

It was a bit disconcerting. For one excited, panicky second the lion fought the clattering dishes, clawing at them and biting vaguely at the atmosphere. Then stung by hot soup, half blinded by the pounding of crockery as it descended upon his eye and skull bones, he leaped at random and ran for a new place of hiding. And his path led toward the kitchen also!

The chef went out a window. Also the waiter. The dishwasher, deafened by the clattering of the crockery which he was massaging, had not received the warning in time to avail himself of a method of exit. He turned, saw a lion entering his domain, and did the only natural thing, opened a small door leading to the drain pipes beneath the sink, and dived in. Just then, some excited person appeared in the front of the restaurant with a shotgun, and fired.

The charge went wild except for a few shots which did no more than sting the lion's hide, but the noise was enough. Befuddled, bewildered, in the midst of a strange world and a conglomeration of annoying surroundings, the beast leaped again and sought retreat.

Happiness! A hole! Something to crawl into, some place where he might hide! It was the opening beneath the sink. And there the animal men of the circus found them, a fear-whitened, speechless negro, and an amazement-stricken lion, wedged in together, side by side, and neither making the first move to come out. The lion didn't want to. He was safe in a hole. The negro dishwasher couldn't. Even after the lion had been lassoed, pulled forth and dragged like some great, shaggy, recalcitrant dog into a shifting den, the dishwasher could do nothing but gasp and sit there beneath the sink. And between the two the lion was perhaps the more frightened!

Talk to the animal trainer, and he will tell you that as a rule it is not the maliciousness of an escaped animal which causes trouble. It's the panic of the crowd about him and the fright of the animal himself. The fear in a beast's mind when he suddenly becomes free is all pervading. He does not know that everyone else is afraid of him; he believes that he is in a world surrounded by enemies, that the safety of the cage has vanished, and that he must fight—if fight there be—for his very existence. It was during such a case as this that a tiger which escaped from a circus at Twin Falls, Idaho, a number of years ago, killed a child, and was in turn killed by Frank Tammen, the manager of the show, with a revolver. In his native state, a revolver shot would mean nothing to an eight-foot, four-hundred-pound tiger. It would simply bring a charge and the death of the hunter. But in the circus, the tiger was killed simply because he was out of his element, he was frightened, dazed, and he had not been loose sufficiently long to gain the natural savagery which time would bring him by the sheer command of instinct.

In fact, panic is the ruling power of the suddenly loosed animal. In elephants this is almost invariably true. Yet in spite of it, there is always an indication that the ruling sense of humor which appears always to be present in the elephantine mind, is there even in the frenzy of flight. And when the elephants break loose, there is this to remember: keep out of the way! For an elephant does not know how to go around anything. His ideas run along straight lines, and his paths follow his ideas.

In Winnipeg, for instance, several years ago, a circus was showing on the fairgrounds. A severe storm came up, and the elephants became frightened. They decided to run, the whole herd of them, and some thirty tons of elephantine flesh suddenly broke loose and headed for new and open fields where there was no thunder, no lightning and no wind.

Before them was one of the buildings of the fair association. It was a solid structure, built to stand year after year. At least, that was the idea in the minds of those who had erected it. But the path of the escaping pachyderms was on a line that included the building! The head of the herd, leading the chase, could have turned to the right some fifty or seventy-five feet and gone on without an obstruction. Was it done? It was not. A building showed ahead of her; she lowered her head, and hunching her shoulders, went on. A crash, the splintering of wood, the flying dust of mortar and the clattering of brick. Where the wall had been was now a hole, with the rear end of an elephant disappearing within, followed closely, by the rest of the thundering herd, each one taking out a bit more as it went through.

The other side—and a repetition. When the runaway was over, the building contained a perfect tunnel. As for the elephants, they ran until they became tired, breaking down a few fences and wooden sheds and other inconsequential impediments which had arisen in their path; then they stopped at a haystack and gorged themselves until the trainers arrived, gave them all a good berating and hustled them back to the show again.

The same was true in Riverside, California. There it was the same herd, led by the same old elephant, old enough, one would think, to have better sense, since one hundred and twenty-five circus seasons had passed since she was a bouncing baby of some three hundred pounds. This time Old Mamma led the way through a barber shop, taking with her, draped over her shoulders, the mug rack which hung at one end, and distributing along the street the vari-colored shaving-soap receptacles with their gaudy lettering and resplendent flowers, while the rest of the herd, trumpeting and bellowing, clattered along in the rear. From there the course led down the street, where, a bit tired, Mamma stopped at a fruit stand, the rest of the herd nudging up beside her, while the proprietors yelled for the police,—and departed.

The oranges and apples were great. Mamma enjoyed 'em. Also Alice and Floto and Frieda and the rest of the bulky runaways. In the rear the crowd, recovering a bit from its fright, began to close in. Just then, however, Mamma happened to notice that within the store hung a beautiful bunch of bananas. So she went in, taking the door with her. After that a new panic, for the floor was breaking, and an elephant hates an unsound footing. So she and the rest of the herd went out again,— through the wall on the other side!

Once more a runaway, which led to the free and open country. An hour or so of wandering about. Then the herd grew tired. Back into town it came, and a few minutes later, a yelping livery-stable owner scurried down the street with the announcement that his place of business had just been visited by a flock of elephants that was eating up everything in the barn!

There the animal men found them, peaceable, glad to obey their commands, happy and squealing and grunting as they answered the shout of "mule up" and trudged back once more to the circus. And the animal men will tell you that when the elephants dropped in at that livery stable they were doing their pachydermic best to get back to the show. They were through with their panic, they realized that they were lost, and they had but one thing to guide them,—the smell of fresh hay which would indicate to them the menagerie. They found that odor in a livery stable, and there they stopped. It wasn't exactly home, but it was a good substitute.

It is indeed seldom that the escape of any animal in a circus is a premeditated thing. The accidental opening of a door, the breaking of bars, or a wreck of some sort is the thing which usually leads to the cry "Th' lions is loose!" or the scurrying of a wild beast through the menagerie. But premeditated escapes have happened, and among them is the story of Fuller, a gigantic black-faced chimpanzee, whose mind, according to the scientists, was but a few notches below that of the human.

Fuller once had been the pet of a Pasadena millionaire and had been allowed to run loose about the estate. However, that brought complications. Residents of the neighborhood began to complain that their houses were being burglarized, ice boxes robbed, and in one instance an elderly man who affected a silk hat, Prince Albert and cane, investigated a noise in the hallway to find a six-foot chimpanzee just making his exit with his cane in one hand and the silk topper slanted over one eye. Then Fuller began to invite himself to breakfast rooms, even bedrooms, loping in the windows at inopportune times and causing everything from hysteria to riot calls, with the result that he ceased to be a pampered pet and became a circus exhibit. And there, for the first time, Fuller found out what it meant to hate. Not a hundred feet away, in the winter quarters, was the elephant line and that, to Fuller, meant trouble.

The elephant and the chimpanzee are natural enemies. That enmity came into being in the circus winter quarters, and the gigantic Fuller spent most of his time sitting crouched in his cage, grimacing and yowling at the hulking beasts, even repeating one of his tricks of other days,—that of wiggling his fingers at his nose. Day after day he worked at his chains, loosing them, only to have them replaced by the animal men. Then one night the telephone in the winter home of Henry Boucher, head animal trainer of the circus, whirred viciously. He answered to find the night watchman at the other end of the line:

"Get over here as quick as you can!" came the excited message. "Fuller's loose and he's whipping all the elephants! They're about to bust through the building. Hurry!"

Boucher hurried,—to find that the watchman's report had been correct. The herd had broken loose from its picket pins and was crowded in one corner of the building, milling and trumpeting. Only one elephant still was showing fight, a great tusker, and he was about ready to quit. His rushes had availed him nothing; Fuller merely ducked out of the way, and chattering, returned to the attack. The long, heavy tusks had been useless. Their thrusts struck only air as Fuller dodged them. The great blows of the forefeet, aimed at Fuller, had hit nothingness. The sweep of the heavy trunk had inevitably been met by the chimpanzee, who grasped it with his great hands as it circled toward him, then swung upon it until it had lost the force of the blow. Without inflicting a single injury, Fuller had won a "moral" victory simply by tantalizing the great beasts until their frenzy had reached the point of panic. And when Boucher approached him.

A kick, a cuff and a few cusswords. Fuller—his weight was close to two hundred and fifty pounds, and the strength of his great shoulders sufficient to tear a man limb from limb—merely squealed, raised one arm in front of his face like a child afraid of a slapping, then, in obedience to the command, trundled back to his cage. He had achieved his aim. He had wanted to whip those elephants, and he had done it. The object accomplished, he went back to captivity in peace.

But things do not always end as amiably when the circus animals get loose. As is the case with disease, the complications following the escape of jungle beasts often causes more excitement than the escape itself. To wit, the story of Bad Axe, Michigan, and an "escape yarn" that has become laughing history in circusdom. The recital requires a bit of an introduction.

Kaiser and Sultan, two of the lions of the show, were a bit different from the usual run of beasts, inasmuch as they had been led about as pets until almost the last possible moment when their catlike natures could be trusted. Strange as it may be, this often leads to bad temper when the beasts have reached the adult age, and certainly in the case of the two lions, there was little of fear and little of bewilderment when an animal man inadvertently left open a door of their cage and allowed them to wander forth.

The show at this time possessed what it once had believed to be a wonderful feature,—the result of a government experiment which had resulted in the cross-breeding of a Grevy's zebra, from Africa, and a Rocky Mountain "Canary," or burro, from Colorado. The result had been a strange and fearsome beast, possessing the striped body of a zebra, the uncertainty, the viciousness, the meanness and wildness of a jungle animal, combined with the head of a Missouri mule and all that goes with that contrary creature. Long months had been spent in training the things, with the result that they did wonderfully well in rehearsals, and the opposite during the performances. It was nothing at all for the "Five United States Government Hyneys" as they were called, to enter the show tent at a trot,—and keep on trotting. You could find Hyneys scattered all about the circus grounds—and about the town for that matter—trampling gardens, eating up flower beds, kicking the stuffing out of poor, innocent country horses who didn't know enough to kick back, running up damage suits, attachments and causing trouble in general for the circus fixer. It was a dull week indeed when the Hyneys didn't run away at least three times. Often they batted a thousand by pulling a runaway once a day. The result of which was a change in the circus program, from a glowing announcement of these wonderful beasts and the astonishing category of tricks which they had mastered, to the simple announcement:

THE FIVE UNITED STATES GOVERNMENT HYNEYS
WILL NOW PROCEED
TO DO AS THEY PLEASE!

Which they did. And which leads to the opening of the drama of Bad Axe, Michigan. It all happened before the show. The parade had just returned to the lot, the cages had been "spotted" in their regular places in the menagerie, and in the big top, or main tent, the canvas men, the roughnecks, the seat and plank men, the property men and "punks" were busily engaged in putting on the final touches before the opening of the doors for the matinée performance.

Everywhere was the well-greased, smooth-working activity of a circus in its final moment of preparation. From the padroom, a "pony punk" was leading the five recalcitrant Hyneys back to the menagerie from a short and eventful runaway. At one of the forward center poles, "Cow," an assistant boss canvasman, was holding an iron stake which "Fullhouse," a workman, was about to pound into the ground with a sixteen-pound sledge. Everything was traveling along smoothly, beautifully. Then a streaking figure shot from the "connection" or entrance to the menagerie, his arms waving, his eyes wild.

"F'r Gawd's sake, run!" he yelled. "Th' lions is loose! They're right behind me!"

And they were,—Sultan and Kaiser, entering on a trot, perfectly composed through the experience of others days when they had been led about at the end of a leash as cubs, and looking for trouble. The center poles became alive with property men and seat-workers. Two-hundred-pound "Fat," a plank man, made a three-foot leap for a trapeze tape and clambered up it in a far more agile manner than the acrobat himself could have done. Fullhouse dropped his sledge and ran a half mile to a tree where he was found roosting an hour later. "Cow," still holding his iron stake, looked around somewhat hazily, saw Sultan only a few feet away, swung high the stake, walloped the lion in the forehead, knocked him flat and all but unconscious, then did a bit of running himself. Just then Kaiser saw the Hyneys with their zebra stripes, and a new angle of activity started. The zebra forms the lion's natural meat in the wild state.

It all seemed to come back to Kaiser,—the old call of the veldt. He roared, with a note strange to the circus menagerie. Then he leaped, claws extended, mouth wide, straight for the rumps of the nearest Hyney.

But that was all. Out came vicious heels that caught the beast in the chest and knocked him back. He came on once more, only to find the world filled with kicking, sharp hoofs that battled him in the face and head and chest, that knocked the wind out of his lungs, that cut and whanged and battered him until at last, whimpering and bleeding, he turned and sought flight, the animal men after him, leaving behind a mulish, contrary creature that allowed his ears to go flat, and his raucous voice to raise in a long hee-haw of victory.

One lion was blinking in the daze of returning consciousness, the other was whipped and cowering in a clump of brush near the tent.

Both of them were more than willing to quit. But the excitement still went on, for the elephants had decided to become panic-stricken.

The lions had passed the elephant line before the hulking beasts seemed to realize that the right and proper thing for an occasion like this should be a runaway. Whereupon the head of the herd emitted a bellow of excitement, pulled her stake from the ground, and made a hole in the side wall of the tent for the general exodus. One by one the big creatures ambled forth, squealing and trumpeting, the noise of their exit calling a small contingent of the animal men from the primary business of catching lions. Only one arrived in time, Boucher, the menagerie superintendent, and he got there just as the rear of the last elephant was disappearing.

A leap and he caught the hulking, squealing beast by its piglike tail and sought to run along behind it until his shouts could bring the head of the herd to her senses. He was wrong. The elephant herd merely rounded into express-train speed and kept going, while Boucher, his feet touching the ground once in a while, still clung to the last elephant's tail and yelled himself hoarse, in vain. Then—more complications!

An eight-horse team, harnessed to an empty pole wagon, was just crossing the lot, quietly, peaceably, without any knowledge of what had gone on in the tent. Then came the elephants! Swarms of elephants, trumpeting, squealing, and thundering, as they came up from behind, alongside the wagon and its eight horses. It was too much. The driver pulled and tugged his best. It was useless. The horses, all eight of them, with the pole wagon clattering along behind, ran away also. Their idea was to evade the elephants. The result was that they stayed side by side, neither gaining on the other, while in the rear, Boucher still hung to an elephant's tail.

Half across the lot and another element entered,—a man in an automobile. Glancing over his shoulder, he saw a world full of elephants and horses, all coming toward him at once. So he decided to move faster than they. He didn't. Just as his machine got into its speed on the rough, rutty ground, the elephants and horses came alongside.

And side by side the race began, the queerest race, so circus men say, in history,—a herd of elephants, an eight-horse team attached to a wagon, and a human being in an automobile. The elephants bellowed. The horses did all but scream. The man on the pole wagon yelled, and so did Boucher and the driver of the automobile.

Just before them stood the cook house. The automobile, under the guidance of a human being, ran halfway through the tent before it could be stopped. The elephants slid on their haunches and decided to quit. The horses, with a sudden swerve, ran around the end and finally came to a halt. The race was over. And the queer part of it all was that by this time the lions were back in their cages, both of them whipped to a standstill, and both of them glad to be home again where there were no hoofs or iron bars, and where life ran on the level!

And so goes the usual animal escape. There is often more to cause laughter than tragedy. For it is the good luck of the circus that most escapes happen when the tent is empty, during the cleaning time of the cages, or during a storm when the performance has been abandoned. And it is seldom that the audience itself suffers as a result. There have even been cases where animals have escaped during the performance of a circus and been recaptured, without a person in the great throng knowing anything of the occurrence!

Circus Day at Mancos

BY EDGAR BEECHER BRONSON

Why not mix two great American myths together? Marry a circus story to a great cowboy tale and you've really got something. Add a young galloot, a posse of kibitzers, and a mysterious girl with fiery red hair, and the ole magic really begins to happen. Climax the whole thing with a shoot-out in the shadow of a big top, and you have something approaching the sublime. Also a darn good read.

Edgar Beecher Bronson (1856-1917) was a Nebraska rancher, a West Texas cattleman, an African big-game hunter, a serious photographer and a very fine writer. Though he came to this last fairly late in his life. He published *Reminiscences of a Ranchman* in 1908, and on the strength of its success, published *The Red-Blooded Heroes of the Frontier* (from which this story is taken) and *In Closed Territory* (with nearly 100 illustrations from photos by the author) in 1910. In 1914 he published his final work *The Vanguard*.

○ ○ ○

Cowboys were seldom respecters of the feelings of their fellows. Few topics were so sacred or incidents so grave they were not made the subject of the rawest jests. Leading a life of such stirring adventure that few days passed without some more or less serious mishap, reckless of life, unheedful alike of time and eternity, they made the smallest trifles and the biggest tragedies the subjects of chaff and badinage till the next diverting occurrence. But to the Cross Cañon outfit Mat Barlow's love for Netty Nevins was so obviously a downright worship, an all-absorbing, dominating cult, that, in a way, and all unknown to her, she became the nearest thing to a religion the Cross Cañonites ever had.

Eight years before Mat had come among them a green tenderfoot from a South Missouri village, picked up in Durango by Tom McTigh, the foreman, on a glint of the eye and set of the jaw that suggested workable material. Nor was McTigh mistaken. Mat took to range work like a duck to water. Within a year he could rope and tie a mossback with the best, and in scraps with Mancos Jim's Pah-Ute horse raiders had proved himself as careless a dare-devil as the oldest and toughest trigger-twitcher of the lot.

But persuade and cajole as much as they liked, none of the outfit were ever able to induce Mat to pursue his education as a cowboy beyond the details incident to work and frolic on the open range. Old past-masters in the classics of cowboy town deportment, expert light shooters, monte players, dance-hall beaux, elbow-crookers, and red-eye riot-starters labored faithfully with Mat, but all to no purpose. To town with them he went, but with them in their debauches he never joined; indeed as a rule he even refused to discuss such incidents with them academically. Thus he delicately but plainly made it known to the outfit that he proposed to keep his mind as clean as his conduct.

Such a curiosity as Mat was naturally closely studied. The combined intelligence of the outfit was trained upon him, for some time without result. He was the knottiest puzzle that ever hit Cross Cañon. At first he was suspected of religious scruples and nicknamed "Circuit Rider." But presently it became apparent that he owned ability and will to curse a fighting outlaw bronco till the burning desert air felt chill, and it became plain he feared God as little as man. Mat had joined the outfit in the Autumn, when for several weeks it was on the jump; first gathering and shipping beeves, then branding calves, lastly moving the herd down to its Winter range on the San Juan. Throughout this period Cross Cañon's puzzle remained hopeless; but the very first evening after the outfit went into Winter quarters at the home ranch, the puzzle was solved.

Ranch mails were always small, no matter how infrequent their coming or how large the outfit. The owner's business involved little correspondence, the boys' sentiments inspired less. Few with close hometies exiled themselves on the range. Many were "on the scout" from the scene of some remote shooting scrape and known by no other than a nickname. For most of them such was the rarity of letters that often have I seen a cowboy turning and studying an unopened envelope for a half-day or more, wondering whoever it was from and guessing whatever its contents could be. Thus it was one of the great sensations of the season for McTigh and his red-sashers, when the ranch cook produced five letters for Circuit Rider, all addressed in the same neat feminine hand, all bearing the same postmark. And when, while the rest were washing for supper, disposing of war sacks, or "making down" blankets, Mat squatted in the chimney corner to read his letters, Lee Skeats impressively whispered to Priest:

"Ben, I jest nachally hope never to cock another gun ef that thar little ol' Circuit hain't got a gal that 's stuck to him tighter'n a tick makin' a gotch ear, or that ain't got airy damn thing to do to hum but write letters. Size o' them five he 's got must 'a kept her settin' up nights to make 'em ever since Circuit jumped the hum reservation. Did you *ever* hear of a feller gettin' five letters from a gal to wonst?"

"I shore never did," answered Ben; "Circuit must 'a been 'prentice to some big Medicine Man back among his tribe and have a bagful o' hoodoos hid out somewhere. He ain't so damn hijus to look at, but he shore never knocked no gal plum loco that away with his p'rsn'l beauty. Must be some sort o' Injun medicine he works."

"Cain't be from his mother," cogitated Lee. "Writin' ain't trembly none—looks like it was writ by a school-marm, an' a lally-cooler at that. Circuit will have to git one o' them pianer-like writin' makers and keep poundin' it on the back till it hollers, ef he allows to lope close up in that gal's writin' class.

"Lord! but won't thar be fun for us all Winter he'pin' him 'tend to his correspondence!

"Let's you an' me slip round and tip off the outfit to shet up till after supper, an' then all be ready with a hot line o' useful hints 'bout his answerin' her."

Ben joyously fell in with Lee's plan. The tips were quickly passed round. But none of the hints were ever given, not a single one. A facer lay ahead of them beside which the mere receipt of the five letters was nothing. To be sure, the letters were the greatest sensation the outfit had enjoyed since they stood off successfully two troops of U.S. Cavalry, come to arrest them for killing twenty marauding Utes. But what soon followed filled them with an astonishment that stilled their mischievous tongues, stirred sentiments long dormant, and ultimately, in a measure, tuned their own heart-strings into chord with the sweet melody ringing over Circuit's own.

Supper was called, and upon it the outfit fell—all but Circuit. They attacked it wolf-fashion according to their habit, bolting the steaming food in a silence absolute but for the crunching of jaws and the shrill hiss of sipped coffee. The meal was half over before Circuit, the last letter finished, tucked his five treasures inside his shirt, stepped over the bench to a vacant place at the table, and hastily swallowed a light meal; in fact he rose while the rest were still busy gorging themselves. And before Lee or the others were ready to launch at Circuit any shafts of their rude wit, his maneuvers struck them dumb with curiosity.

Having hurried from the table direct to his bunk, Circuit was observed delving in the depths of his war sack, out of which he produced a set of clean underclothing, complete from shirt to socks, and a razor. Besides these he carefully laid out his best suit of store clothes, and from beneath the "heading" of the bunk he pulled a new pair of boots. All this was done with a rapidity and method that evinced some set purpose which the outfit could not fathom, a purpose become the more puzzling when, five minutes later, Circuit returned from the kitchen bearing the cook's wash-tub and a pail of warm water. The tub he deposited and filled in an obscure corner of the bunk-room, and shortly thereafter was stripped to the buff, laboriously bathing himself. The bath finished, Circuit carefully shaved, combed his hair, and dressed himself in his cleanest and best.

While he was dressing, Bill Ball caught breath enough to whisper to Lee: "By cripes! I've got it. Circuit 's got a hunch some feller 's tryin' to rope an' hobble his gal, an' he 's goin' to ask Tom for his time, fork a cayuse, an' hit a lope for a railroad that'll take him to whatever little ol' humanyville his gal lives at."

"Lope hell," answered Lee; "it 's a run he 's goin' to hit, with one spur in the shoulder an' th' other in th' flank. Why, th' way he 's throwin' that whiskercutter at his face, he 's plumb shore to dewlap and wattle his fool self till you could spot him in airy herd o' humans as fer as you could see him."

But Bill's guess proved wide of the mark.

As soon as Circuit's dressing was finished and he had received assurance from the angular fragment of mirror nailed above the washbasin that his hair was smoothly combed and a new neckerchief neatly knotted, he produced paper and an envelope from his war sack, seated himself at the end of the long dinner-table, farthest from the fireplace, lighted a fresh candle, spread out his five treasures, carefully sharpened a stub pencil, and duly set its lead end a-soak in his mouth, preparatory to the composition of a letter. The surprise was complete. Such painstaking preparation and elaborate costuming for the mere writing of a letter none present—or absent, for that matter—had ever heard of. But it was all so obviously eloquent of a most tender respect for his correspondent that boisterous voices were hushed, and for at least a quarter of an hour the Cross Cañonites sat covertly watching the puckered brows, drawn mouth, and awkwardly crawling pencil of the writer.

Presently Lee gently nudged Ball and passed a wink to the rest; then all rose and softly tiptoed their way to the kitchen.

Comfortably squatted on his heels before the cook's fireplace, Lee quietly observed:"Fellers, I allow it 's up to us to hold a inquest on th' remains o' my idee about stringin' Circuit over that thar gal o' his'n. I moves that th' idee 's done died a-bornin', an' that we bury her. All that agrees, say so; any agin it, say so, 'n' then git their guns an' come outside."

There were no dissenting votes, Lee's motion was unanimously carried.

"Lee 's plumb right," whispered McTigh; "that kid 's got it harder an' worse than airy feller I ever heerd tell of, too hard for us to lite in stringin' him 'bout it. Never had no gal myself; leastways, no good one; been allus like a old buffalo bull whipped out o' th' herd, sorta flockin' by my lonesome, an'—an'—" with a husky catch of the voice,"an' that thar kid 'minds me I must a' been missin' a *hell* of a lot hit 'pears to me I would n't have no great trouble gittin' to like."

Then for a time there was silence in the kitchen.

Crouching over his pots, the black cook stared in surprised inquiry at the semicircle of grim bronzed faces, now dimly lit by the flickering embers and then for a moment sharply outlined by the flash of a cigarette deeply inhaled by nervous lips. The situation was tense. In each man emotions long dormant, or perhaps by some never before experienced, were tumultuously surging; surging the more tumultuously for their long dormancy or first recognition. Presently in a low, hoarse voice that scarcely carried round the semicircle, Chillili Jim spoke:

"Fellers, Circuit shore 'minds me pow'ful strong o' my ol' mammy. She was monstrous lovin' to we-uns; an' th' way she scrubbed an' fixed up my ol' pa when he comes home from the break-up o' Terry's Rangers, with his ol' carcass 'bout as full o' rents an' holes as his ragged gray war clothes! Allus have tho't ef I could git to find a gal stuck on me like mammy on pa, I'd drop my rope on her, throw her into th' home ranch pasture, an' nail up th' gate fer keeps."

"'Minds me o' goin' to meetin' when I was a six-year-old," mused Mancos Mitch; "when Circuit's pencil got to smokin' over th' paper an' we-uns got so dedburned still, 'peared to me like I was back in th' little ol' meetin'-house in th' mosquito clearin', on th' banks o' th' Leona in ol' Uvalde County. Th' air got that quar sort o' dead smell 'ligion allus 'pears to give to meetin'-houses, an' I could hear th' ol' pa's on a-tellin' us how it 's th' lovinest that allus gits th' longest end o' th' rope o' life. Hits me now that ther ol' sky scout was 'bout right. Feller cain't possibly keep busy *all* th' love in his system, workin' it off on nothin' but a pet hoss or gun; thar 's allus a hell of a lot you did n't know you had comes oozin' out when a proper piece o' calico lets you next."

"Boys," cut in Bill Ball, the dean of the outfit's shooters-up of town and shooters-out of dance-hall lights; "boys, I allow it 's up to me to 'pologize to Circuit. Ef I was n't such a damned o'nery kiyote I'd o' caught on befo'. But I hain't been runnin' with th' drags o' th' she herd so long that I can't 'preciate th' feelin's o' a feller that 's got a good gal stuck on him, like Circuit. Ef I had one, you-all kin gamble yer *alce* all bets would be off with them painted dance-hall beer jerkers, an' it would be out in th' brush fo' me while th' corks was poppin', gals cussin', red-eye flowin', an' chips rattlin'. That thar little ol' kid has my 'spects, an' ef airy o' th' Blue Mountain outfit tries to string him 'bout not runnin' with them oreide propositions, I'll hand 'em lead till my belt 's empty."

Ensued a long silence; at length, by common consent the inquest was adjourned, and the members of the jury returned to the bunk-room, quiet and solemn as men entering a death chamber. There at the table before the guttering candle still sat Circuit, his hair now badly tousled, his upper lip blackened with pencil lead, his brows more deeply puckered, his entire underlip apparently swallowed, the table littered with rudely scrawled sheets.

Slipping softly to their respective bunks, the boys peeled and climbed into their blankets. And there they all lay, wide-awake but silent, for an hour or two, some watching Circuit curiously, some enviously, others staring fixedly into the dying fire until from its dull-glowing embers there rose for some visions of bare-footed, nut-brown, fustian-clad maids, and for others the finer lines of silk and lace draped figures, now long since passed forever out of their lives. Those longest awake were privileged to witness Circuit's final offering at the shrine of his love.

His letter finished, enclosed, addressed, and stamped, he kissed it and laid it aside, apparently all unconscious of the presence of his mates, as he had been since beginning his letter. Then he drew from beneath his shirt something none of them had seen before, a buckskin bag, out of which he pulled a fat blank memorandum book, *into which he proceeded to copy, in as small a hand as he could write, every line of his sweetheart's letters*. Later they learned that this bag and its contents never left Circuit's body, nestled always over his heart, suspended by a buckskin thong!

Out of the close intimacies cow-camp life promotes, it was not long before the well-nigh overmastering curiosity of the outfit was satisfied. They learned how the "little ol' blue-eyed sorrel top," as Bill Ball had christened her, had vowed to wait faithfully till Circuit could earn and save enough to make them a home, and how Circuit had sworn to look into no woman's eyes till he could again look into hers. Before many months had passed, Circuit's regular weekly letter to Netty—regular when on the ranch—and the ceremonial purification and personal decking that preceded it, had become for the Cross Cañon outfit a public ceremony all studiously observed. None were ever too tired, none too grumpy, to wash, shave, and "slick up" of letter nights, scrupulously as Moslems bathe their feet before approaching the shrine of Mahomet; and still as Moslems before their shrine all sat about the bunk-room while Circuit wrote his letter and copied Netty's last. Indeed, more than one well-started wild town orgy was stopped short by one of the boys remarking: "Cut it, you kiyotes! Netty would n't like it!"

And thus the months rolled on till they stacked up into years, but the interchange of letters never ceased and the burden of Circuit's buckskin bag grew heavier.

Twice Circuit ventured a financial *coup*, and both times lost—invested his savings in horses, losing one band to Arizona rustlers, and the other to Mancos Jim's Pah-Utes. After the last experience he took no further chances and settled down to the slow but sure plan of hoarding his wages.

Come the Fall of the eighth year of his exile from Netty, Circuit had accumulated two thousand dollars, and it was unanimously voted by the Cross Cañon outfit, gathered in solemn conclave at Circuit's request, that he might venture to return to claim her. And before the conclave was adjourned, Lee Skeats, the chairman, remarked: "Circuit, ef Netty shows airy sign o' balkin' at th' size o' your bank roll, you kin jes' tell her that thar 's a bunch out here in Cross Cañon that's been lovin' her sort o' by proxy, that'll chip into your matrimonial play, plumb double the size o' your stack, jest fo' th' hono' o' meetin' up wi' her an' th' pleasure o' seein' their pardner hitched."

The season's work done and the herd turned loose on its Winter range on the San Juan, the outfit decided to escort Circuit into Mancos and there celebrate his coming nuptials. For them the one hundred and seventy intervening miles of alternating cañon and mesa, much of the journey over trails deadly dangerous for any creature less sure-footed than a goat, was no more than a pleasant *pasear*. Thus it was barely high noon of the third day when the thirty Cross Cañonites reached their destination.

Deep down in a mighty gorge, nestled beside the stream that gave its name alike to cañon and to town, Mancos stewed contentedly in a temperature that would try the strength and temper of any unaccustomed to the climate of southwestern Colorado. Framed in Franciscan-gray sage brush, itself gray as the sage with the dust of pounding hoofs and rushing whirlwinds, at a little distance Mancos looked like an aggregation of dead ash heaps, save where, here and there, dabs of faded paint lent a semblance of patches of dying embers.

While raw, uninviting, and even melancholy in its every aspect, for the scattered denizens of a vast region round about Mancos's principal street was the local Great White Way that furnished all the fun and frolic most of them ever knew. To it flocked miners from their dusky, pine-clad gorges in the north, grangers from the then new farming settlement in the Montezuma Valley, cowboys from Blue Mountain, the Dolores, and the San Juan; Navajos from Chillili, Utes from their reservation—a motley lot burning with untamed elemental passions that called for pleasure "straight."

Joyously descending upon the town at a breakneck lope before a following high wind that completely shrouded them in clouds of dust, it was not until they pulled up before their favorite feed corral that the outfit learned that Mancos was revelling in quite the reddest red-letter day of its existence, the day of its first visitation by a circus—and also its last for many a year thereafter.

In the eighties Mancos was forty miles from the nearest railway, but news of the reckless extravagances of its visiting miners and cowboys tempted Fells Brothers' "Greatest Aggregation on Earth of Ring Artists and Monsters" to visit it. Dusted and costumed outside of town, down the main street of Mancos the circus bravely paraded that morning, its red enameled paint and gilt, its many-tinted tights and spangles, making a perfect riot of brilliant colors over the prevailing dull gray of valley and town.

Streets, stores, saloons, and dance halls were swarming with the outpouring of the ranches and the mines, men who drank abundantly but in the main a rollicking, good-natured lot.

While the Cross Cañonites were liquoring at the Fashion Bar (Circuit drinking sarsaparilla), Lame Johny, the barkeeper, remarked: "You-uns missed it a lot, not seein' the pr'cesh. She were a ring-tailed tooter for fair, with the damnedest biggest noisemakin' band you ever heard, an' th' p'rformers wearin' more pr'tys than I ever allowed was made. An' say, they've got a gal in th' bunch, rider I reckon, that's jest that damned good to look at it *hurts*. Damned ef I kin git her outen my eyes yet. Say, she's shore prittier than airy red wagon in th' show—built like a quarter horse, got eyes like a doe, and a sorrel mane she could hide in. She 's sure a *chile con carne* proposition, if I ever see one."

"Huh!" grunted Lee; "may be a good-looker, but I'll gamble she ain't in it with our Sorrel-top; hey, boys? Here 's to *our* Sorrel-top, fellers, an' th' day Circuit prances into Mancos wi' her."

Several who tried to drink and cheer at the same time lost much of their liquor, but none of their enthusiasm. After dinner at Charpiot's, a wretched counterfeit of the splendid old Denver restaurant of that name, the Cross Cañonites joined the throng streaming toward the circus.

For his sobriety designated treasurer of the outfit for the day and night, Circuit marched up to the ticket wagon, passed in a hundred dollar bill and asked for thirty tickets. The tickets and change were promptly handed him. On the first count the change appeared to be correct, but on a recount Circuit found the ticket-seller had cunningly folded one twenty double, so that it appeared as two bills instead of one. Turning immediately to the ticket-seller, Circuit showed the deception and demanded correction.

"Change was right; you can't dope and roll me; gwan!" growled the ticket-agent.

"But it's plumb wrong, an' you can't rob me none, you kiyote," answered Circuit; "hand out another twenty, and do it sudden!"

"Chase yourself to hell, you bow-legged hold-up," threatened the ticket-seller.

When, a moment later, the ticket man plunged out of the door of his wagon wildly yelling for his clan, it was with eyes flooding with blood from a gash in his forehead due to a resentful tap from the barrel of Circuit's gun.

Almost in an instant pandemonium reigned and a massacre was imminent. Stalwart canvasmen rushed to their chief's call till Circuit's bunch were outnumbered three to one by tough trained battlers on many a tented field, armed with hand weapons of all sorts. Victors these men usually were over the town roughs it was customarily theirs to handle; but here before them was a bunch not to be trifled with, a

quiet group of thirty bronzed faces, some grinning with the antici-
pated joy of the combat they loved, some grim as death itself, each af-
fectionately twirling a gleaming gun. One overt act on the part of the
circus men, and down they would go like ninepins, and they knew
it—knew it so well that, within two minutes after they had assembled,
all dodged into and lost themselves in the throng of onlookers like
rabbits darting into their warrens.

"Mighty pore 'pology for real men, them elephant busters,"
disgustedly observed Bill Ball. "Come on, fellers, le's go in."

"Nix for me," spoke up Circuit; "I'm that hot in the collar over
him tryin' to rob me I've got no use for their old show. You all go in, an'
I'll go down to Chapps' and fix my traps to hit the trail for the railroad
in the mornin'."

On the crest of a jutting bastion of the lofty escarpment that
formed the west wall of the cañon, the sun lingered for a good-night
kiss of the eastern cliffs which it loved to paint every evening with all
the brilliant colors of the spectrum; it lingered over loving memories of
ancient days when every niche of the Mancos cliffs held its little
bronze-hued line of primitive worshippers, old and young, devout,
prostrate, fearful of their Red God's nightly absences, suppliant of his
return and continued largess; over memories of ceremonials and pas-
times barbaric in their elemental violence, but none more primitively
savage than the new moon looked down upon an hour later.

Supper over, on motion of Lee Skeats the Cross Cañonites had
adjourned to the feed corral and gone into executive session.

Lee called the meeting to order.

"Fellers," he said, "that dod-burned show makes my back tired.
A few geezers an' gals flipfloopin' in swings an' a bunch o' dead ones on
ol' broad-backed work hosses that calls theirselves riders! Shucks! thar
hain't one o' th' lot could sit a real twister long enough to git his seat
warm; about th' second jump would have 'em clawin' sand.

"Only thing in their hull circus wo'th lookin' at is that red-
maned gal, an' she looks that sweet an' innercent she don't 'pear to
rightly belong in that thar bare-legged bunch o' she dido-cutters. They-
all must 'a mavericked her recent. Looks like a pr'ty ripe red apple
among a lot o' rotten ones.

"Hated like hell to see her thar, specially with next to nothin' on, fer somehow I could n't help her 'mindin' me o' our Sorrel-top. Reckon ef we busted up their damn show, that gal'd git to stay a while in a decent woman's sort o' clothes. What say, shall we bust her?"

"Fer one, I sits in an' draw cards in your play cheerful," promptly responded Bill Ball; "kind o' hurt me too to see Reddy thar. An' then them animiles hain't gittin' no squar' deal. Never did believe in cagin' animiles more'n men. Ef they need it bad, kill 'em; ef they don't, give 'm a run fo' their money, way ol' Mahster meant 'em to have when He made 'em. Let's all saddle up, ride down thar, tie onto their tents, an' pull 'em down, an' then bust open them cages an' give every dod-blamed animile th' liberty I allows he loves same as humans! An' then, jest to make sure she's a good job, le's whoop all their hosses ove' to th' Dolores an' scatter 'em through th' piñons!"

Bill's motion was unanimously carried, even Circuit cheerfully consenting, from memories of the outrage attempted upon him earlier in the day. Ten minutes later the outfit charged down upon the circus at top speed, arriving among the first comers for the evening perform-ance. Flaming oil torches lit the scene, making it bright almost as day.

By united action, thirty lariats were quickly looped round guy ropes and snubbed to saddle horns, and then, incited by simultaneous spur digs and yells, thirty fractious broncos bounded away from the tent, fetching it down in sheets and ribbons, ropes popping like pistols, the rent canvas shrieking like a creature in pain, startled animals thresh-ing about their cages and crying their alarm. Cowboys were never slow at anything they undertook. In three minutes more the side shows were tentless, the dwarfs trying to swarm up the giant's sturdy legs to safety or to hide among the adipose wrinkles of the fat lady, and the outfit tackled the cages.

In another three minutes the elephant, with a sociable shot through his off ear to make sure he should not tarry, was thundering down Mancos's main street, trumpeting at every jump, followed by the lion, the great tuft of hair at the end of his tail converted, by a happy thought of Lee Skeats, into a brightly blazing torch that, so long as the fuel lasted, lighted the shortest cut to freedom for his escaping mates— for the lion hit as close a beeline as possible trying to outrun his own tail. For the outfit, it was the lark of their lives. Crashing pistol shots and ringing yells bore practical testimony to their joy. But they were not to have it entirely their own way.

Just as they were all balled up before the rhinoceros, staggered a bit by his great bulk and threatening horn, out upon them charged a body of canvasmen, all the manager could contrive to rally, for a desperate effort to stop the damage and avenge the outrage. In their lead ran the ticket-seller, armed with a pistol and keen for evening up things with the man who had hit him, dashing straight for Circuit. Circuit did not see him, but Lee did; and thus in the very instant Circuit staggered and dropped to the crack of his pistol, down beside Circuit pitched the ticket man with a ball through his head. Then for two minutes, perhaps, a hell of fierce hand-to-hand battle raged, cowboy skulls crunching beneath fierce blows, circus men falling like autumn leaves before the cowboys' fire. And so the fight might have lasted till all were down but for a startling diversion.

Suddenly, just as Circuit had struggled to his feet, out from among the wrecked wagons sprang a dainty figure in tulle and tights, masses of hair red as the blood of the battlers streaming in waves behind her, and fired at the nearest of the common enemy, which happened to be poor Circuit. Swaying for a moment with the shock of the wound, down to the ground he settled like an empty sack, falling across the legs of the ticket-seller.

Startled and shocked, it seemed, by the consequences of her deed, the woman approached and for a moment gazed down, horror-stricken, into Circuit's face. Then suddenly, with a shriek of agony, she dropped beside him, drew his head into her lap, wiped the gathering foam from his lips, fondled and kissed him. Ripping his shirt open at the neck to find his wound, she uncovered Circuit's buckskin bag and memorandum book, showing through its center the track of a bullet that had finally spent itself in fracturing a rib over Circuit's heart, the ticket-seller's shot, that would have killed him instantly but for the shielding bulk Netty's treasured letters interposed. Moved, perhaps, by some subtle instinctive suspicion of its contents, she glanced within the book, started to remove it from Circuit's neck, and then gently laid it back above the heart it so long had lain next and so lately had shielded.

Meantime about this little group gathered such of the Cross Cañonites as were still upon their legs, while, glad of the diversion, their enemies hurriedly withdrew; round about the outfit stood, their fingers still clutching smoking guns, but pale and sobered.

Circuit lay with eyes closed, feebly gasping for breath, and just as the girl's nervous fingers further rent his shirt and exposed the mortal wound through the right lung made by her own tiny pistol, Circuit half rose on one elbow and whispered: "Boys, write—write Netty I was tryin' to git to her."

And then he fell back and lay still.

For five minutes, perhaps, the girl crouched silent over the body, gazing wide-eyed into the dead face, stunned, every faculty paralyzed.

Presently Lee softly spoke:

"Sis, if, as I allows, you're Netty, you shore did Mat a good turn killin' him 'fore he saw you. Would 'a hurt him pow'ful to see you in this bunch; hurts us 'bout enough, I reckon."

Roused from contemplation of her deed, the girl rose to her knees, still clinging to Circuit's stiffening fingers, and sobbingly murmured, in a voice so low the awed group had to bend to hear her:

"Yes, I'm Netty, and every day while I live I shall thank God Mat never knew. This is my husband lying dead beneath Mat. They made me do it—my family—nagged me to marry Tom, then a rich horse-breeder of our county, till home was such a hell I could n't stand it. It was four long years ago, and never since have I had the heart to own to Mat the truth. His letters were my greatest joy, and they breathed a love I little have deserved."

"Reckon that 's dead right, Netty," broke in Bill Ball; "hain't a bit shore myself airy critter that ever stood up in petticoats deserved a love big as Circuit's. Excuse *us*, please."

And at a sign from Bill, six bent and gently lifted the body and bore it away into the town.

In the twilight of an Autumn day that happened to be the twenty-second anniversary of Circuit's death, two grizzled old ranchmen, ambling slowly out of Mancos along the Dolores trail, rode softly up to a corner of the burying ground and stopped. There within, hard by, a woman bent and gnarled and gray as the sage-brush about her, was tenderly decking a grave with piñon wreaths.

"Hope to never cock another gun, Bill Ball, ef she ain't thar ag'in!"

"She shore is, Lee," answered Bill; "provin' we-all mislaid no bets reconsiderin', an' stakin' Sorrel-top to a little ranch and brand."

Thus, happily, does time sweeten the bitterest memories.

Inside the Training Den

BY C. R. COOPER

I don't know. Except for the guys on the elephant crew, I never really warmed to the animal trainers. It's not that I have anything against them. I never saw one really abuse his or her animal, quite the contrary. Every one I knew fairly lavished their animals with care and attention. It's not that. It's just we failed to see eye to eye, and not one of them ever seemed to be on the same frequency as I was. I've heard other circus people say the same thing. I used to think that people who are very good with animals are often not much good with other people. It's not that they beat their spouses and bully their children. It's just they don't seem to be able to connect with the rest of humanity. Their talents lie elsewhere. This may be judged a failure or a flaw in their characters, or it may be a great gift. Take your pick.

This terrific selection is excerpted from C. R. Cooper's "Lions 'n' Tigers 'n' Everything." It doesn't really bear directly on the dysfunction I've outlined, but at least I've had my say.

○ ○ ○

I remember, rather distinctly, the first time I ever went into the steel arena. I was to meet three lions and an equal number of tigers, all full-grown, and unintroduced, so far, to any one but their original trainer. Naturally, I believed I knew beforehand just about what would happen.

Outside the arena, on one side, would be three or four men with long iron rods, the points of which were heated white hot,—sufficient to halt any beast in the attack. On the other side would be an equal number of attendants, equipped with an invention which I never had seen, but which I knew all about, a thing called an "electric prod rod," coupled up with the electric light wires and capable of spitting thousands of volts of electricity at the lion or tiger which might seek to devour me. I, personally, would have two revolvers, one loaded with blank cartridges, for use during the ordinary course of the visit and to cow the beasts into a knowledge that I was their superior; the other equipped with steel-jacketed bullets in case of a real emergency.

There was a certain amount of foundation for my beliefs. Back in childhood days, when I had been a runaway clown with a small, tatterdemalion circus, the menagerie had consisted of one lion, vicious to the extreme and permanently blinded by blows from a leaden-tipped whip, and three scarred and scurvy-appearing leopards which hated humans with enthusiastic passion, and which eventually accomplished their much desired ambition of killing the trainer who had beaten them daily for years. From that menagerie experience I knew that all animals were beaten unmercifully, that they were burned and tortured and shot, and that the training of any jungle animal could be carried out in only one way—that of breaking the spirit of the beast and holding it in a constant subjection of fear. But—

Only one man was in the menagerie house of the circus winter quarters when I entered—the trainer. The steel arena stood, already erected, in the center of the big building, but I looked in vain for the attendants with the electric prod rods, and the men with the white-hot irons. As for the trainer himself, I failed to notice any bulges in his pockets which might denote revolvers; in fact, he carried nothing except two cheap, innocent-appearing buggy whips. One of these he handed me in nonchalant style, then motioned toward the arena.

"All right," he ordered, pulling back the steel door, "get in."

"Get in?" Everything was all wrong, and I knew it. "Where are the animal men?"

"Over at the cookhouse, eating dinner. I'll let the cats into the chute. Go ahead inside so I can strap the door."

"But—"

"I'll come in after I've let the cats through from the permanent cages. I want you in there first, though, so they can see you the minute they start into the chute. Then you won't surprise 'em, see, and scare 'em. Just stand still in the center as they come in. If any of 'em get excited, just say 'seats!' in a good, strong voice, and tap 'em with that buggy whip. By that time I'll be in there."

"But where's my gun? And aren't we going to have any of the men around with hot irons or electric prods—"

"Electric what?" The trainer cocked his head.

"Electric prod rods—you know, that throw electricity."

"Cut the comedy," came briefly; "you've been readin' them Fred Fearnot stories! Nope," he continued, "there ain't going to be any hot irons or electric prods, whatever they are, or nothin'. Just you an' me an' the cats an' a couple of buggy whips!"

Whereupon, somewhat dazed, I allowed myself to be shunted into the arena. The door was closed behind me—and strapped. Shorty, the animal trainer went to the line of permanent cages, shifted a few doors, then opened the one leading to the chute. A tiger traveled slowly toward me, while I juggled myself in my shoes, and wondered why the buggy whip had suddenly become so slippery in my clenched hand. While this was happening, the Bengal looked me over, dismissed me with a mild hiss, and walked to the pedestal. Then, almost before I knew it, the den was occupied by three tigers and three lions, none of which had done anything more than greet me with a perfunctory hiss as they entered! Already Shorty was unstrapping the door, himself to enter the den. Then, one by one, the animals went through their routine, roaring and bellowing and clawing at Shorty, but paying no attention whatever to me!

"Part of the act," explained the little trainer as he came beside me for a moment, "trained 'em that way. Audience likes to see cats act vicious, like they was going to eat up their trainer. But a lot of it's bunk. Just for instance—"

Then he turned to the lion which had fought him the hardest.

"Meo-w-w-w-w-w-w-w!" he said.

"Meo-w-w-w-w-w-w-w!" answered the lion, somewhat after the fashion of an overgrown house-cat.

Following which, a loose purring issued from Shorty's lips, to be echoed by the tigers.

"That's their pay!" came laconically as the trainer walked to the chute. Then, "All right, Kids! Work's over!"

Whereupon the great cats bounded through the doors for their permanent cages again, and still somewhat hazy, I left the steel arena. Everything had gone wrong! There had been no firing of a revolver, no lashing of steel-tipped whips; something radical had happened since the old days when Pop Jensen had beaten those three leopards about on the Old Clattertrap Shows. Either that or Pop Jensen had been an exception!

Since that first introduction, I've learned a few things about animals. A great many of these little facts have been gained by personal visits, often in as narrow a space as an eight-foot permanent cage in which the other occupant was anything from a leopard to a lion. And I've learned incidentally that Pop Jensen wasn't an exception. He just belonged to another day, that is all, and his day is past. The animal trainer of the present is a different sort, with a different attitude toward the beasts under his control, different theories, different methods, and different ideas. Ask a present-day trainer about hot irons and all you'll gain is a blank look. He wouldn't know how to use them, and if he did, he wouldn't admit it. He wants to hold his job, and with present-day circuses; hot irons or anything like them are barred. All for one very simple reason besides the humanitarian qualities. Jungle animals cost about eight times as much today as they did twenty or twenty-five years ago. No circus owner is going to mar a thousand-dollar bill if he can help it—and hot irons produce scars.

Which represents the business side of animal training as it exists today. There are two reasons; one being that the whole fabric of the circus business had changed in the last score of years from the low-browed "grifting" owner and his "grifting," thieving, fighting personnel to a new generation of men who have higher ideals and who have realized that the circus is as much of an institution as a dry-goods store or the post-office department.

Where the canvassmen and "roughnecks" and "razorbacks," the laborers of the circus, once were forced to sleep beneath the wagons, or at best upon makeshift bunks, they now have sanitary berths, car porters, and sheets and pillow cases. Where they once ate the leftovers of stores; stale bread, old meat, and "puffed" canned goods, they now have food that is far better than that served in the United States Army. Where they formerly were the victims of hundred percent loan sharks, feeding upon them like so many human leeches; forcing them to pay double prices for every commodity and bit of clothing, and practically at the mercy of brutal bosses, their lot has been bettered until there is now at least one circus where the lot superintendent never allows his men to be commanded without a prefix unknown in a great many business institutions. He doesn't swear at them, for instance, when he orders the tents strengthened against a possible blow. Instead, it is:

"All right, *gentlemen*, take up them guy ropes!"

When the weather is foul, and the circus lot is hip-deep in mud, when men have struggled to their utmost and can go no longer on their own power, he doesn't brace them with bootleg whisky. Instead, he keeps a man on the pay roll whose job is to laugh and sing in such times as this—the superintendent knowing full well that one laugh begets another, that singing engenders singing, and that the psychological value of that laughing man is worth barrels of booze. It has saved the show more times than one!

Just as conditions have improved with the human personnel of the circus, so have they progressed in the menagerie. The circus animal trainer of today is not chosen for his brutality, or his cunning, or his so-called bravery. He is hired because he has studied and knows animals—even to talking their various "languages!" There are few real animal trainers who cannot gain an answer from their charges, talking to them as the ordinary person talks to a dog and receiving as intelligent attention. It is by this method that cat animals are trained for the most part, it being about the only way, outside of catnip, in which they can be rewarded.

In that last word comes the whole explanation of the theory of present-day animal training, a theory of rewards. Animal men have learned that the brute isn't any different from the human; the surest way to make him work is to pay him for his trouble. In the steel arena today, the same fundamentals exist as in any big factory, or business house, or office. The animals are just so many hired hands. When they do their work, they get their pay envelope—and they know it. Beyond this lies, however, another fundamental principle, by which in the last score or so of years the whole animal-training system has been revolutionized. The present-day trainer doesn't cow the animal or make it afraid of him. On the contrary, the first thing he does is to conquer all fear and make friends with the beast!

A study of jungle animals has taught him that they exist through fear; that the elephant fears, and therefore hates the chimpanzee, the gorilla and any other member of the big ape tribes that can attack from above, and therefore, simply through instinct, will kill any of these beasts at the first opportunity. In like manner does the hyena or the zebra fear the lion, the tiger fear the elephant, the leopard fear the python. It has taken little deduction to find that with this fear, hatred is inevitably linked, and that if an animal fears a trainer, it also hates him and will "get" him at the first opportunity. Therefore, the first thing to be eliminated is not fear on the part of the trainer, but on the part of the animal! I am no animal trainer. Yet, as I say, I've occupied some mighty close quarters with every form of jungle beast. Nor was it bravery. It was simply because I knew the great cats wouldn't be afraid of me, and that, having nothing to fear, they would simply ignore me. Which happened.

Perhaps the best example of the change in training tactics lies in the story of a soft-hearted, millionaire circus owner who is somewhat of a crank about his animals being well treated. One day, several years ago, we happened to be together at a vaudeville theater, in which an old-time trainer was exhibiting a supposed "trained" monkey band. The audience seemed to enjoy the affair; but there were two who didn't. All for the reason that we could see the cruelty of it.

The unfortunate monkeys were tied to their chairs. To their arms were attached invisible piano wires which ran to a succession of pulleys above and thence to the wings, where they were pulled and jerked by an assistant to create the illusion that the beasts were obeying commands. By an elaborate network of wires, the monkeys were made to raise horns, which also were tied to their hands, and apparently play them. Time after time, as he watched, the circus owner snorted his displeasure, and, at last, the act finished, rose from his chair and sought the stage entrance.

"Swell act you got!" he announced to the owner. "What do you want for it? You know, I own a circus; I'd kind of like to have that layout in the kid show."

It was the beginning of a series of bickerings, which ended in the purchase of the act—why, I could not quite understand. So I asked the reason. The eccentric little owner waved a hand.

"Going to have it in my show."

"But with those wires—that's torture, Boss!"

"Now, nix, Kid! Nix. Wait till I've got my bill of sale."

Incidentally, when he received that, the new owner of the monkey band gave to the old-time trainer a tongue lashing as artistic as anything I ever heard, a little masterpiece on cruelty, on the cowardice of the human, and on decency in general. Following which, he bundled up his newly purchased monkeys, together with the properties which went with the act, and took them to winter quarters.

The next day I went out there with him. The monkeys were in their chairs, apparently waiting for something exceedingly important. No wires were visible. At a signal, an attendant ran forward with a small table, upon which were heaped the band instruments which at one time had represented so much torture to the little prisoners. Instantly there was chattering and excitement. The simians leaped from their chairs, scrambled toward the table, grasped a band instrument apiece and ran back to their places, each holding the musical apparatus tight to his lips and producing faint sounds that bore the resemblance of music! Yet the cruelty was gone! The wires had vanished! The monkeys were doing all this of their own accord and actually taking a delight in it! Like a pleased boy, the little circus owner walked to one of the simians and, against the monkey's squealing protests, took away his horn.

"There," he said, with a shrug of his shoulders, "that's all you have to do."

The mouthpiece of the horn had been refashioned overnight. Extending slightly outward from the interior was a metal standard bearing a thin reed; which would sound at the slightest suction, while just beyond this, at a point which would necessitate some effort on the part of the monkey to reach it, was an ordinary piece of old-fashioned, striped stick candy! When the monkey sucked on the candy, the reed sounded. By such a simple method had cruelty been changed to pleasure!

The same thing holds true for practically every other animal act. Instead of making animals pretend to work because they are afraid, they merely work for wages now. For years, in the old days, trainers had kicked and mauled and beaten a slow-thinking, lunk-headed hippopotamus in an effort to make him perform. It was impossible. The hip neither fought nor obeyed. It didn't have enough sense to know that it could escape punishment by doing a few tricks. Then, with the coming of the newer régime into the circus business, the effort was discontinued. For years the big river hog merely wallowed in his trough. Then, one day, an animal trainer slanted his head and stood for a long time in thought.

"Believe I'll work that hip," he announced. And a week later, the miracle happened!

"Ladies-s-s-s-s and gentlemen-n-n-n" came the bawling outcry of the official announcer, "I take great pleasuah in announcing to you a featuah not on the program, a race between a swift-footed human being-g-g-g and a real, living, breathing hippopotamus-s-s, or sweating be-hemoth of Holy Writ. Wa-a-a-tch them!"

Into the hippodrome track from the menagerie connection came the trainer, running at a fair gait, while striving his best; seemingly, to outpace him, was a goggle-eyed hippopotamus, trotting as swiftly as his wobbly avoirdupois would permit. All the way around they went, the hippopotamus gaining for an instant, then the trainer taking the lead again, finally passing once more into the menagerie. The audience applauded delightedly. It was the first time it ever had seen a trained hippopotamus. Nor had it noticed the fact that, about fifty yards in advance of the racing pair, was a menagerie attendant, also running. The important thing about this person was that he carried a bucket of bran mash, and the hippopotamus knew that it was for him! He wasn't racing the trainer, he was merely following a good meal; the old, old story of the donkey and the ear of corn!

Likewise the pig which you've seen squealing in the wake of the clown in the circus. The secret? Simply that His Hoglets has been taken from his mother at birth and raised on a bottle. His feeding has been timed so that it comes during circus hours. The pig follows the clown because he knows he's going to get a square meal. At certain places in the circuit of the big top the clown pauses and gives him a few nips from the bottle. Then he goes on again and the pig runs squealing after. Simple, isn't it?

In the same manner is the "follow goose" trained. The person he trails has food, and the goose knows he's going to get it. Likewise the pigs which you've seen "shooting the chutes."

A pig isn't supposed to have much intelligence. Perhaps he hasn't—but you can have a trained-pig act all your own very easily.

Simply build a pen leading to a set of stairs which lead in turn to a chute, the chute traveling down into another closely netted enclosure. In this enclosure put a bucket of favorite pig food. Then turn the hogs loose and let then make their own deductions.

First of all, the pigs will try to reach the food by going through the netting. That's impossible. So at last they turn to the runway, go up the steps, hesitate a long while, then finally slide down the chute and get what they're after. Then—here's the strange part of it: after a week or so, remove the food. The pigs will keep on shooting the chutes just the same. By some strange form of animal reasoning, the pleasure of food has become associated with that exercise of sliding down that incline. Like a dog that gains a form of stomachic satisfaction from the sight of food, so do the pigs derive a certain amount of pleasure from going where the food ought to be! And they'll shoot the chutes for you as often as you please. Particularly if you feed them directly after it's done!

In fact, the system of rewards and payment for work holds true through every form of trained animal life. Sugar for dogs, carrots for elephants, fish for seals, stale bread for the polar bears, a bit of honey or candy for the ordinary species of bear, pieces of apple or lumps of sugar for horses; every animal has his reward, for which he'll work a hundred times harder than ever he did in the old and almost obsolete days of fear. Even lions, tigers and leopards have their likes, but with them the payment comes in a different fashion.

Jungle cats are primeval in their instincts. They're unable to control themselves at the sight of food, and a few strips of meat distributed in the training den might lead to a fight. Therefore the new style of trainer has a different method. He talks to the cats!

Nor is that so difficult as it sounds. A short association with animals and one easily can learn the particular intonation by which they express pleasure. With the lion, this takes form in a long drawn-out meow of satisfaction; with the leopard and the tiger it is evinced by purring, as with house cats. The trainer simply practices an imitation of these sounds until he masters them, with the result that he is almost invariably answered by the beast when he emits them! The animal seems to understand that the trainer is seeking to convey the fact that he is pleased, and the beast appears pleased also. As to the reward extraordinary, there is the joy of joys—catnip!

To a house cat, catnip is a thing of ecstasy. To a jungle cat it holds as much allurement as morphine to a dope user, or whisky to a drunkard. A catnip ball and the world immediately becomes rosy; the great cats roll in it, toss it about their cages, purr and arch their backs, all in a perfect frenzy of delight. Therefore, when they do their work, they get their catnip. When they don't work they're simply docked their week's wages; that's all.

Old principles, naturally, and perhaps all the more efficacious for their age. In fact, there is one circus in the West which regularly depends upon this age-worn idea of food to save itself in wet weather. It possesses one of the largest and strongest elephants existent in the United States, an animal capable of pulling any of the show's wagons from hub-deep mud with but little effort. There is only one trouble. When Nature made that elephant, it put concrete where the brains should be. Training is next to impossible. The elephant simply doesn't seem able to assimilate a command. Which worries the circus not at all.

When bad weather comes, they simply bring out "Old Bonehead" and hitch him with a rope harness to whichever wagon happens to be stuck. Then a workman takes his position slightly in front of the beast, with a bucketful of carrots, and practices a little animal Coueism. He holds out a carrot. The elephant reaches for it but can't quite achieve his object. Whereupon he takes a step forward—and drags the wagon with him. Which forms the end of that particular vehicle's troubles. He is unhitched and taken to the next scene of difficulty. For every wagon a carrot, and the circus counts it rather cheap motive power at that!

However, the training of animals does not mean that they're simply given food, in return for which, by some magical process, they realize that they are to do certain work. Far from it. It is a long, patient progress,

in which the trainer, if he is a good one, grits his teeth to hold his temper
and smiles many and many a time when he would like to swear. He has
three jobs which must be synchronized into one objective—to teach the
animal that there is nothing to fear from this strange human who has
suddenly made his entry into the beast's life, to plant certain routines into
the beast's mind, and to place there at the same time the knowledge that,
for doing these things, the animal is to be rewarded. But there is this consolation: once a single trick is learned, the whole avenue is unlocked; and
the way to other stunts made easier. Here and here alone is the whip
used, but for the most part it is only the light, cheap affair which once
adorned that ancient vehicle, the buggy.

The lessons start in much the same manner in which those of a
human child begin; the primary object being to accustom the charges
to the fact that they are going to school. And so the lion tamer merely
takes his position in the center of the arena and calls for the attendants
to release the animals from their permanent cages.

Often the lesson consists of nothing more than that. The beasts
have become accustomed to mankind through seeing them every day
in the menagerie and through being fed by them. Therefore they cata-
logue them as merely other animals which are harmless and upon
which the beasts themselves depend for a livelihood. Again is the road
to the brain opened through the path to the stomach!

However, there also are times when the cats seem to realize
that they no longer are protected by intervening bars, and the old instincts of fright and self-preservation overcome them. One by one
they attempt to rush their trainer. The answer is a swift, accurately
placed blow of the whip, usually on the nostrils. In force it corresponds
to a sharp slap on the lips, such as happens to more than one child,
stinging it for the moment and causing it to recoil. Unless the beast is
intractable, an inbred or a "bad actor," about two of these blows are
sufficient to teach the animal its first combined lesson: that a whip
hurts, that the man in the arena commands that whip but, most important of all, he uses it only as a means of self-protection. The good
trainer only strikes an animal to break up an attack; he has a specified
task, to make the beast respect the whip, but not to fear it. After the
first few minutes, the trainer can sit down in the center of the arena

and wait in peace. His charges have ceased attacking and now are merely roaming the big enclosure, accustoming themselves to the larger space of their quarters and assuring themselves that they have nothing to fear. So ends the first lesson.

After which comes the second and most important period of all. The animal already has learned three things, that the trainer will not hurt him unless the animal tries to hurt the trainer, that the whip is something that can sting and it is best to keep away from it, and that there will be a reward for doing what the trainer desires, and that, taken all in all, he's a pretty good sort of a being after all. Therefore, the trainer selects one beast at a time and falls into a routine. He cracks his whip just behind the beast, not striking the animal, but close enough to make his charge move away from it. At the same time, he keeps repeating his rote:

"Seats, Rajah! Seats—seats!"

Which the beast doesn't understand at all. But by "crowding," by the constant repetition of that command, and by desisting with the whip when the animal moves in the right direction and cracking it to hold him from the wrong course, the trainer gradually works the cat to its pedestal. Once this lesson is implanted in the mind of the beast, the whole door to a trained act is unlocked, for everything else is accomplished in the same manner.

More than once I have happened into a menagerie house to find the arena full of cat animals and a trainer seemingly nowhere about. The animals were doing as they pleased, some lolling in the spots of sunlight which came from the high windows, others playing, still others merely pacing. It was as though a recess had been called at school and the teacher had departed. Instead, however, he was hiding!

Hiding and watching the animals with hawklike eagerness, as, left to themselves, they followed the dictates of their own likes and dislikes. It was not a recess; on the contrary, it was one of the most important features of present-day animal training, that of allowing the animals themselves to choose their own acts! In other words, the trainer was playing the part of a hidden observer, watching his tawny charges, and from his unseen point of vantage learning their true natures and the things which they liked best to do.

Some animals are natural climbers and balancers; others are not. Weeks could be wasted in an effort to teach a beast to walk a tightrope, for instance, when the power of balance simply was not in his brain. So the trainer of today, being a believer in efficiency, allows his animals to volunteer for the various services of the performing arena. During the recess time, in which the animals are left to their own resources, their every mannerism is catalogued. In their play, for instance, it may be found that two lions or two tigers will box each other in mock fighting; two pals of the feline race that have selected each other as playmates. Naturally, there is fierce growling and a sprinkling of flying fur. The trainer notes it all, and when the show goes on the road, the audience gets a thrill out of two great cats which leap at each other in a seeming battle of death. For the trainer has taken advantage of this play instinct and made it a part of the show. The audience doesn't know that the big beasts are growling and hissing in good humor, and wouldn't believe it if the trainer announced the fact.

Another animal will be found to have a love for climbing and for balancing himself about the thin rails of the arena. This is the beast which is turned into the "tightrope walking tiger" or the "Leonine Blondin." Another will be a humorist, cavorting about in comical fashion, and he becomes the "only-y-y-y, living-g-g-g, breathing-g-g-g cat clown in existence." In fact, the animal trainer has learned one great truth, that animals have tempers, likes, dislikes, moods, frailties and mannerisms just as a human has them, and that the easiest way to present a pleasing act is to take advantage of the natural "histrionic talent" of the beast. For instance, on one of the big shows was an "untamable lion." At the very sight of the trainer, he would hiss and claw and roar and appear obsessed with a mad desire to eat that trainer alive at the first opportunity. His act was a constant thing of cracking whips, of shouts, of barking revolver shots, and of scurrying attendants outside the arena, on the alert every instant for the leap of death. Old Duke, to tell the truth, seemed one of the fiercest beasts that ever went into a steel arena. His every mannerism carried the hint of death; he hated humans; you could see the malevolent glare in his eyes, the deadly threat of naked teeth, the—

By the way, did you ever play with a dog that mocked fierceness? A dog that growled and barked and pretended every moment that he was going to take off an arm or a leg, while you, in turn, pretended just as hard as that you were fighting for your very life? Of course, I shouldn't reveal circus secrets, but I once spent half an hour with Old Duke in a cage so small that he slapped me in the face with his tail every time he turned round, and I didn't even have the customary buggy whip!

The explanation is simply the fact that it was discovered early in Duke's training days that he was an animal humorist. Pompous appearing, dignified in mien, yet possessed with a funny streak, which the trainer soon recognized and realized, Old Duke played his rôle so excellently that upon his death a short time ago, a large newspaper published an editorial regarding him, and the laugh that he, the lion, had on the "smart" human beings who had watched him!

"If Old Duke only had possessed a sleeve," said the editorial, "he would have placed many a snicker in it during his long and useful show days. For Duke had a mission, that of showing at least a few persons who really understood him and who knew, that we who call ourselves humans are only super-egoists, that because we can talk, and build edifices and go scurrying about this ant hill we call life, we think we are the only beings existent who possess a brain. That was Duke's mission, to prove, after all, that we are only wonderful because we think we are wonderful, that we believe animals are soulless things because we do not understand them. No doubt there are many Old Dukes in the animal kingdom, supposedly our inferiors, that go through life tickling our egoism, and quietly, to themselves, giving us the laugh!"

In the old days of animal training, Duke would have been just a lion doing routine things, because the trainers of those days didn't know enough to realize that animals might possess individuality. But those days are gone. It is a different deal now; far more acts are suggested by the animals themselves than by any trainer. The man in circus demand is the person who knows enough to stand at one side and watch, then take advantage of what he has seen.

Which explains perhaps a sight many circus-goers have noticed—of a herd of young elephants romping in the mud of a show lot, and an interested group of men standing at one side, cataloguing every move. Mud makes elephants actors. From a beginning of mud and rain come the balance artists of the elephant herd, the dancers, the "hootchie-kootchie" experts, and the comedians. All for the reason that mud to an elephant is like catnip to a lion or tiger. It is part of an elephant herd's routine of health to send it forth into the mire and rain of a "wet lot" and let the members play like so many tremendous puppies. And while they play, the trainer observes.

No two do the same thing in the same way; the individuality is as marked as in the members of any human kindergarten class. The trainer therefore has simply to pick his "bulls" for the various things he wants them to do when they have graduated into performers, one to walk upon his hind legs, another to dance in the ring as he danced in the happiness of sticky mud, one more to sit on still another's head, and so on through out the routine. There is hardly an elephant act that has not been first done voluntarily at some time in the antics of a play-fest in the mud.

However, after learning an elephant's aptitudes comes the real job, that of making him know that he is to do these tricks as a part of his livelihood, and to recognize them by cues. An elephant doesn't measure his weight by pounds; he runs to tons, and to teach him the rudiments of his lifework under canvass is a matter of everything from blocks and tackle to lifting-cranes.

Combined with one ultra-essential point: the elimination of pain. There is no braver beast than an elephant, and no greater coward; no better friend and no worse enemy. Injure an elephant when he is a baby, combine the thought of pain with the idea of work, and some day it all will come back in a furious, thundering engine of destruction that not only wrecks the circus, but signs his own death warrant. Bad elephants must be killed; and when that happens a circus checks off anything from $4,000 to $10,000 on the wrong side of the ledger.

Therefore, the early training of a pachyderm is a delicate affair. First of all, the student is led to the "class-room" accompanied by an older and more experienced "bull." Then, while the new applicant for performing honors watches, the older elephant is padded about the legs and tied; following which the blocks and tackles are pulled taut, causing the beast to lose its balance and fall on its side, the trainer meanwhile repeating and re-repeating the "lay-down" command. At the end of which the performer is allowed to rise and is given a carrot. Time after time is this done, while the student watches—especially that part where the feeding comes in. It all has its purpose—to attempt to fix in the new performer's mind the fact that, in the first place, this schooling won't hurt, and secondly that all a "bull" has to do to earn a nice, fresh carrot is to have a couple of ropes hooked to his legs and be pulled over on his side. So quick is the intelligence of some elephants that instances have been known of the beasts learning their primary lesson on the first attempt. Others, hampered by fear, have required a month.

In the same way is every other rudimentary trick taught. The elephant is shown how to stand on his head by having his trunk pulled under him and his hind legs raised. After which he receives carrots. The reverse system is used for teaching him "the hind-leg stand"—and again the carrots appear. After this, the block and tackle is not a necessity except as a means of support, while hitherto unused muscles are strengthened. The animal has learned his alphabet; now it is simply a matter of putting the letters together, the words themselves being furnished largely by his own antics.

Incidentally, this new order of things in the training field has led to a different relationship between the man and the beast. There was a time when animals were only animals, to be taken from their cages, pushed through their tricks, then shunted back into their cages and forgotten. Things are different now. The average menagerie has become more of an animal hotel, with conveniences. The superintendent must be a person who has studied not only the beasts themselves, but their anatomy, in other words, a jungle veterinarian.

The boss of the circus menagerie of today doesn't merely content himself with seeing that his charges are well fed. By a glance at the coat of a lion or tiger he can tell whether that beast has indigestion; ventilation is watched carefully to dispel the ammonia smell of the cat animals and thereby prevent headaches on the part of the beasts; teeth are pulled, ingrown toe nails doctored, operations performed, and every disease from rickets to pneumonia treated and cured. And the fact that man at last has learned that beasts possess temperaments, individuality, emotions and a good many things that humans brag about has seemed to place them on a different plane. Where there once was cruelty there now is often affection, both on the part of the trainer, and also on that of the animal!

In the Al G. Barnes Circus, in California, for instance, is a great, sleek-muscled, four hundred pound tiger, that is ever watching, watching, his eyes constantly on the crowds about his den, seeking but one person. At the sight of any blond-haired woman, he rises excitedly, hurries close to the bars, growling in gruff, yet pleased fashion. Then, with a second look, he turns and slumps to the floor again. It is not the person he seeks!

That tiger is a killer. He has murdered four other cat animals, two lions and two tigers, yet if the woman he awaits should appear, she could tie a cord string about his neck and lead him around the tent in perfect safety.

He is one of the few wrestling tigers in captivity. Twice a day for two years, in the steel arena, his claws unguarded, his great jaws unmuzzled, this four hundred pound Bengal wrestled in almost human fashion with Mabel Stark, the woman who had raised him from cubhood, and whom he loved with a genuine affection. Once, in a motion picture, when it was necessary for the "double" of the heroine to appear as though she were almost killed by a tiger, Mabel Stark took the job. The tiger leaped and knocked her down. Then, while the cameras ground, he seemingly crushed her skull in his giant jaws. Yet those who watched saw that those jaws were closed so carefully, in spite of the swiftness of their action, that they barely dishevelled the trainer's hair.

There came the time when Mabel Stark was called away to become one of the featured trainers for the combined Ringling Brothers-Barnum and Bailey Circus, the biggest circus of them all. Mabel Stark is far better known today than she was back in the days with Al G. Barnes. But with the circus she left behind, that tiger still watches, still waits and seeks constantly for one woman out of the crowds which daily throng through the menagerie, rising with hope, then dropping forlornly again to the floor, while, in the midst of her greater fame, Mabel Stark smiles and sighs, and talks of how wonderful it would be if she could only have her wrestling tiger!

It's only one instance of hundreds. Up in Bridgeport, Connecticut, at the winter quarters of the Barnum show, lives Captain "Dutch"

Ricardo, "the man of a thousand scars." There was a time when they called "Cap" the biggest fool in the animal business—for "Cap" was one of the pioneers of the newer methods of animal training. It was he, for instance, who once walked into the office of H. H. Tammen, then owner of the Sells-Floto Circus, and made him a proposition.

"I understand," he said, "that you've got a bunch of bad cats. Been beaten, ain't they?"

"Yep," came the answer. "Just about ruined too. That idiot I had got 'em so flighty they'll kill anybody that goes into the arena with 'em."

"I'll fix 'em up for you," announced "Cap," laconically. "Say the word and I'll go out there and start in on 'em."

The circus owner swallowed quickly then reached for a liability contract.

"Er—just sign this first," he announced, and "Cap" signed, releasing the circus from any possible damages for his death. Then together they went to winter quarters, Ricardo to make his first effort at training, Tammen to see a new trainer get killed.

"Want any help?" he asked.

"Nope—just two kitchen chairs."

"Kitchen chairs? What for?"

"To train 'em with."

Whereupon "Cap" got his chairs and a buggy whip. Then he ordered one lion into the arena, where he awaited it.

The lion took one look and sprang. Midway in the air, it struck something, roared in victorious fashion, then settled to chew it to pieces. But it wasn't a man—it was that chair. He disentangled himself and leaped again, only to tangle himself with the second chair which "Cap" had tossed in his path. A third time, while again Ricardo broke the leap with the first chair which he had retrieved while the lion was breaking away from the second; then the cat paused to look his new antagonist over. So far he hadn't been hurt at all. Merely foiled. Here was some one who could outwit him, and who really had him at his mercy, who didn't beat him, but who, instead, talked and purred and meowed continually in friendly fashion. The lion didn't leap again.

One by one the whole group was introduced to its new trainer. Not once was a gun fired. Not once was a cat struck, other than a sharp tap with that buggy whip. That season the "hopeless" act once more went on the road, and "Cap" Ricardo worked it!

In fact, "Cap" is a man of individual theories. Just as his kitchen chair was an idea of his own, so there are others.

"I'll stick my head in any lion's mouth on earth," he says. "But," with a wink, "I got a trick about it. Always chew tobacco, see? If the lion should happen to close down, I'd just let that tobacco go in his mouth. Ever notice how you'll open your jaws sudden-like when you've got hold o' something that tastes bad? Huh? Well, it'd be the same way with a lion. He'd turn loose and I'd take my head out."

Which is an optimistic manner in which to look at things. The billing of "Cap" as "the man of a thousand scars" is only a slight exaggeration. He possesses them by the hundreds, for "Cap" is a specialist on undoing the misdeeds of others.

"It's just this here old principle of red-hot coals, or coals of fire, or whatever you call 'em," he explains. "Now, for instance, if you hit a man that's tryin' to be good to you, you're goin' to feel bad about it, ain't you? Well, a cat, when he's clawing you up—he knows what he's doin'. Don't ever get it in your head that he don't. Particularly a tiger cat. I always did like tiger cats better'n I liked lion cats, at that. 'Course, lots of trainers will tell you different, but I've seen 'em all; I've been among the slums and I've been among the aristocrats, and what I claim is, the lions ain't the king of beasts. But, be that as it may, a cat knows what he's doing. And when he finds out he's done a friend dirt, ain't he goin' to be sorry about it and do his best to make up? That's my theory, and it works out too."

Incidentally, one of these little coals of fire took shape one day while "Cap" was standing on the ballyhoo stand of a circus side-show, a lion by his side. Inadvertently, he poked the lion in an eye, and the lion in turn bit off the middle finger of "Cap's" right hand.

"But he didn't mean to," says "Cap". "Figure yourself how surprised a guy gets when he bumps his face into a door in the dark. He never meant it."

Which may sound as an unusual example. To a certain extent it is, for "Cap" and his theories have an outstanding place in the show world, the surprising thing about them being the fact that they have worked out to such an extent that he "breaks" a great many of the animal acts for the biggest circus in the world. However, there are other instances of affection between trainer and animal, almost as remarkable.

Out on a ranch in Colorado live a man and a woman who once were featured on the billboards of every city in the country. He was a menagerie superintendent, she a trainer of lions, tigers and elephants. But they troupe no more.

The circus does not represent to them what it once did. There seems a certain bitterness about it, a grimness which they are unable to dispel, and so they remain away. The elephant which they raised together from a three-year-old "punk" to one of the really great performers among pachyderms in America is dead, felled by volley after volley of steel-jacketed bullets during a rampage at Salina, Kansas, several years ago, in which he all but wrecked the menagerie and endangered the lives of hundreds of persons.

Loneliness on the part of the elephant for his old trainers is commonly accredited for his "badness." But the circus had no other recourse; there were human lives to guard and only one thing was possible, to slay the maddened beast before it, in turn, became a slayer. But that argument doesn't go with his former trainers.

"They surely could have found some way of holding him quiet until we got there," is their plaint, "they just didn't understand him! If they had even told him that we were coming, he'd have quieted down. He just wanted us, and we weren't there, and he went out of his head for a while. If they'd only penned him up in the cars and then wired us, we'd have come; we'd have gotten there somehow!"

In answer to which the circus points to pictures of wrecked wagons, smashed ticket boxes, torn side-walling, and overturned animal dens—in vain. The trainers can't accept the argument.

"The circus wouldn't be the same—without Snyder," is their reply, and the big tops go traveling on without two stellar performers.

A similar incident came in Texas, during the necessary killing of another elephant on the same show, which had become maddened through "*must*," and was virtually insane. He had torn the menagerie almost to shreds, injured one man, and was holding a whole town at bay. And while circus men hastened for army rifles, the executive staff struggled with a woman who strove by every means of feminine aggressiveness to break from their grasp, and go to that elephant.

"Let me go, you idiots!" she screamed in hysterical fashion. "I can handle him! I'm not afraid—let me go! Let me go!"

She had trained the elephant for two years, and it had obeyed her every command. With any other pachyderm, she would have understood that the natural condition of "must" brings insanity, and that, when in this condition, it recognizes no one, understands no command, and knows nothing save the wildest sort of maniacal antagonism toward everything, animate or inanimate, which may come into its path. But her faith in this particular beast had transgressed even beyond good sense. It was necessary to drag her from the circus grounds by main force before the first shot could be fired at the unfortunate beast!

Nor does the love of animals always confine itself to the trainer. Workmen of the circus are shadowy beings; few persons know whence they come, what their life before they drifted into the nomadic, grim life of the "razorback," the "canvassman" or the "big top roughneck." There are stories by the scores in the unshaven beings who sleep about the lot in the afternoons; stories of men whose finer cast of features tells of a time when all was not work and long hours, hints of hidden things in the shadows; they are men who seldom write a letter or receive one. And they are lonely.

Human companionship often does not appeal to them. But the friendship of animals is a different thing. Perhaps it is because they can talk to these beasts during the long hours of the night, as the circus train rocks along on its journey from town to town, knowing that their confidences will not be revealed. Nevertheless, the fact remains that more than one workman has been left behind in an alien burial ground, with no close human friend to know of his death, and with only a lion or tiger or elephant to watch for a companion who never again appears.

More than once also I have seen laborers of the circus volunteer to "sit up" with a dying orangutan or chimpanzee, doing their work by day, remaining awake at night and nursing the beast in the hours of darkness; at last, lonely again, tears in their eyes, to shuffle on

out to their hard, grim, dangerous labors, while a still form remains behind, to be buried behind the big top, after the matinée. It was such a
case as this that formed a story which a certain circus owner likes to
tell, as he explains one of the reasons why the workmen of his show are
better treated than they were in other days, and furnished with more
conveniences and accommodations. For in this case it was the man and
not the animal that suffered tragedy.

No one around the show even remembers his name. They only
know that his loyalty and devotion in a strange friendship caused a soft-
hearted circus owner to become far more interested in the workmen than
ever before, almost to the point of sentimental solicitude. The recipient
of that loyalty, incidentally, was rather grotesque,—Bon, the baby hippo,
or, in circus language, "the blood-sweating behemoth of Holy Writ."

Four men carried Bon to the show when he arrived, a fat
aimless-appearing baby river hog from the Nile Country. The press
agents properly exploited him. Which Bon didn't seem to relish whatever, for all that the baby hippopotamus did was whine. One day the
menagerie superintendent received an inspiration.

"That hip's lonesome," he announced to an assistant. "Round
up one of them there 'roughnecks' and put him in with it—see if that
does any good."

The "roughneck," known only as Mike, was obtained, and paid
a few dollars extra a week for the discomfort of sleeping in the same
cage with a hippopotamus. A silent, taciturn individual, he had told
nothing of himself when he came on the show; his name had been
plainly a makeshift, and the circus, with other things to think about, had
made no inquiries.

The baby hippo ceased to whine. Gradually, it was noticed that
the "hippopotamus nurse," was taking more and more interest in his
charge, pilfering bread for him from the cookhouse, or cutting fresh
grass from around the circus lot, when he should have been resting during matinée hours. A month passed. The hippo seemed cured.

"Guess you can go back to your bunk now," said the menagerie
superintendent.

The "hippo nurse" nodded. But the next morning, the superintendent found him again in the behemoth's den.

"Just thought I'd sneak out an' see how he was gettin' along," came the explanation. "An' he was whinin'—so I stuck with him."

The superintendent winked—to himself. Two dollars a week extra is a fortune to a circus roughneck.

"Nix on that stuff," came finally; "the pay's stopped."

"Yeh. I know it."

And Mike continued to sleep in the hippopotamus den—without pay. Another month passed. Two more after that. The circus rounded into its trip down the west coast, for its final effort at possible dollars before the cold weather closed in. Then, one night, the emergencies suddenly clamped hard. There had come a shrieking cry from the shrouded wagons atop the flat cars, the warning of that feared thing of the circus:

"Fire! F-i-r-e!"

Hurrying men "spotted" the cage where a red glow had shown for an instant, then faded—the hippopotamus den, evidently set afire by a spark from the engine. The train stopped. Workmen and performers rushed forward.

The den was dripping with water, evidently carried from the circus water-cart just ahead. A bucket lay beside the cage. But Mike the "hippo nurse" was not to be found.

Then came a shout. They had discovered him by the right of way, his neck broken; in the fight for his grotesque comrade's life, he evidently had tripped on the top of the den and fallen from the train. Death had been instantaneous.

But that last bucket of water had extinguished the fire.

The Elephant People

BY GEORGE CONKLIN

I love elephant people. In my experience there was nobody on the circus like them. I don't know why this was. Maybe their constant working proximity to what is after all the most amazing beast on the planet, endowed them all with a kind of grace. And even people who were generally pretty awful human beings seemed to change when they got a bull-hook in their hands. It is as though, mysteriously, they have assumed an almost holy aura and a miracle occurs, the quick-tempered became patient, the foolish, wise.

When I first met the Elephant Boss on our show, I didn't much like what I saw. We called him "The Colonel." (He had another name, but I don't remember what it was—or won't say.) He was a bull-necked, shaved-headed, man with a beet-red complexion and a fierce scowl. But after I got to know him a little, it was clear I'd been all wrong about him. I discovered a gentle man, honest and funny, with a vulnerability that was almost painful to behold; a sweet man.

His assistant was a young fellow with a wife and a daughter and a pair of oversized handle-bar mustaches. It was he who really ran the Department, and there was no more honest, capable man on the lot. And, his way with the bulls was a thing to see.

Finally there were the grooms, three of them I think. Actually, they were ordinary workingmen on permanent assignment to the elephant crew, and they tended to be a little older than the others on our show. These guys were my heroes, absolutely. One in particular (I've mentioned him elsewhere) became a close friend. Late at night, after the show had gone to sleep, we'd sit around smoking, and drink a few beers, and he'd tell me tall stories drawn from his lifetime on various shows.

Now don't get me wrong. My admiration for elephant people does not extend to their charges. One day I was walking down the elephant line, minding my own business, when one old she-bull did her very best to kill me—swinging out at me with her trunk and knocking me to the ground, and then proceeding to try to step on me. The shock of this attempted assassination rankles still, and I hold the whole race of pachyderms responsible.

I've also been peed on by tigers and bitten and spat upon by a camel—and mooned by monkeys—but who hasn't?

○ ○ ○

Much of my first knowledge of training elephants I got from Stuart Craven. Without any exception I consider him the best all-round elephant man there ever was in this country. I had been with Pogey O'Brien for two or three years when Craven came to O'Brien's winter quarters for the first time, to train an elephant for him. He came three different winters for the same purpose, and in helping and watching him I picked up a good many points.

Craven was a big, slim, rawboned fellow, very strong and very determined. He was the only man I ever knew who could ride an elephant standing up. In my younger days, when I was supple, I tried and tried to learn the trick myself. I even arranged ropes and one thing and another to steady me, but no use. I never succeeded. One not familiar with elephants, and thinking of their great size, might wonder what there would be difficult about it. The secret of the difficulty is that an elephant's skin is loose and as soon as he begins to move the skin rolls all round, giving a man a footing about as secure as water; but in spite of this Stuart Craven would ride clear round the ring balanced on one foot.

Craven once trained a troop of elephants for Cooper & Bailey. Old Ad Forepaugh was so much taken with their act that he told Craven that if he would train him a troop that could do as well he would pay him as much as Cooper & Bailey did, and if he trained them so they were better than Cooper & Bailey's he would give him a thousand dollars extra. So Craven went to work, and he succeeded in training some that were much better than the ones Cooper & Bailey had. He turned them over to Forepaugh, who was pleased enough with them, but when it came to paying for them he refused to give Craven the extra thousand dollars, claiming that the elephants were no better than those of Cooper & Bailey.

Forepaugh and Craven had some hot words and Craven went away without his thousand dollars, but he had not given up. He waited until Forepaugh's show went out on the road. Then he employed a clever lawyer. The first thing they did was to send some strangers to attend one or two of Forepaugh's performances, and they came back and reported that the showman was boasting to the public how much better his elephants were and how much more they could do than those of Cooper & Bailey. The next move of the lawyer was to go himself with two or three witnesses to the show, and after the performance was over they managed to get round to where Forepaugh was, engaged him in conversation, and began to praise his elephants.

"Those are pretty fine elephants you've got, Mr. Forepaugh. Their act was simply great."

"Yes, you bet they are!" Forepaugh replied. "They are 'nuff sight better than those things that Cooper & Bailey have got, an' they ought to be, too, for I paid good money to have them trained and I paid a thousand dollars extra to be sure they were better."

This was all Craven's lawyer needed and it was not very long before Forepaugh was obliged to hand over the thousand dollars.

It was only the next winter, though, that Forepaugh had to get Craven to help him out of trouble. Forepaugh had a big elephant by the name of Romeo, which began to be ugly, and all his help got afraid of him. Finally it got so that none of them dared to go near him, not even to clean out his paddock, and all his food and water had to be put down through a hole in the floor over him. At last they got Craven to come and see if he could do anything with Romeo.

Craven took a shotgun and went in where the elephant was, and began to give him orders. The elephant showed no disposition to pay any attention to them, so Craven began to fill his hide with buckshot. Romeo did not care much about this, either, until one of the shots hit him in an eye. Then he gave in and Craven could do anything he wanted with him. Craven taught young George Forepaugh to handle Romeo after that, and the Forepaughs had him for a good many years longer.

Not long afterward Craven gave up handling elephants, went South, and bought a great deal of land. The last time I saw him was a number of years later. He was very anxious for me to buy a lot of his land and offered to let me have it for twenty-five cents an acre.

I had only been with Pogey O'Brien's show a few years when I trained my first elephant. She was called Queen Anne, and at the time I took her in hand she was about thirty-five years old, stood some seven feet high, and weighed about four tons and a half. When I went into the ring to perform her I had a black-velvet suit, with gold stripes running down the sides of the pants.

The first thing I taught her to do was to walk round the ring nicely. After that I trained her to do what we called the Spanish trot. In teaching her this I placed a man on either side of her with an elephant hook, while I stood in front with my whip. As I moved the whip they would hook into first one and then the other of her legs, and lift them up. In a very short time she learned what we wanted and the moving of the whip or a stick was all that was necessary to make her lift her feet. After that had been accomplished it was simply a matter of practice to train her so that when I walked beside her and beat time with my stick she would follow its motions with her feet, lifting them high in the air. As we came into the ring this way the band would strike up "Coming Through the Rye," and to the spectators it seemed as if the elephant was really dancing to the music, but as a matter of fact the music was being very carefully played to her dancing.

Another act which I taught her was to fake lameness on first one foot and then another as I walked her round the ring. The crowd on the benches thought she was making the changes to suit herself, but she was strictly following the cues I gave her by my position. If I walked just ahead of her she would go lame in the right front foot. If I dropped back a little by her left side she would go lame in her left front foot; if farther back opposite her hip, in her left hind foot; and if I walked behind her she would go lame in her right hind foot. After doing this I would tie a handkerchief round her ankle, which she would untie and give back to me.

For a grand finish for the act, which usually brought down the house, I had a strip of carpet brought and laid on the ground. I would stretch myself on the carpet, and then Queen Anne would walk over me both ways, straddle me lengthwise, and end by kneeling down over me crosswise until she almost or quite touched me. In teaching her this part of the act I at first used a dummy, then after she had become accustomed to doing it I lay down myself. I taught her to do the act very slowly, to increase the impression that it was very difficult. It was not so dangerous for me as it seemed, for I had my hook in my hands all the time, and if Queen Anne had settled down a little too heavy a touch from that would have raised her very quickly.

When I went to the Cole show he had an Indian elephant by the name of Tom. He was an especially intelligent fellow and became my second elephant pupil. The first thing I taught him was to walk a tight rope. He was about thirty-five years old at the time and weighed three tons. We were all winter teaching him the trick. It made quite a hit when we brought it out, and so far as I know I was the first man to teach it to an elephant.

The first step in getting him to walk the rope was having him walk a six-inch plank we laid on the floor. It took us a good many days to accomplish this, but after a while he could do it easily and carry a balance pole in his trunk. Then we began and blocked the plank up a little bit higher each day. When we had got up high enough so we could, we exchanged the plank for a six-inch timber. Gradually we got him accustomed to walking the timber at quite a height. On either end of the timber we placed an inclined platform for him to walk up to the timber and away from it. After he had become thoroughly trained in the act we took pieces of rope and bound them to the timber so that at a little distance it looked like a huge rope. When we put it up we set four jacks under it to make it solid. We found that we could only have him do the act in a building where the floor was very solid. When he attempted to do it on the ground some of the jacks would settle in the earth and throw him off. This happened two or three times. It did not hurt him, but it frightened him and made him trumpet in great shape.

One season in winter quarters Tom was placed just by the door which opened out into the yard and through which the men wheeled out all the manure from the place. He used to watch the men come behind him with wheelbarrow loads of manure, turn the key, open the door, and go out into the yard. One day he tried turning the key and opening the door. He found he could do it, and he did it so much that we had to stop leaving the key in the door.

One day a stableman came and unlocked the door and left the key in the lock while he went out in the yard. When he came in he could find no key. All hands took hold and helped him hunt for it. Finally, after more than an hour's hunt we discovered that Tom was calmly standing on it and watching us. He had evidently taken it out of the door, dropped it on the floor, and put his foot on it. I always thought that if we had gone away without finding it he would have picked it up again and opened the door with it.

Tom was taught a mean trick by the canvasmen. Fortunately, no one was ever hurt by it, but it might easily have been the cause of someone's death. How they came to do it or what their object was I never knew, but if a sledge hammer or a large stone or a wheelbarrow were left anywhere within Tom's reach he would pick it up and throw it at whoever happened to be in sight.

We had an amusing experience with Tom once out in Seattle. We had to go to the next place by boat, and the pier was quite large, built out over the water quite a distance, and it shook a good deal when we tried to walk Tom over it. This frightened him so much that we had to coax him to make him move at all. To make matters worse, some of the planks broke and let his hind legs through. By the time we got him up out of the hole he had no use for piers and plank floors, so he bolted and ran.

On one side of the pier was a great sugar warehouse, and into this he went just as far as the barrels and sacks would let him. No amount of urging could get him to stir. Something had to be done, for the show had to travel soon and he had to go with it. In thinking of some way to get him started I spied one of the boat's hawsers. I took an end of it across the pier into the warehouse and fastened it round one of Tom's hind feet. Then I put the other end round the drum of the windlass and had the men turn on it slowly while I went and talked to Tom. He was in his place on board all right when the show was ready to start. Cole kept Tom until after he bought into the Barnum show, and then he sold him to Frank Lemon, who changed his name to Rajah.

I once had an elephant that was very sick as the result of eating tobacco. Her name was Lalla Rookh. At that time the show was traveling by train. We had a car on purpose for the elephants. Built into one end of it was a stateroom for the use of myself and my head elephant keeper, an Englishman who went by the name of Printer. Printer sold tobacco to the rest of the men in the menagerie, and he had hidden away in the straw of his mattress his stock of five pounds of plug. One morning when we went to breakfast Printer forgot and left the door from the stateroom into the elephant's quarters unfastened. While we were away Lalla Rookh got her trunk through the door into the stateroom and ate up the straw in Printer's mattress, tobacco and all.

I did not know about it. We took her over to the show grounds with the rest of the elephants and began dressing her for parade. I noticed that she did not act right, and soon she was all of a tremble and could hardly stand up. We could not get her to move and I was considerably alarmed. I had another elephant push her into the tent, where she lay down. Her eyes were rolled down until you could see nothing but the whites. I gave her such treatment as I could and after a time she began to seem relieved and presently got over it, but it was not until fall that I knew what was the matter with her.

We were going into winter quarters in St. Louis when Printer said to me one day, "You never knew what ailed Lalla Rookh that time, did yer, Mr. Conklin?"

"No," I said. "Did you?"

"Yes. She ate five pounds of my tobacco," he answered, and then he told me the whole story.

The tobacco must have been a kind of medicine for her, for in spite of its making her so sick it seemed to do her good. She began to pick up right away after it, and from then on she was in better flesh and general condition than she had ever been before.

When I went to California the first time with Cole he had a little elephant that he called Tom Thumb. He was a bright, good-natured youngster, but small—so small that Mrs. Cole had made a big tick stuffed with straw, which we fastened under his blanket when on parade, to increase his apparent size. It worked all right if it stayed tight, but sometimes the fastenings would work loose, and then the pad got out of place and made the elephant look lopsided.

Cole had advertised in San Francisco that he would exhibit a trained elephant. As a matter of fact he did not have one, but he thought if we just walked an elephant round the ring the public would be satisfied.

We showed in Woodward's Garden, and when I saw the great amphitheater crowded to its limit I realized that it was going to hurt the show if we did not put up some kind of a bluff for a trained elephant, and determined to see if I could not make one that would get by. I had little Tom Thumb all brushed up and I told one of my men—John Hadley, a red-headed Irishman from Pennsylvania—to get ready to go into the ring with me. John had no idea what I wanted, and when our turn came to go in he went along quite willingly. I walked Tom Thumb round the ring a couple of times and into it. Then I told John to lie down, and, taking the elephant by the ear and trunk, I walked him over the man two or three times lengthwise and crosswise. It satisfied the crowd, but Hadley was a scared man and swore roundly after we got out of the ring, and declared to me, "I sweat blood, Mr. Conklin, I'm sure I did."

In teaching elephants to do various tricks and acts the first and principal thing to accomplish is to make them understand clearly what you want and to associate that particular action with a certain command or cue. Once the big fellows grasp your meaning it is seldom that they will deliberately refuse to do what you wish them to. In fact, the more intelligent ones seem to take a certain pride in doing their stunts. It will be readily seen, however, that it is a problem not entirely free from perplexities to discover ways to make an elephant understand what you are talking about when, for instance, you ask him to stand on his head.

My method of doing this was to stand him facing a high, strong brick wall, with his front feet securely fastened to a couple of stakes driven in the ground. A heavy rope sling was put round his hind quarters, and from this a rope was run up to and over a pulley high above him on the wall, then down through a snatch block near the ground, and the end fastened to a harness on another elephant. When all was ready I would take my place by him, strike him on the flank, and say, "Stand on your head." At the same time an assistant would start up the other elephant and draw the pupil's hind quarters up until he stood squarely on his head. The wall kept him from going over forward. After a moment or two I would tell him to get down. The assistant would slack off on the rope and let him settle back on to his feet. Then I would give him a carrot, or something of the kind. I did this two or three times every morning and afternoon. It was not long before it was possible to do away with the rigging, and at the word of command he would put his head down and throw his hind quarters into the air. Of course the longer he practiced the more easily and surely he did it.

To teach an elephant to lie down, which one would expect to be an easy matter, is, in fact, one of the most difficult things for a trainer to accomplish. It is usually necessary to fasten the animal's feet to stakes and pull him over on his side with tackle, at the same time giving him the proper command, and repeat the lesson many times before he is ready to do it without help when he is told.

Sometimes I used to arrange so an elephant could earn certain things by himself. I used this method in teaching them to let my horses alone. I always kept my horse in the menagerie, saddled and ready in case I needed it suddenly for anything. Every time I had a new horse I had to get it and the elephants acquainted with one another and teach the elephants to leave the horse alone.

The first few days I tied the horse in front of the elephants, but just out of their reach. Then I lengthened his hitch so the elephant could just touch him with the end of his trunk, and after a day or two so he could feel the horse over. When he began to do this the horse would usually kick and bite him. In this way the elephant found out that it was better to leave the horse alone, and the horse discovered that he could master the elephant. It did not take the horse long to learn to bite the elephant if it interfered with him, and it was possible then to put the horse alongside of the elephant. After being together for a month or two the elephant and horse would become the best of friends.

One winter in Utica I broke four elephants to do a military drill—march, halt, wheel, and a few things of that sort. In teaching them the meaning of the different commands I had a driver by each one at first, who made them go and stop as I gave the commands. After a while the elephants began to understand what was wanted and the drivers had to guide them less and less, until all they had to do was to walk behind them and prod them when they did not do their part promptly, and then finally they were not needed at all.

While with the Cole show I taught one of his elephants to sit at a table and do an act. Before I went into the ring with him for the act there was placed in it a table. On the table was a fan and a bell, and beside it were two heavy chairs. When we reached the table the elephant would sit on one of the chairs, pick up the bell, and ring it, and then fan himself until a clown dressed as a waiter appeared. I would explain to the waiter that the elephant wanted a drink, and he would go for it. While the waiter was gone the elephant would ring again impatiently. The clown would come back with a big bottle made of tin, and weighted so it would always stand up. This was filled with molasses and water, and the elephant would take it up and pour the contents into his mouth. He was always eager for this part of the act, as he liked the sweet water.

After he had emptied the bottle he always rang again vigorously, and I would get up and explain to him that there was no more. As I did so I took off my tall hat and put it on my chair. Then I moved round to the side of the table with my back toward the elephant. This was his cue to get up quickly and sit on my chair, crushing my hat, which always brought down the house.

In teaching this act I first got the elephant to sit in the chair. This was done by placing the chair next the side of the building, backing the animal up to it and fastening his hind feet, and then working him down into the chair with a hook. After he found the chair was solid he willingly settled his weight into it. After a few times he found out what I wanted, and then by rewarding him each time with a carrot or a lump of sugar it was easy to get him to practice until he was perfect. All that was needed to teach him to ring the bell was to place it in his trunk and shake it. This he learned in three lessons, but the complete act took an entire winter's training.

We had an elephant with the O'Brien show called Don, who would run at the drop of a hat. I was taking the menagerie from the train to the show grounds in Albany once, and in some way Don found an opportunity to bolt, and started off down a road which led to a rolling mill. A big gang of half-naked men were busy rolling out and handling great bars of white-hot iron, and a lot of red-hot bars lay scattered round the floor. Seeing an elephant coming toward them on the run, they simply dropped everything and got out. Don was not fazed in the least by having the mill left to himself, nor did he stop running, but went in one end, came out the other, and kept going. We found him later back in the yards, hanging round the animal cars, and the singular thing was that in going through the rolling mill among so much hot iron he had not so much as singed a toe.

This same elephant was a part of the Barnum & Bailey show when it went to England. Over there he had several ugly turns, and Mr. Bailey, who never was inclined to take any chances, ordered him killed in Stoke-on-Trent. This I did by choking him. I had found this to be the easiest and most humane way to bring about the death of one of the big animals.

In my first attempt to kill an elephant I tried poison, but he simply ran his trunk down his throat and pumped the poison all out, and that was all there was to it.

In an open field I had two strong stakes driven firmly into the ground. To these I securely fastened Don's front feet. Three or four rods away on either side of him I had another stake driven. Then my men brought a couple of ropes an inch and a half in diameter. On one end of each of them I had made a strong slip noose and thoroughly soaped it so it worked freely and easily. These nooses I put round the elephant's throat and carried the ends of the ropes to the stakes at either side of him. The one on the left I put round the stake, drew up snugly, and fastened. On the right I secured a snatch block to the stake, and, passing the rope through the block, carried the end back to where I had another elephant waiting, and fastened the rope to his harness. When all was ready I gave the word, and the elephant began to pull on the rope, which caused both nooses to close round Don's throat with tremendous force. As he felt the ropes tighten, instead of trying to pull away he threw the whole of his weight against them. There was nothing to indicate that the sensation was even disagreeable to him, and in a few minutes, with no struggle or apparent suffering, he gently settled down into a big heap and it was all over.

When I went to the Barnum & Bailey show they had a very intelligent elephant by the name of Fritz. He was the largest in the country at the time and weighed five tons. I won a bet by teaching him in three teaching periods to sit up, hold up his forelegs and stretch his trunk straight up in the air, let me climb up his back, stand on his head, and hold on to trunk.

One of my most popular acts was with this elephant. He had a leading part with some other elephants in a waltz and some pedestal work, after which I lined them all up behind him. Then the one next behind Fritz would put his front feet on Fritz's hips. The next one would place his front feet on that one's back, and so on until each elephant except Fritz had its front feet on another elephant. When they were all in position I would speak to Fritz. He then put his head down for me to step on his tusks, and when he had straightened up again I gave the word and the whole line traveled to the exit, where all went out except Fritz. He and I would start round the ring again, and every little way I would stop him, lift my hat to the spectators in acknowledgment of the applause, at the same time saying, "Down," to Fritz, who would lower his head and raise it again, making it seem as though we were both bowing to the crowd.

Fritz had the principal part in several acts and I used to ride out of the ring on his tusks. One night in Madison Square Garden I had got the rest of the elephants in line and was going to give Fritz the word to lower his head for me to get on his tusks, when I noticed that he was about to go for me. I did not wait a second, but dodged between all four of his legs and made my way out of the ring. My helper, who was beside the row of elephants to keep them in line, saw that something was wrong, came up to Fritz, started the line in motion, and marched them out of the ring to their quarters without anything happening. So quick had I been in dodging between Fritz's legs, and so prompt was the helper in marching them out, that no one outside the show people mistrusted that anything was wrong. The next day while he was tied up I gave Fritz a good punishing, and for a long while his behavior was above suspicion.

A few years later, however, he displayed his temper in such a way that he got his death warrant. It happened in Tours, France. The evening show had commenced and I was getting the menagerie down to the train. We had at the time some two dozen elephants, and I was sending them down chained together in twos and threes. Fritz was in the lead, with Babe and Columbia chained on either side of him and in charge of driver George Bates. I was on my horse, just behind the elephants and in front of the line of cage wagons.

We were about halfway to the railroad and just passing through a little park, with everything going nicely, when all of a sudden Fritz made for Bates as best he could with the other two elephants hitched to him. At once the whole band of elephants was in a mix-up. The road was more than full and the whole outfit came to a stop. Bates ran for his life. There were a half dozen other men with the elephants, but at the first indication of trouble they all disappeared, each looking for a hole. The only man who stayed by me was a fellow known about the show as Deafy. I rode up in front of Fritz as quickly as I could and tried to calm him down, but I saw at once it was no use, so I told Deafy to get some chains, and be quick about it.

The chains we wanted were under some other stuff, which had to be unloaded to get at them, so it was quite a few minutes before he came back with them. Meanwhile I was doing what I could to keep Fritz from bolting. I had done a good deal of work with one of the elephants chained to him, called Babe, and she would do anything I told her. So, keeping Fritz's attention on trying to get me, I had Babe pull round in the opposite direction, and in this way hampered him and took up his attention until Deafy came with the chains.

Then by the same methods I worked Fritz round near a tree and gave Deafy a chance to get a chain round his hind leg and the tree. The tree was some inches in diameter, but Fritz snapped it off immediately, and I had to work him round to a larger one. Deafy managed to get a hitch round this, and it held. With one leg fast, it was a simple matter to fasten the other one. As soon as Fritz's hind feet were fastened the men began to appear from various directions and I had plenty of help. Still keeping Fritz's attention directed to me, I had Deafy, with some of those who were now willing to help him, get chains on Fritz's front feet and unfasten and take away Babe and Columbia. Then with tackle I pulled him to the ground.

By this time word had reached Mr. Bailey of the trouble with Fritz, and he ordered him killed. I tried to convince McCaddon, one of the directors, who had brought the word from Mr. Bailey, that it was unnecessary, and begged him to leave the elephant to me. I told him that, now I had him down, I could punish and regain control of him, and would guarantee to have him on board the train before the show was ready to start away in the morning. But Mr. Bailey's orders were imperative, and McCaddon insisted that Fritz be killed where he lay.

As there was no choice in the matter, I went about preparing nooses. I had considerable difficulty in getting them round the animal's neck, but after a while I got them properly placed. By this time every-one had plenty of courage and it was no trouble to get upward of a hundred men to pull on the rope with all their strength, and in less than fifteen minutes after I gave the word poor Fritz was dead.

Mr. Bailey made a present of Fritz's body to a scientific society of Tours. It sent men to take charge as soon as he was dead. The body was carefully skinned, and afterward the skin was stuffed and placed in the local museum. I suppose it is still there.

Fritz's tusks grew very rapidly and I cut about six inches off them each year. A tuba player in the band wanted me to give him a piece of one of them, out of which to have a couple of mouthpieces turned for his instrument. I gave him enough on condition that he would have an elephant carved for me, which he did, and I still have the little ivory, image three or four inches high, cut from a piece of Fritz's tusk.

Not long before we came back to New York from England I was in the animal quarters of the Olympia, in London, talking with some carpenters who were eating their lunch, when one of the ele-phant men we called Red came in and began to clean up round a big elephant named Mandarin. For some reason the elephant did not feel friendly toward him and suddenly struck him a blow with his trunk that sent him against the wall, and before any of us could do anything had crushed the life out of the poor fellow with his great head. Man-darin was about forty-five years old, all of eight feet high, and heavy in proportion. We brought him to New York in a big crate on the upper deck of the boat. On the way over Mr. Bailey decided to have him killed, so instead of unloading him on to the pier Mr. Bailey had a big seagoing tug come alongside, and the crate, elephant and all, was swung down to the deck of the tug, which then put out to sea. When far enough outside the crate was loaded down with pig iron, swung out over the water, and let go. And so ended Mandarin.

Elephants can be taught useful tricks as well as others. I always had at least one which I could use for pushing wagons round and helping to lift them out of the mud, and when I was in Australia, where transportation conditions were bad, I used to hitch seven and eight wagons together, put a man on each to work the brake, and then had three elephants broken to draw them, and a fourth to help by pushing in the rear. I also used an elephant to move cars on the sidings in the yards of the Bridgeport winter quarters.

The elephant is the only animal that will make an effort by itself to learn a trick. I have often noticed, after I had been showing an intelligent elephant a new trick and he thought he was alone, that he would keep trying it, and seemed really pleased if he mastered it.

Most of the various harnesses, hobbles, tackle, and so on, used in the handling and training of elephants are either inventions of mine or adaptations of them.

An elephant lives to a great age and comes to maturity slowly, not being full grown until from thirty-five to forty years old. It is a mistake to think an elephant is clumsy because he looks so. In proportion to its size an elephant is much lighter on its feet than a horse and can outrun most horses for a short distance, and there is no one of an elephant's four feet with which he cannot strike or kick quickly and accurately. An easy rule to remember for an elephant's height is that twice the circumference of his front foot at the ground equals his height at the shoulder.

An elephant can stand considerable cold if he is kept moving. I have taken elephants in Bridgeport, fitted bags over their ears and tails, and worked them up to their bellies in the snow, pushing cars, without its doing them any harm. On the other hand, I lost a fine elephant once as a result of exposure to the cold.

It happened with the Cole show. We were in the west near Denver, and had to go over the mountains on a narrow-gauge road over which we could not run our elephant car. Cole had us take one of the narrow-gauge flat cars, put stakes up round the sides, and stretch canvas on them. On to this car we put Pete and another elephant. During the night, while we were in the mountains, there came on a very sudden and unusual storm of rain, hail, and snow. There was no cover over the top of the car to shield the animals and we were delayed and did not get to our destination until several hours after we expected to. In the morning, when we were able to take Pete off the car, he was so cold and stiff that he could hardly move, and in spite of all we could do he died almost immediately; but strange to say the other one did not seem to mind it.

The elephant is the most affectionate of animals and will watch over and protect a favorite keeper, and he will also hold a grudge against one for some time, watching for an opportunity to get even with him. But I do not believe those popular stories of elephants that have remembered being cheated by a stranger and squirted water over him when they had an opportunity after the lapse of years.

An angry elephant, however, is a dangerous thing, and an elephant keeper who is rough is always running a risk. A cross elephant is usually made so by the keeper. Some men are naturally cruel and are willing to do anything to satisfy their desire to show off. This is apt to be a fault of new men round elephants. They disobey instructions, and if nothing worse happens are quite likely in a short time to get a blow from some elephant's trunk that bowls them along the ground and calls their attention pretty forcibly to their bad manners. Quite often they do not get off so easily.

I knew of the case of a fellow called Bayo Bill, who was with the Jerry Mabie show. An elephant put her trunk round his shoulders, pulled him off his horse, and before anyone could prevent it she put one of her feet on his legs, pulled him in two, and threw the pieces over her back. I have also known many instances of men being squeezed to death between a wall and an elephant's head or under its foot. But from a keeper or trainer who treats him properly an elephant will accept punishment, and when he has given in the man can do anything with him and the animal will not lay it up against him.

In spite of his great size the elephant is quite timid. A strange animal or an unfamiliar noise will start him in a panic. Once Today

Hamilton, the Barnum & Bailey press agent, had me demonstrate to a group of New York reporters how easy it was to frighten an elephant. It was at the winter quarters in Bridgeport. We had at the time some two or three dozen elephants and I let a pig loose among them. There was a commotion at once. They snorted and squealed and kicked—and by the way, they can use their hind legs like Gatling guns. I also put some rats in among them and they were just as afraid of them. If they had not all been well chained the whole bunch of them would have run away.

Elephants are driven from the near, or left, side, like oxen. The driver tells them to "shy" when he wants them to go to the right, and says "come in" to bring them toward him. "Mile" means to go fast, "mule up" to trot, and when he wants them to stop the driver calls out "tut."

In driving elephants on the road it is very necessary to look out for their feet or they will get sore. If the roads are very soft and sandy the driver is sometimes compelled to put boots on them, otherwise the motion of the foot on the sand, with the pressure from the great weight of the animal, would soon grind through the skin.

The careful keeper will also lay the elephant down on its side twice a year, and with a great drawing knife cut the toenails. Each spring, too, he gives the elephant a thick coat of neat's-foot oil. This keeps the skin in good shape, and if there are any lice on the animal it kills them as well. An elephant louse is a very tiny thing, red in color, much smaller than those which sometimes get on humans, and it lives in the cracks and crevices of the skin round the elephant's ears. Imported elephants are almost always lousy, but those in this country are usually almost or entirely free from them.

Elephants are now fed nothing but hay. In the old days, when they were driven from town to town, they were fed grain in addition to the hay. The ordinary elephant will eat about a hundred and fifty pounds of hay a day. Each Sunday I used to give my elephants a bran mash, using about five sacks of bran to each dozen elephants.

It has always been a popular and paying thing for a circus to advertise the birth of a baby elephant in its quarters, and later on when the show goes on the road the little elephant is always a drawing card; but as a matter of fact, while there have been plenty of very young elephants exhibited, there were never but two actually born in the United States. The first one was born in Philadelphia and belonged to the Cooper & Bailey show. It was named Columbia, and its mother was Babe. The mother is still alive and owned by the Ringling Brothers. The father was Mandarin. The keepers became afraid of Columbia and she was killed in Bridgeport in 1907. The other young elephant was born at the quarters of the Barnum show in Bridgeport.

During the last year I was with the Barnum & Bailey show some New York animal dealer brought over from the other side a baby elephant and sold it to the show. It was smuggled up to Bridgeport and then it was announced in the papers that it had been born there. When the show went down to Madison Square Garden in New York a few weeks later for its opening we took the youngster along. He was still being fed on milk and I could pick him up in my arms. I do not believe he was more than thirty inches high. We had named him Abe.

One day I got orders to take him over to St. Mary's Free Hospital for Children in West Thirty-fourth Street, so I put Abe in a taxi and over we went. When we got there I helped him out on to the street, and then, taking him by the trunk and ear, led him up the long flight of steps into the building, and then into the wards and up and down between the rows of beds, stopping a moment beside each one. Those of the youngsters who were able to reached out and touched the little fellow, and then followed him with their eyes as he went on down the ward. From St. Mary's we took him up to the New York Orthopædic Hospital in East Fifty-ninth Street, and led him through the wards there before we took him back to the Garden.

In all my experience I do not remember a more touching sight than the wonder and happiness on the faces of the two hundred children in those hospitals as they watched that little elephant.

During my forty years in charge of circus menageries I have handled more so-called bad elephants than any man in the United States, and have killed five of them. However, in my opinion it is a mistake to kill them, for the bad elephant is only bad for a few weeks in a year, and a clever keeper can detect the change in the animal's manner soon enough to make it possible to confine him by himself until he is good-natured again. As a usual thing elephants do not have bad spells before they are twenty-five or thirty years old. The elephant that is bad first, last, and all the time exists only in fiction.

The liveliest and most serious time I ever had with an elephant occurred in Hailey, Idaho. He was named Samson, and Cole had bought him from a New York animal dealer in the fall before we went into winter quarters at Utica. We had to have a special car made for him in order to get him up to Utica. There during the winter I got acquainted with him, taught him some new tricks, and broke in a fellow to drive him. As near as we could make out, he was between forty and fifty years old at the time Cole bought him, and he weighed almost five tons. Previous to his purchase by Cole he had been at Coney Island, carrying children on his back. His owners for some reason had become afraid of him and sold him.

At that time Barnum had a big elephant which he called Jumbo and was billing extensively as the largest elephant in the world. As soon as Cole bought Samson he at once began to bill him as the largest one in existence. I think probably Cole's statement came nearer the truth, for while Barnum's elephant may have measured a little more in height and had larger ears, Cole's had by far the greater bulk and weight. In addition he was much more intelligent, being an Indian elephant, than the Barnum elephant, which was African. Some years later he became a part of the Barnum show, Cole having bought an interest in it.

Jack Shumake was Samson's driver and I always had Jack follow in the parade directly behind the cage of lions in which I rode, so that I might keep an eye on the elephant and tell Jack what to do if anything happened, or even get out and help if it was necessary. We had had no trouble with him, and this day in Hailey we had put fifteen or twenty of the children of the place on Samson's back and taken them round on the parade. Just on the outskirts of the town we had stopped and taken the children off.

The parade had reached the show grounds and was breaking up. The other cages of animals had been driven under the canvas ahead of mine, but the horses had not been taken away. My cage had no more than stopped and I jumped out than Samson reached under it and threw it over on its side. Jack tried to get him away, but I saw at once that he had lost control of him. Samson turned from the cage to the horses and knocked over four of them. To save the horses I seized a pitchfork and began jabbing the elephant in the hind legs. He immediately turned on me and to save myself I dodged behind a cage. He threw this into the air with no apparent effort and I realized that he must be got outside at once or he would wreck the whole menagerie.

I shouted to Cole, the owner of the show, who was trying to help, to get me my horse and gun. He was only a few moments doing it, but in the meantime Samson had thrown over twelve cages, trying to get me. I jumped on the broncho and started out of the door, and the elephant followed me, just as I wanted him to do.

A few rods from the tent was a blacksmith shop, and standing in front of it, waiting to be repaired, was one of the huge gondola wagons used in that section to haul ore in. Samson stopped long enough to give this a shove, which sent one end of it crashing through the side of the shop, and then he turned and followed me. I headed for the open fields, and as soon as I got away from the horses and crowd I turned in my saddle and opened fire on him with charges of buckshot. I hit him squarely in the trunk five or six times, but he paid no more attention to it than he would to so many raindrops. Two or three cowboys came following on and fired at him with their rifles, but all they succeeded in doing was to make a slight flesh wound in his back.

I have often laughed when I have thought of the spectacle we must have made. I was dressed in a suit of tights covered with shining spangles, had a great leopard skin round my waist and hips, and was mounted on a broncho with a Mexican saddle and bridle elaborately ornamented. The elephant had on all his parade trappings and great saddle, and as he ran the colored velvet blanket blew out from both his sides like huge wings.

The broncho was going his best, but the elephant was close behind, and I knew that he would be able to overtake us if we kept the race up much of a distance. When I found that he paid no attention to the buckshot I began to look round for some means of cornering him. Off across the field, something less than a mile away, was the freight yard, and the possibility of stopping him among the cars suggested itself to me, so I headed for them. By the side of the yard was a large water tank, on top of which were a number of people who had been watching the parade. As soon as they saw Samson and me turn and come toward them they climbed down and ran faster than I ever saw anyone run in my life.

As I got near the yard I noticed a lot of cars heavily loaded with ore, standing on two tracks which met in a V shape at one end. Both tracks were full of cars, but at the point of the V the cars did not quite meet. I made for this opening, with Samson right after me. As I had hoped, the broncho and I just squeezed through, but there was not room enough for Samson.

An elephant never goes round anything. He simply tries to push aside or crush whatever gets in his way, and so Samson threw all his weight and strength against the cars in an effort to crowd through the opening and get at me, but the load of ore was so heavy and the cars stood at such an angle to his pressure that they held, and he was blocked. I let him struggle away for a few minutes, and then I began to talk to him. After a little he gave up his efforts and began to calm down. Then I told him to back up and lie down, both of which he did. Finding he would obey me once more, I rode round the cars to where he was, and after making sure I could manage him drove him back to the tent and tied him up.

Cole was very much disturbed over the matter and wanted the animal punished. I remonstrated with him, telling him that it was not necessary, that the elephant had given in and was behaving himself, and that it would do no good. But Cole thought he must be punished until he squealed. It was too near time for the afternoon performance to do anything about it then, so we tied him securely and went on with the show. After that was over I had another talk with Cole and tried to get him to change his mind, but he insisted that the elephant must be punished, so there was nothing left for me to do but go about it.

I had my men drive stout stakes in two rows and made Samson lie down between them. Then with a quantity of inch-and-a-half rope I bound him down to the stakes, passing the rope back and forth over his body so many times that he resembled the picture of Gulliver on the old thread boxes. When at last he was secure I put several men to belaboring him with tent stakes. But though they winded themselves and others took their places, Samson showed no signs of squealing. I heated some large bars of iron red hot and held them within reach of his trunk to see if he was still mad. He reached out and took them, put them into his mouth, and tried to chew them up. After about half an hour of this sort of treatment I was able to convince Cole that the elephant would let us kill him before he would squeal, and Cole gave his consent for us to stop.

When we unfastened the ropes we had a pretty thoroughly done-up elephant. He could hardly stand. His tongue hung out of his mouth like a panting dog's and he could not bend his trunk. For more than a week we had to feed him by hand and give him water with a force pump. I dressed and cared for the buckshot wounds and the burns on his trunk, and the cut on his back where the cowboys had hit him. They all healed rapidly and it was not long before he was as good as ever again. I never had any more trouble with him after that, but he always wanted to get out of my way if possible. He used to have spells of wanting to chase his driver, however, and once when he tried to do it during the next summer he tipped over a load of hay.

After Samson went on his rampage I got a couple of dogs, one a white bull and the other a big fellow, a cross between a St. Bernard and an Irish setter, and broke them to stay near him and keep everyone but myself and the keeper away.

Samson lost his life in the fire that burned the Barnum & Bailey winter quarters in Bridgeport. I was away at the time of the fire and there was no one else who could unchain and get him out of the building, so all they could do was let him burn. After the fire his bones were recovered and mounted and are now on exhibition in the Museum of Natural History in New York City.

I had another lively experience with an elephant in Madison Square Garden in New York City. We called him Tom Thumb. He was young at the time—probably not more than eight years old—and was not very large. During the winter at the quarters in Bridgeport I had been teaching him to walk on a row of big wooden bottles. Toward spring a clown by the name of Reynolds was assigned to work Tom

Thumb in the ring, and he used to come up to Bridgeport from New York every day to go through the act with the elephant.

One day, after he had been coming up for some time, I said to him: "Reynolds, look out you don't get too fresh with that elephant the way you give him orders. If you do when you get down in the Garden he'll knock you out. You won't have all these men sitting round then. It will be new surroundings and he will be excitable."

"You leave that to me," he replied. "I know what I am doing. I've got candy in my pocket and he likes me fust rate."

I said no more to him about it. When we got down to the Garden and ready to open up there was a rehearsal for the benefit of the reporters and a few others. Reynolds went into the ring to do his act with Tom Thumb, but had hardly more than commenced when the elephant hit him a blow that knocked him clear outside the ring. If it had not been for the ring bank he would have been killed. That prevented the elephant from reaching him and crushing him before he got on his feet. Of course Reynolds would have nothing more to do with the act, and it was arranged that another clown, by the name of Billy Burke, should take his place.

Burke was a sort of barroom clown—that is, he was a good deal funnier in a barroom than he was in the ring, but he had unlimited self-confidence. The show was to open to the public the next day, and I took Burke to one side and cautioned him about the elephant; but he paid no attention and told me contemptuously that he could handle him. When it came time for the act I put Tom Thumb's caretaker, Otto Mopus, in the ring, thinking it would help to keep the animal easy.

I watched just outside, and it was well I did, for the elephant had hardly got in the ring before it turned on the two men, and if I had not rushed in and caught him by the ear with my hook he would have killed both of them. He was so excited that instead of allowing me either to put him through his act or take him out, he simply bolted, and while I hung to his ear with my hook he dragged me into the aisle and, before the spectators had time to be frightened, up two flights of stairs and out on to Twenty-sixth Street. There I regained control of him and took him down into the cellar and chained him up.

Later Mr. Bailey came down and told me to chain him to an old elephant and take him up to Central Park—that he was going to make the city a present of him. So that night I fastened him to one of the old elephants and took him up to the Park and delivered him over to Bill Snyder, the head keeper of the Park zoo. Snyder had been connected with a show once and he used to take Tom Thumb out and perform him for the benefit of the crowds on Sunday afternoons, but in a few years the elephant grew so ugly that it was thought best to kill him.

Albany, New York

BY EDWARD HOAGLAND

The circus, qua circus, like many old institutions, is slow to change, and is given to old forms and protocols, hierarchies and caste systems. Management, and the front-of-the-house generally, tends to remain aloof from the rest of the show—even from the artists. The artists, in their turn do not as a rule, socialize with the working people (I never heard them called roustabouts, we called them workingmen, even the women) who are the lowest caste. These are the folk who do the hardest work of the circus, they are the hewers of wood and the drawers of water (as some wag put it). Very often they are young and poor and on the run from something. It might be a bad marriage or some trouble with the law. But whatever it was, something impelled them to leave everything they know and undertake the difficult and often dangerous life (at forty-five 1974 dollars a week) of a circus workingman.

Early on in my time with our show, my brother Andy signed on to the prop crew. His aim was to work his way across the country to the West Coast and then get off the show. Because of this I got to know many of his fellow workers quite well. And they became my friends, some of them, and we did a lot of hanging out together on the move from stand to stand; or after the last show we'd eat together or go to local places to check out what's up. More than once, various performers felt obliged to speak to me about this. It seemed I was letting the side down. But these little chats never did much good, and I continued to choose my own friends. You can have a caste system, only if you can make it stick.

Hoagland's *Cat Man*, from which this selection is excerpted, is the best, the truest circus novel I've ever read.

○ ○ ○

T he rain sheeted down so loud it was hard to think and harder still to hear what anyone said, impossible to hear the show going on. Performers in skimpy costumes made shivery exits a few yards away, wrapping themselves in towels and bathrobes as they ran. David got a side view of several rows of people watching the show muffled in raincoats, reluctant even to bring out their hands to clap. Most of the ground was muck. David's first official job had been to help spread straw on the runway where people would be coming out when the show was over.

It was a pretty bleak beginning. David had been thrown out of his room in the city at five o'clock in the afternoon for not paying his rent and for being a "rummy," his landlady said, who was herself the fattest, whiniest rumdum on Green Street. She'd known he was hungry and didn't have money to eat on and she'd led him into her room on purpose so he could smell all the food she had, see the boxes of candy and the leftovers still on her lunch dishes. She'd shaken a paper under his nose. She'd told him he'd have to find a job if he didn't want to starve, and then, instead of letting him look through the ads himself, she'd caught his finger and brought it to one of them, twisting his finger and smelling so strongly of perfume he thought it would ooze on his head as she bent over him. Scraggling hair, fat, shovy breasts. "I had a boyfriend in the circus," David's landlady had trilled as though she were still young enough to have a boyfriend. She'd pinched his shoulder and arm and bent over him, smelling of perfume, as if she owned him. David remembered feeling crawly, wondering if she really was going to throw him out and wishing he had a drink—she'd give him a drink; if not something to eat, then a drink. But no, she'd stood him on his feet, led him out of the room. "You rummy, you're going to be in the circus like my boyfriend, and you c'n come back and see me when you c'n pay for your room, 'cause I'm a respectable lady. I don't have no men who can't pay for their room."

She'd taken David to a bus stop, flagged a bus and climbed right in with him and paid for him, slapped him on the rear end as if she owned him. "Honey," she told the driver, "take him to the circus and don't let him out before—And you come back and see me some time when you've got something in your pocket besides your pool stick. Hee-hee-hee!" That was the last David saw of her—pulpy, purple-red lips laughing at the big joke.

So David had gotten a job, which was one relief. And so far he hadn't had to do much of anything except keep out of the rain. It had started raining soon after he'd been assigned to the Animal Department and found his way there. He'd helped a couple of the men he'd be working with put canvas over the hay and bags of feed and take some washing off the ropes that held their little top up and "guy out" the ropes to withstand the storm. From then on it had rained, rained and rained. Brownie, the boss, hadn't given David anything to do except scatter straw on the runways for a few minutes. Didn't even sign him up. "You'll quit before we tear down tomorrow if it keeps on raining," Brownie had said.

It kept on raining. It got so that water blanketed the whole ground, every patch of grass. There was no dirt, only mud. But that was okay. If David could have eaten something he wouldn't have minded any amount of rain. If he could have had some milk and eggs and meat and peas and bread. David thought he was reaching the stage of hunger where he could think of nothing but food. He hadn't eaten for forty-eight hours. That wasn't so long really, he knew, but what he knew didn't seem to help the feeling in his belly. It had been too late to get supper when he'd reached the circus—the first show over and the peo-ple gone. "Mealtime! Mealtime! You gotta wait till the next mealtime!" the cookhouse boss had shouted. Brownie had gotten mad at being asked for a loan. The other men in the Animal Department's top said they didn't have any money. And they probably didn't—they looked broke—but they'd eaten.

The evening show had started. David had wandered into the big top to watch, but it wasn't worth it in the rain. He'd been side-tracked to what seemed the dryest spot, next to the elephants and be-hind a big cage-wagon that was humming away like a refrigerator. A group of men were there sitting on gunnysacks and empty peanut packing boxes. It turned out they were Animal men too. But they didn't have any money or food. The one called Robinson seemed to be the leader. He answered all of David's questions in an authoritative voice. David kept asking lots of questions because he couldn't just sit and feel his stomach eating itself, churning and almost climbing up to gnaw his throat.

"What do we have to do?"

"Nothing till the suckers leave," Robinson said.

"Then what?"

"Shut the cages up. Then that's all."

"Then where do we sleep?"

"Wherever you can. We'll be here tomorrow so you stay anywhere you can."

Robinson had the openest, pleasantest face David had seen in the circus yet. He was easy to talk to. The others hadn't deigned to notice David. There was a boy David's age who limped from polio or the war or something. Hopalong was what they called him. He sat facing the wagon, not saying a word. And opposite him a man had hunched himself into the machinery that made the wagon hum. This man didn't once open his mouth either. From cap to shoes he was dressed in black—not rain clothes, black work clothes. And he looked sad enough to be in mourning. Between Hopalong and the man in black Robinson and David sat, and in front of them, in the center limelight, were "Dry Wash" and "Daff."

"He's the creep who really hates the rain. He don't like to get wet—do you, Dry Wash?" Daff demanded. "—He ain't had soap or water on him since he quit wearing diapers." Daff's laughter flapped out of him, harsh as burlap on the ears. He was a board-thin, lank-faced individual with hair dry and long as a clown's wig combed in one direction over the side of his head and a long, Pinnochio nose. He'd been teasing Dry Wash steadily.

"Hitler thought he was smart!" Dry Wash replied. He stuck his little finger in his ear and dug and dug and pulled it out, cleaned it off.

The man in black was chewing his lip and absently watching a woman run toward the cage licking the rain from her lips. She was carrying some fruit, so David immediately became very intent. He could see bananas, grapes and round fruit of some kind, apples, oranges or maybe plums. She was a stumpy gnome of a woman with a crop of dense monkey hair and a wizened, leathery face. An oldtimer obviously. There were all three—apples, oranges and plums, as well as the bananas and green grapes. She had a tattered square of quilt drawn over her shoulders instead of a raincoat. David was not alone in lacking a coat. Nobody had one. But they all had eaten; and she held probably fifteen pounds of fruit heaped in her arms.

"Can you spare an apple, do you think?" David asked, but she was in the wagon. She triggered the latch with one finger and slipped into the wagon without even answering. David caught a glimpse of two baby gorillas or chimps fawning and scrambling up the woman's legs in the lighted cage before the door slammed shut.

"She don't know you," Robinson explained. "But she loves them monks so, you might not have got any if you were her own husband. They're her babies."

"What are they?"

"Gorilla monks. They're valuable. They have to eat right and they're air-conditioned even. It's glassed. They don't hardly breathe the same air we do."

"You ought to see him when he takes a bath," Daff went on.

Dry Wash interrupted, "Listen now, Hitler thought he was smart as hell too"—wringing his little finger in his ear again.

"—First he picks up a couple of rolls of toilet paper somewhere, from a can, in a gas station or some place, a can. And then he goes into the giraffe wagon, just like anybody else—that's where we clean up. So he strips like anybody else. So, so then he takes the paper an' wipes himself with it! you know, hard, all over his body, all over, everywhere, with a handful of can paper! I spied on him once. Hah, hah, hah!"

"Listen now, some people think they can get away with anything, but they're not so smart as what they suppose!" Dry Wash interrupted again. That ear-rubbing seemed to be something he did every time he spoke.

"And the poor giraffe man"—Daff pointed at Hopalong—"he's got to clean it up. It's like after a spitball fight. Kids roll up little balls. The paper does that; all filthy balls from being rubbed on him, all over him."

Dry Wash did seem to be unusually miserable in the rain, and the water had washed white streaks on his face. He was under a particularly bad leak, although anywhere you sat (except scrunched into machinery like the man in black) you were bound to get wet. The rope ribbing of the big top stood out gaunt and skeletal between huge hanging pouches of trapped water. Water dripped from most of the pouches; some places it poured. Just outside, an unbroken sheet clattered off the big top into the lake that was the ground. Even if you could keep your clothes dry, by having eyes on top of your head and jumping-jack legs, you couldn't keep your shoes from getting wet. There was no possibility of that. David tried to remind himself how uncomfortable the rain was—as in his mind he stared through that boarded-up back side of the gorilla cage.

"What time do they have breakfast?"

"Food, food, food. The first thing you said was about food. What's the matter, you miss a few meals?" Robinson laughed jokingly.

"He looks like it," jeered Daff. "I'll make your mouth water. I'll tell you what we had. We had liver-and-onions and roast-beef-and-brown-gravy. We could choose."

"Why don't you keep your mind on little girls?" Robinson told him. "—He always has to be starting fights with somebody.—You've missed a few yourself, Daff. And there's one now." Robinson pointed.

Daff strained forward, stretched flat in the mud to leer at the legs of a little girl who was crossing the runway with her father, to look up her skirts.

Robinson warned him. "Some day some kid's going to have a paratrooper for a father, and he's going to stomp the eyes right out of your head and bust up your hands like a sonofabitch!" He turned to David. "He's awful! He'll give us all a bad name—if he don't get us all arrested! 'Molesting children.' These town cops will kill you for that!"

The gorilla woman emerged, with three apples left! David didn't say anything. He knew she'd saved them for him. And when she kept right on going, he waited to catch her eye. She was almost out of hearing before he really realized the apples were not for him. She went to where the elephants were chained. She walked along the row until she came to one sprawled sick on the ground, its trunk a grotesque fifth leg and its bloated side heaved up like a hill. Feebly the trunk reached, took the apples and flopped back down in the mud before groping its way to deposit them in the mouth. David envied the elephant. The others trumpeted forlornly.

"Here's Brownie." Robinson was on his feet.

Brownie shouted, "We're gonna close these cages. It's wet; it's leaking. Nobody'll look at 'em anyhow." David, not knowing what to do, stood up and started toward the boss immediately, then stopped and waited for the others and went with them. He stepped in mud ankle-deep. He had a pair of cracked, cast-off shoes that were about like cardboard for keeping out water. "Close 'em up! What a sonofabitching night this is going to be! Close 'em up! They ought to tear down and blow the town." Brownie had a terrible-looking left eye. He slogged away, muttering. He wore rubber boots which covered him to his knees and a long black fireman's coat and even a hat. He shouldn't complain.

"Get up top, kid, will you?" said Robinson.

"Where?"

"Behind the cages. There's things to climb up. Here's Chief. He's got the pole."

Obediently David went around behind a wagon that said GNU—*Africa* and contained a strange, horned, striped cross between a zebra and a cow. He looked in vain for a ladder behind the cage, under the cage. At last on the end of the wagon he saw rungs going up and he climbed. They were very slippery, as if coated with ice. The roof of the wagon had nothing to hold on to except a flap which David was made to understand he should unhook and let down in "Just a minute for Jesus Christ sake! Wait! We gotta close the bottom!" David waited, kneeling, spacing out the weight of his body to keep his balance and avoid sliding off. It was slick as ice up there. Water had leaked in buckets onto the metal roof. Daff and Hopalong slammed up the bottom flap and the third guy, Chief, a big, dark, Indian-looking guy, stuck a pole against the flap David was holding and David let it go down. Then Daff and Hopalong slammed the two side flaps shut with a bang that shook the wagon. Robinson stood off to the side as if he were a sort of supervisor who didn't have to work.

Robinson shouted, "Jump, kid, jump!" Daff and Hopalong had closed the bottom flap of the next cage in line.

David hesitated. "What do you mean?"

"You're s'posed to be up there!" Chief roared at Robinson. "Why ain't you up there?"

"Hurry up. They're waiting on you. Jump!" Robinson repeated. It was only seven feet or so to the next wagon, but both surfaces gleamed treacherous with rain, with a ten-foot drop in between and the wagonpole to land across. David jumped, skidding, beating his arms. Then there was another wagon to jump to, and another; ten more. The arc lights swung high off the quarterpoles and made the wagon tops gleam silver. Great sinister pockets of canvas bellied down overhead, incessantly trickling water and making the footing even more slippery. People in nearby seats turned around to watch David instead of the show. And he put on an exhibition with his leaps, sliding all over the place, clutching at air, juggling himself on the balls of his feet. He certainly couldn't get drunk on this job!

When he got on the ground again, unhurt, Brownie beckoned and said, "None of these bums can do anything. Here," and gave him the pole Chief had used to lower the flaps.

"What do I do?"

"Chase those bastards in. Get up on the cage."

It was the giraffe pen Brownie was talking about. It was open and two wagons were parked in the entrance. The giraffes were supposed to go in the wagons. David shinnied up the fence and brandished the pole like a wild westerner. The giraffes bucked and protested, but not very vigorously because they were getting rained on through holes in the canvas. They seemed to know that being shut up for the night would be comfortable. Hind legs gangling like rudders and necks bold stalks out in front, they vaulted into the wagons.

Brownie was already gone. David had intended asking him where to sleep.

"Where does he sleep?"

"Huh?" said Daff.

"Where does the boss sleep?"

"In the wagon."

"In the wagon with the giraffes?"

"No! Hah, hah, hah, hah! No, our wagon, Number 12, the department wagon. He's got a cot he uses."

"Would there be room for me in there?"

"In the wagon with Brownie? Hell, no! He don't let nobody in there." Daff had to share the joke with the others.—"This kid wanted to know if Brownie slept with the giraffes and he wanted to sleep with him! Hah, hah, hah!"

Hopalong laughed. Robinson smiled. "There's tons of flops around here," Robinson explained. "Don't worry about it. You'll have ten thousand seats in there when the suckers get out." Hopalong, Daff and Robinson went under the sidewall and outside. David tagged along.

"Where do you sleep?"

"Kid, I sleep in the orang cage, me and Hopalong and Robinson and the orang," said Daff, although David hadn't been talking to him. "There ain't no room for nobody else."

The rain had softened. David could almost feel it letting up. The wind seemed to be blowing the very drops away. And the circus was going strong. The music not only was audible; it oompahed in the grandest fashion. The midway lights blasted up at the smothering cushions of sopping clouds, staining them orange and yellow and red. Wind sissed on a row of trees somewhere and water plopped instead of spilling off the big top. The little wagon and top the department used looked exceedingly small. They entered the top, to be greeted with— "Don't nobody touch that bed. That's my bed!"—and a jabbing arm and a very grumpy Indian face. A canvas laid over a bale of hay was Chief's "bed."

"It'll be pouring again in five minutes, you'll see," Brownie was saying as he poked a flashlight around trying to find something. When the beam happened to hit David Brownie exclaimed, "Goddam, what'uve we got, another queer? Your hair's as long as a goddam—as a goddam violinist!"

"I don't have any money," David said angrily.

Hopalong, Daff and Robinson opened their boxes and picked out an assortment of torn pants and scraps of quilt and army blanket which they could wrap themselves in for the night. They cursed because their belongings had gotten wet—the boxes like everything else were sitting in puddles of water. That was one thing David didn't have to worry about, belongings. Then the three of them headed back to the big top. David followed, not knowing what else to do. They went to a cage, opened a barred door in the front and crawled inside. This time David couldn't come along, because Hopalong closed the door in his face and clicked the padlock.

"See, we don't wanna get rolled. We lock it."

Behind Hopalong an ape was cavorting, trying to entertain and postpone being caught. Daff and Robinson were after it and there wasn't much room. The chase was short. Once caught, the thing buttered up to them, hugging and whimpering and sentimental. But Robinson worked it over to a box in the corner and stuffed it in. Its arms were long, grabbing in all directions to escape from the box. Robinson rammed in the door and fixed the padlock. Daff and Hopalong were smoothing the straw in the cage to sleep on.

"Now he's locked in and we're locked in and you're the only one that's free!" Robinson said to David, laughing. "But you want to sleep with us, do you?"

—"There ain't no space!" Daff broke in.

Robinson's pleasant brown eyes looked very deeply into David's. A smile crept over his lips persuasively. "Look, when they clear those suckers out of here you'll have ten thousand seats to sleep on." Robinson's hair was awfully long too. It was a wavy type that didn't look as bad long as David's straight hair. But David wondered what Robinson would do if Brownie ever said he looked like a queer and a violinist. David looked at the hair again and began to see that actually it was freshly cut, cut long around the ears deliberately.

"Not tonight, honey," whispered Robinson with eyes moistening and a mincing smile.

Chilled with disgust, David left.

There was still the problem of getting a bed of some kind. He might have to forget he was hungry until tomorrow, but sleep he was determined to find. And he didn't want to sit in one of those folding show chairs all night.

The man in black was squeezed into the compartment of the gorilla wagon with the machinery like before. But now he was asleep. It looked dangerous. David noticed that, although on three sides the guy didn't have an inch to spare, he wasn't quite touching any of the apparatus.

He seemed to be in precisely the same position as when he'd been awake. He hadn't slumped a bit. So maybe he always slept there, without getting burned or caught in the gears! Maybe there wasn't any place else to sleep!

A family of performers was gathered in a corner jabbering to itself in some foreign language and trying to wipe dry the springboard and seesaw contraptions it used in its act.

David went back out to the department's top.

"What do you want, boy?" Chief demanded grumpily.

"I'm looking for a place to sleep and I'm looking for something to eat. I haven't eaten for two days."

Chief was seated on his canvas-covered bale of hay with water trickling all around him, sewing what looked like a string of beads on to what appeared to be a belt. David couldn't imagine how he could see in the slight glimmering of light which penetrated the tent.

"What am I s'posed to do about it?"

"I thought you could give me some help." David felt willing to grasp at any straw.

"Jesus Christ! Help? Jesus Christ, boy! What d'ya mean, help? Everybody wants help. Who the hell doesn't want help when they come on this show. When I come on this show I had my head beat open so you could see the brains! What d'ja say, you're hungry? Everybody's hungry when they come on this show! If I helped one-hundredth the people who come on this department in a year, I wouldn't have a STITCH! Two days you haven't eaten? I've seen men go without eatin' eight, ten days! Didja tell the boss you was hungry? He'd have given you some of the animals' food. Carrots, apples. Didja? No, you was ashamed. 'Can you lend me a dollar?'—I heardja. That's all you said. I don't know where he is now. What have you got to be ashamed of? You're as good as anybody—anybody watchin' that show!"

Chief got up blustering and beefing and loud. David followed him toward the big top. "When I come on this show I had my head beat open so bad you could see my brains! Hah, hah, hah, hah, I had to comb my hair specially to hide them when I was gettin' a job! They don't want to see your brains on this show. Hah, hah, hah, hah!" He put his hand in his pocket. "You see how much money I got, all together?"

It was eighty or ninety cents. "That's all I got. That's all. And that's more than anybody else in this department has to his name! Everybody's hungry when they come on this show."

Chief stood in the entryway to the seats, surveying the eager-beaver butchers who bustled up and down the aisles waving their wares.

"Doggie, doggie. Hey, red hot! Hey, doggie, doggie. Red hot! Hey, doggie, doggie. Hey, red hot!"

Chief called to the kid selling hot dogs, "C'mere."

"How many?" asked the kid.

"One."

"Mustard?"

Chief turned to David. "Mustard?"

"Yes, thanks."

"That's fifteen."

"It's a dime. I'm with the show," Chief told the kid.

"We charge fifteen for a frank. I don't care who you're with."

"Come on. You pay ten if you're in the show. Come on!" Chief's voice menaced and he reached out, extracted the hot dog from the kid's hand and put two nickels in its place. "Come on!" he had to say again, even though the transaction had been completed. The kid was holding his tray with one hand and seemed to be debating whether to put it down and try to take the hot dog back by force. It took still one more "Come on!" before the kid gave up and walked sneeringly away.

"Those guys, they make a nickel profit, see? They're rich. But they shouldn't make no profit off of people in the show!" Chief explained. Then he called over one of the Coca-Cola butchers and worked the same deal, getting less of a protest this time because the guy was older and more cynical.

"Okay, okay," he said sarcastically, accepting Chief's dime.

"Now you want a place to sleep." Chief sloshed off through the mud with his heavy work boots, expecting David to keep up in cardboard shoes. Chief took him to the giraffe pen. "Them giraffes are gone and they've got straw. You can sleep there. Find a place where it don't leak and pile it up there and sleep there. —You got a friend!" Somebody was already sleeping in the pen. "He's Rabbit. He's got big ears. Hah, hah,

hah, hah, he loves the fat lady. You know what she says? 'You're only in the creases,' she says to him. She kicked him out. Hah, hah, hah, hah, didja ever hear of a thing like that!"

David smiled. "Okay. Thanks a hell of a lot, Chief, a real lot. Soon as I can get some money I'll pay you back."

"You'll be warm. Get a lot of straw and get in it." Chief went under the sidewall and out of sight.

First David ate his supper slowly, religiously. Then, pretending to himself that he was full, he tramped over every part of the pen with his hands and eyes raised as if he were praying, looking for the largest space between leaks. When he found it he was very disappointed to see giraffe manure in the straw underneath. He had to separate all the dirty straw from the clean and crawl around feeling for dry straw to add to what little he had. It didn't really seem to matter, though, whether he slept in dry straw or not, since his clothes were wringing wet. And he could hear it beginning to rain harder. David's penmate, Rabbit, hadn't picked much of a place to bed down. He was being dripped on; and he lay so still that David wondered if the guy was alive, when he didn't forget about him. Finally, as David was ready to stretch out and sleep, a shirt landed on his head.

"You'll be warm," said Chief decisively. The sidewall slammed down. He was gone again.

David snuggled into the straw, using the shirt as a pillow to keep the straw from scratching against his face. The band played and played; people clapped, cheered. The tempo of the rain increased. The storm began to renew. David couldn't get to sleep because the sound was not steady. A hard rain might have been lulling, so long as its noise stayed the same. But the rain drummed harder, faster, louder. By degrees the wind grew until it flayed the canvas. The whole big top shivered and pliantly gave with the wind; quarterpoles creaked, and every fourth or fifth sidepole was lifted bodily by the canvas and swung like a stick from its mooring. David sat up uneasily to watch.

The elephants couldn't stand to have the sidepoles swinging loose behind them, cracking them on the rump. They whistled, caterwauled, growled like lions, bawled like bears. They were chained by the legs to stakes, and the chains went taut as piano wire, heaved and went taut again. Men came running with hooks and clubs—David lay down again—he was in the circus, after all, and should be used to such things, and he was tired, hungry; the whole night was a mess. By the time curiosity had got the better of him and he sat up for another look the chains were being stripped from the elephants' feet. They were being rushed in single file out through a lift in the sidewall, protesting with growls and whistles and bawls. Dimly David saw the water pouring off the big top splash on the elephants' backs as if they were going under a waterfall. The men got doused too. Even yet David could taste mud spatters on his own lips and remember the mud outside. Mud the consistency of cereal, mud you could skate through, then in places mud that would try to suck off your shoes!—your socks!—your *toes!*

The gap between the bleachers and grandstand gave David a view of one of the rings. When he saw the elephants again they were standing on their heads, streaming mud and water, and partly climbing on each other's backs, desperately being driven through all their repertoire of tricks. It looked like a finale. The big top resounded to the spanking of the storm. The wind whooped and punished the canvas. Rain drummed; lashes of it sounded like cloth tearing and ran down straining into a thousand holes or swashing over the sidepoles onto the ground. Some of the spectators had drawn their raincoats over their heads so that they looked like turtles. The men who handled the elephants had got so soaking wet they were sleek and shone like seals in the spotlights. And they barked like seals. Light glared off the wet ring curbing and the steel sides of the bleachers and silver quarterpoles.

David squirmed into the straw as far as he could, wrapping his face in Chief's shirt. Circus noises were deadened, but not the rain's lambasting. That kept him awake. It wasn't like rain on a roof. It was Niagara, the sky falling in. It was the kind of roar that made you feel like an ant. Water was flooding the straw; David knew he was going to be wet. Pretty soon he heard voices, high-pitched and quavering. The show was over. The people were coming out. He poked his head from under the shirt. The straw they had spread on the runways had vanished in mud, and people had no choice of routes but had to wade right through it. The ones in front wouldn't go until they were pushed by the ones behind, who couldn't see. And by the time the ones behind had sighted the bogs of mud they could scarcely even hesitate because *they* were being shoved forward.

"They've got their troubles too!" David laughed out loud. He turned to see if Rabbit was awake. But no, the guy still lay motionless on his stomach, his face pressed so deep in the straw David wondered if he was breathing. At least one of his ears was certainly very big.

Ushers shepherded the people out. The elephants returned to their chains and stakes and shrieked only once in a while. The elephant men piled hay in strategic spots, bedded down in front of their animals. The lights went off. The wind quit walloping quite so hard and the rain gentled. But Rabbit didn't stir. He didn't even seem to shiver, while the lights were on and David could see. David shivered, though—so strenuously he couldn't get to sleep. The rain became only a soothing patter, but everything he touched was cold and drenched. He didn't worry about covering his face any more; he wrapped the shirt around his belly. Then, just as exhaustion was slipping him to sleep, Rabbit started coughing. They were horrible, sob-sounding coughs. David was afraid now he'd never be able to sleep.

"Did you ever taste blood in your spit? It ain't like a goober. It don't hold together," Rabbit said. He sounded frightened.

David did manage to fall asleep. Only once he woke, and found his legs and arms coated in congealed mud. Behind the elephants, under the loop in the sidewall, moonlight was fingered on pools left outside. Rabbit lay clutching straw in both hands, again silent and prone.

On the High Wire

BY PHILIPPE PETIT,
TRANSLATED BY PAUL AUSTER

I remember being surprised the first time I saw the high-wire walker work. Where was the net? When I put this to the artist himself—concern no doubt evident in my voice, he grinned, embraced me, and whispered in my ear "You fall on the wire."

Well, of course! I had supposed, in my vague sort of way, that any aerialist, anyone in mortal danger of falling from a great height needed a net, or a line, or something to keep him or her from bouncing on the hard earth. But this is not so. Only the trapeze acts take this precaution. There, if you miss your catch, or your grip loosens and you fall, you have only air to snatch at.

Before too long I grew to be good friends with this daring gentleman, and often I would help him rig his act. He traveled with his small family and they frequently had me to their trailer for the midday meal. At some point he decided to teach his five-year-old son to walk a low-wire, and I was invited to join them for their early morning practice sessions. A low-wire is rigged only four or five feet off the ground, and the wire itself is much thinner than the cable used for the high wire, and it is usually cinched much tighter. For week after week we practiced.

The five-year-old boy got very good, able to leap up off the wire, turn completely around and land, perfectly balanced, like a bird on the wire. This was considerably beyond what I was to achieve, but after some time I was able to manage a slow progress across the wire, over my shallow void; and if I fell, I fell on the wire. I was very good at that. I never missed. One morning my friend suggested I try the high wire. Let me tell you how I felt about this.

My heart said, *What an amazing opportunity! What a thing to accomplish!*

My gut said, *What!? Are you crazy?! You'll smash yourself like an egg!*

And my head—that betrayer—said, *What a mark of confidence this is. You can at least try—and if you fall, just fall on the wire.*

I crossed the ring and began to ascend the little cable ladder. Up and up the pole I climbed, my eyes on the rungs, looking neither left nor right, never looking down. At near forty feet up I reached the tiny platform the walker is to step out from; I carefully edged myself around the pole onto it. And you know what? I couldn't let go of the pole. My heart and my gut and my head all shouted, *Don't let go! Whatever you do, don't let go!*

For some time, I remained high on my perch, my arms clasped around the pole, until eventually my friend came up and helped me down.

I cannot even begin to say how proud I am to be able to include Paul Auster's wonderful translation of a work by Philippe Petit in this anthology. Many remember Petit as the young man who, once upon a time, strung his wire between the two World Trade Towers and for a couple hours treated the people of New York to a sublime exploit. Petit is that very rare man, a real artist who is also a true hero. Read "On the High Wire" and you'll recognize also the storyteller, technician, teacher, poet, and mystic.

O O O

Definitions

Whoever walks, dances, or performs
on a rope raised several yards from the ground
is not a high-wire walker.
His wire can be tight or slack; it can bounce
or be completely loose. He works with or without a balancing pole.
He is called the ropedancer.

Whoever uses a thin wire of brass or steel
in the same way
becomes a low-wire artist.

There remains the one whose performance is a game of chance.
The one who is proud of his fear.
He dares to stretch his cable over precipices,
he attacks bell towers,
he separates mountains and brings them together.
His steel cable, his rope, must be extremely tight.
He uses a balancing pole for great crossings.
He is the *Voleur* of the Middle Ages,
the *Ascensioniste* of Blondin's time,
the *Funambule*.

In English we call him the High-Wire Walker.

Warning

No, the high wire is not what you think it is.
It is not a realm of lightness, space, and smiles.
It is a job.
Grim, tough, deceptive.

And whoever does not want to struggle
against failure, against danger,
whoever is not prepared to give everything
to feel that he is alive,
does not need to be a high-wire walker.
Nor could he ever become one.

As for this book—
the study of the high wire is not rigorous,
it is useless.

244 . The Greatest Circus Stories Ever Told

Setting Up the Wire

There are ropes made of natural fibers, artificial fibers, and metal fibers. When they are stretched, twisted, rolled, compressed, or submitted to rapidly changing temperatures, these fibers create a wire.

The wires are put together to form a strand. Several strands braided, twisted, or sheathed together become a rope. A rope often has in its center a strand of some other material. This is usually called the core, the "soul."

Wires, strands, and soul are assembled according to methods whose laws are as rigorous as they are varied.

The number of ropes, therefore, is infinite.

Whoever intends to master the art of walking on them must take on the task of seeking them out. Of comparing them. Of keeping those whose properties correspond to his aspirations. Of learning how to knot them. Of knowing how to tighten them.

Acquiring this knowledge is the work of a lifetime.

For now, take a metal rope of clear steel, composed of six, seven, or eight strands, with a diameter of between twelve and twenty-six millimeters.

With a soul of hemp.

Today, one no longer finds high-wire walkers who use thick ropes of Italian hemp. For reasons of convenience, the steel cable has replaced the rope.

This cable must be free of all traces of grease.

Each steel cable is lubricated when it is manufactured. The first operation, therefore, is to remove this grease. The best method is to stretch out the cable in the corner of a garden and to leave it there for several years. At the end of that time, you will hunt through the tall grass to retake possession of the "old" cable. To make it new again, wash it in gasoline and rub it with emery until it is clean and gray. It is a good idea to leave a considerable length of cable exposed in this fashion, perhaps five hundred meters. Walk-lengths can then be cut off when needed.

If you are not in a position to age a new cable in this manner, an alternative is to repeat the cleaning process as many times as necessary—to wipe each strand, one after the other, and to go through the operation again and again until the wire is absolutely dry. This method is not entirely satisfactory, however, since the grease that lurks in the soul can sometimes spill forth abundantly when a tightly stretched cable has been exposed to the sun for a prolonged period.

A rusted cable can be made excellent once it has been brushed and wiped.

A cable must be in good condition. Without kinks or meat hooks. Kinks are the traces left by an old loop or hook: the cable has been twisted, and when it is stretched out, a barely perceptible bump remains that even the greatest tension cannot eliminate. Meat hooks are the wires of a broken strand; they bristle up like splinters. To make sure that the cable is not concealing any meat hooks, run a cloth along the entire length of the wire in both directions.

When setting up for the first time, use a simple wire ten meters long, stretched out two and a half meters off the ground between two small poles—two X's of wood or metal—or, even more simply, between two trees. Preferably, trees with character. Attach one end with wire clamps; on the other end attach a tightening device (a large turn-buckle or a level hoist) to a sling. At the tip of the cable make a spliced eye with a thimble inside it. Draw the eye toward the hoist hook with the help of a pulley block. Fasten to the hoist and tighten. Be careful to wrap the tree trunks with large jute cloths so they are not hurt by the wire.

The First Steps

The first steps, of course, can be made on a small wire stretched out just two inches from the ground. But then, you could just as easily close this book and become a weekend wire walker.

★★★

Don't look for a ladder; leap up onto the wire. Slippers and balancing pole are for later.

Right away, balance yourself on one foot, facing the tree. Quick. Try to hold on as long as possible before grabbing the tree again.

Do no jump. Do not walk. The leg is fixed. The foot is poised along the wire.

Your arms will wave about wildly. Pay no attention to them. Look for balance. Enough! Change feet. Just a little try. Change again. In this way you will find your better foot, the one that will later become your "balancing foot." Then you will stop these stupid gymnastics, turn around, and lean your back against the tree.

High-wire walking is not a solution to the problem of balance. Look intensely at what stretches out before you.

You are facing the cable.

That's it.

Everything changes now that the wire is there.

Fix your eyes on the target—the end—and try a crossing.

Don't look for the bark behind you, but jump down the moment you lose your balance. In this way, the crossing will be a series of balancings: on one foot, on the other foot, again, and again, and again.

You must not fall.

When you lose your balance, resist for a long time before turning yourself toward the earth. Then jump.

You must not force yourself to stay steady. You must move forward.

You must win.

The wire trembles. The tendency is to want to calm it by force. In fact, you must move with grace and suppleness to avoid disturbing the song of the cable.

It is better to take your first steps without a balancing pole. Above all, it is natural. This cumbersome bar can help an experienced walker to make an effortless crossing, but it is utterly useless to the beginner. You should not begin to think about a balancing pole until you have mastered balancing on one foot and have been able to make a partial crossing without losing your composure.

The balancing pole is generally a wooden rod or a metal tube with a diameter that allows for easy handling; it is five to eight meters in length. Its weight varies according to the situation: the exercise balancing pole weighs twenty pounds; the balancing pole used in great crossings can be as heavy as fifty pounds. The way it is made is the wire walker's secret. Assemble your own and do not tell anyone how you did it.

So that the foot will feel the cable and not lend itself to accidental slips, buffalo-hide slippers are recommended, though in rainy weather these should be replaced by slippers with rubber soles. But any reinforced shoes with the main sole removed, or even thick socks—several on each foot—will do the job quite well. In the same way, a twisted green branch or an old rusty pipe will be perfectly adequate for the first balancing pole.

Don't waste your time on the ground.

Work without stopping. Little by little, the wire must belong to you.

Hold the balancing pole firmly, arms spread. Never dip it. It is moved to the left, to the right, in a horizontal gesture. The body does not lean. The hips do not move. The leg is rigid without being dead. But you discover that on your own.

By the end of the day, you will have made your first crossing.

Walking

The horseman knows the pleasure of working his horse at a slow pace. He leaves galloping to the frenzied knight.

Perfectly calm, the high-wire walker will endlessly practice "the Time of the Rope." This consists of traveling the length of his cable slowly, one step at a time. This is the first exercise with the balancing pole. It is also the most important and the most ancient. After a great number of crossings back and forth, you will know what it is to go and what it is to return. Continue to do this for a long time before attempting a real walk. For a walk on the wire must be slow and careful, like a line pulled tight by the strength of your eyes: the body straight, the foot firmly inside the wire with each step, the balancing pole motionless.

To put your whole foot on the wire all at once produces a sure though heavy king of walking, but if you first slide your toes, then your sole, and finally your heel onto the wire, you will be able to experience the intoxicating lightness that is so magnificent at great heights. And then people will say of you: "He is strolling on his wire!" Dismount and pace off nine meters holding the balancing pole: that is the perfect walk! This test is necessary: you were beginning to feel like a high-wire walker.

Walking is the soul of the wire. There are an infinite number of styles.

There is the walk that glides, like that of a bullfighter who slowly approaches his adversary, the presence of danger growing with each new step, his body arched outrageously, hypnotized.

There is the unbroken, continuous walk, without the least concern for balance, the pole on your shoulder, your arm swinging and your eyes turned upward, as if you were looking for your thoughts in the sky; this is the solid walk of a man of the earth returning home, a tool over his shoulder, satisfied with this day's work.

These walks happen to be mine.

Discover your own. Work on them until they are perfect.

Running

Running?

Ah! Yes, running is entertaining.

It's fresh, it's tempting, it's joyous, it's distracting.

All running is joyful.
Ah! How he runs on his wire!

You are running to a certain fall.

Running will come naturally from a light and rapid way of walking.
Let is come by itself.

When you walk, the foot follows the line of the wire: in this way you can do extremely rapid crossing and brief runs. But to run vigorously on a cable, you must put your feet sideways across the wire, like a duck. To begin, run on the wire thinking only of regularity; running will be difficult. Add speed, and it will become impossible.

You must set your eyes so that they take in the whole length of the wire. You must feel it in space. Measure its extension. The distance is too great to hazard without courage: hold the balancing pole in front of you and take off with a sure and straight step. With the help of your open arms, clear a path for yourself, push you hips along the wire to the very end; your feet will follow, your body will get through. You want your steps to control this length of steel. Launch yourself then, and cross it with three long strides.

To understand running is to harmonize the wind of your steps with the breath of the wire—without asking questions.

Running is not the way to go quickly from one end of the wire to the other.

Running? It's the acrobat's laughter!

The Quest for Immobility

This is the mystery of the rope dance. The essence, the secret. Time plays no part in achieving it.

Or perhaps I should say "in approaching it."

To approach it, the high-wire walker turns himself into an al-chemist. Again and again, he attempts it along the wire, but without ever entering the Domain of Immobility—where, I was told, the arms become useless, hanging alongside a body that is ten times heavier than before.

The feeling of a second of immobility—if the wire grants it to you—is an intimate happiness.

Come to the middle of the wire with the most beautiful of your walks.

Achieve a state of balance, and then wait. All by itself, the balancing pole will become horizontal, your body will settle on two fixed and solid legs. Immobility will come promptly. Or so you would think.

You will feel yourself immobile: I'm not moving, therefore I'm immobile.

And what about your eyes that watch and wander?

I saw your eyes climbing up through the trees.

And those thoughts in your skull, stammering back and forth?

And the blood rushing through your veins? And the wind in your hair? And the bobbing wire? And all this air your eat and chew?

What a racket!

No, the tiny inhabitants of the weeds have never seen such an agitated being.

The quest for immobility is even more deceptive if you give up the balancing pole, but it is absolutely essential.

You must devote yourself to it.

Balanced on one foot, the balancing foot, slowly bring your arm and leg to rest. Hold this position. This is the first point. Then put your free leg into contact with the other, your two feet on the wire; your arms will serve as a balancing pole, you will gradually move them less and less. This is the second point. Now you must get rid of these arms: by crossing them in front of you, by letting them hang naturally, or by putting them behind your back. All this happens in surreptitious ways. Clandestinely. This is the third point.

It is now a matter of patience. It is between the wire and you.

Approach. Feel how balance no longer exists. Be on the lookout for the moment when you will suddenly stop breathing. An otherworldly heaviness will anchor you to the cable. You will breathe along it: the air will surge from the end of the wire, work its way slowly along it, pierce the soles of your feet, climb up through your legs, inundate your body, and in the end reach your nostrils. You will exhale without any pause, and your breath will travel back along the same path: softly, from your lips, you will expel the air, and it will go down, flow around each muscle, trace the outline of your feet, and then reenter the wire. . . .

Do not abandon your breath halfway. Pursue it until it escapes through the end of your wire, in the same way it came.

Your breathing will become slow, distended, long like a thread.

You and the rigging will become a single body, solid as a rock.

You will feel yourself a thing of balance. You will become wire.

Once you have built this flawless balance, so fleeting and fragile, it will be as dense for you as granite.

If no thought came to disturb this miracle, it would go on and on. But man, who is astonished by everything, himself included, quickly loses hold of it.

The minute point of balance hovers above the wire, knocks against the wire walker, and navigates like a feather in the wind of his efforts.

Let this wind slacken, let it die, and the feather will soon enter the wire walker and come to rest in his center of gravity.

This is the way it happens then: first, you reach a relative calm; then, you achieve a second, finer balance; and finally, if only rarely, you attain a brief instant of absolute immobility.

For the wind of our thoughts is more violent than the wind of balance and will soon set this delicate feather fluttering again.

Barefoot

I am nostalgic for the old ropes.

You walked on them with bare feet. Not so on the cable.

How proud the tightrope walker was. On the bottom of each foot there was an astonishing tattoo, a mark made far above the crowds. It was the sign of his art and his daring, and only he knew it was there. Its hardness was proof to him that he was Emperor of the Air, and even on the ground he continued to walk on these tough, callused lines.

The foot lived well when it lived with hemp.

The steel cable has replaced the rope, and if it breathes it is only because its soul is made of hemp. And even though the foot can never merge with the metal, you must go back often to working barefoot. This is indispensable. The foot can then find its place on the cable, and the cable can find its place in the foot.

But that must be attempted delicately.

The wire penetrates between the big toe and the second toe, crosses the foot along the whole length of the sole, and escapes behind the middle of the heel. One can also make the wire enter along the bottom of the big toe; the sole is then traversed obliquely, and the cable leaves slightly to one side of the heel. If this second method is acceptable for certain walks, the first is nevertheless essential. You must be able to use the big toe and the second toe to grip the wire and hang on to it (this is the only way to avoid a slip during a Death Walk).

Remain balanced on one foot until the pain is no longer bearable, and then prolong this suffering for another minute before changing feet.

Repeat the exercise, then attempt a series of walks. Wait until the foot is perfectly placed before taking the next step.

When the positioning of each foot has become quite natural, the legs will have gained their independence, and your step will have become noble and sure.

You won't get results from a few hours of serious work. You must continue until your flesh understands it.

But I promise that when your feet slide to rest on a cable bed, you will astonish yourself with a smile of deep weariness.

Look: on you sole there is what my friend Fouad calls the Line of Laughter. It corresponds to the mark of the wire.

The High-Wire Walker's Salute

Before entering the last phase of combat,
the bullfighter removes his montera
and, in a neat circling gesture, presents it to the crowd.
Then he throws it onto the sand.
The matador's salute is a dedication.

When the balloon is ready, the pilot orders: "Hands off!"
Rising above a forest of arms, he flourishes his cap
in broad figure eights and disappears.
The aeronaut's salute is a farewell.

The wire walker, after setting foot on the cable,
walks halfway across, stops, and slides down to one knee.
He removes one hand from his balancing pole.
The wire walker's salute is a dedication.
Of strength, of magnificence.
He thrusts his fist into the teeth of the wind,
and in that same movement his fist opens to receive the answer.
The wire walker reads it in his own hand, there, resting
on one knee, in the middle of the wire.
News of death, a promise of joy:
he lets nothing escape
of what he has learned.

★★★

Except for the Time of the Rope, the Salute is the first exercise the high-wire walker must learn.

There is the standing salute, the kneeling salute, and the sitting salute.

The first is made on one leg, balancing pole resting horizontally on the raised thigh, the arm up.

The second is the true high-wire walker's salute. So that it will be perfect, a part of the body's weight must rest on the top of the foot where it joins the ankle, and the whole top of the foot must be touching the cable—not just the knuckles of the foot. You often see this, and it is a disgrace.

The sitting salute is the same as the standing, except that the wire passes under the thigh and the middle of the buttocks.

You can achieve the sitting salute unexpectedly—by jumping onto the wire from the standing position. The leg muscles will absorb the vibrations of this sudden encounter with the cable.

There are numerous variations to the high-wire walker's salute.

I have discovered old engravings in which the acrobat is kneeling, but only the knee is touching the rope; the rest of the leg is in the air perpendicular to the wire.

A salute is made when you step onto the wire, but there is also the salute that concludes a performance, and as a general rule the strongest moment of any exercise can be accompanied by an appropriate salute. There is no particular salute without a balancing pole. One possibility would be to imitate those gymnasts with big mustaches who posed for the earliest cameras: standing proudly and simply, arms crossed, head held high, feet almost at right angles, the torso inflated. I do this. I call it the Salute in the Old Style.

But there is nothing, it seems to me, more gravely majestic than the moment when the high-wire walker, with admirable reverence, takes leave of his wire.

Exercises

Walking, running, and the salute precede a multitude of exercises; an infinite number, in fact, if one were to include all the variants. Often the balancing pole is required; sometimes special equipment must be used. One must also mention the net, the belt, and other safety systems. They guarantee the conquest of the impossible—but at the same time they cheapen the victory. A rule of thumb would be the following: anything that can be done on the ground can be done on the wire, although sometimes necessarily in a slightly different form. To draw up the complete list of exercises for rope, cable, and low wire would be as impossible as pretending to draw up a list of newly invented exercises, exercises that have not yet been done, or exercises that are unheard of, that defy execution.

Here, in any case, is a list—presented more or less in order of appearance:

The Time of the Rope.
Walking.
Running.
The salute.
Dancing.
Splits.
The pretend fall.
The headstand (with or without balancing pole).
Resting on the wire, in a supine position.
The genuflection; walking while genuflecting.
Balancing on one knee.
The planche: balancing on one leg.
One-arm handstand.
The cartwheel.
Balancing, facing the audience.
High-bar exercises.
Descending an inclined cable by sliding on the stomach (a specialty of the Middle Ages); hanging from the back of the neck, or with one foot attached to a pulley.
The Death Walk (up or down an inclined cable, with or without the balancing pole).
Blindfolded: walking with the head covered, walking in a sack.
Dancing in wooden shoes.
Dancing with scythes, sickles, or daggers attached to the ankles.
Walking with feet in baskets (with wicker bottoms or fake bottoms made of cloth).
The bound walk: ankles chained together.

Jumping through a paper hoop.

Walking with a pennant, crossing with flags.

With a pitcher and glass of water: refreshments on the rope.

Walking with a candlestick or sword (the prop is balanced on the chin, the nose, or even the forehead, for the length of a balancing, or for wire walkers of great heights, for the length of a crossing with the balancing pole—without the balancing pole for slack-rope walkers).

Tricks with a Chinese umbrella or an Indian fan (often on an inclined rope).

The half-turn without the balancing pole.

The half-turn jump without the balancing pole.

The half-turn with the balancing pole (the wire walker turns; his balancing pole does not move).

Juggling (usually with balls, clubs, torches, or hoops), with or without the balancing pole. The pole can be balanced off-center on the wire with the help of the balancing foot.

Walking in a hoop (the hoop rolls on the wire and is kept in a vertical position by the feet of the wire walker, who walks on the inside).

Hoop around the ankles (the hoop is kept in a horizontal position by the ankles, which means the wire walker must take broad, semicircular steps so as to not to lose the hoop).

Passing a hoop over the body and stepping out.

Walking with the balancing pole behind the back.

Walking with the balancing pole above the head, arms fully extended.

With the balancing pole on the shoulders.

Putting the balancing pole behind the back (over the shoulders or under the legs).

Walking backward.

Wearing disguises.

Imitating characters, animals.

Wearing armor.

Doing comedy routines on the wire.

Playing a musical instrument (in all positions).

Balancing on a small wooden plank (motionless, or with tiny leaps forward).

Balancing on a ladder, or on a step ladder.

Balancing on a chair, its strut or legs resting on the rope.

With a table and chair: a meal on the wire.

With a stove and kitchen equipment: cooking an omelette on the wire.

Pistol dancing, sword dancing. Knife throwing.

Precision shooting on the wire, shooting at a moving target, shooting balloons.

On a velocipede, bicycle.

On a unicycle (regular-size, giant).

Walking on stilts.

High jumping. Hurdling a table.

Jumping rope. Double, triple, crisscross, while moving forward.

Jumping over a riding crop held in both hands, frontward and backward.

High-wire walker's somersault (forward roll with jump start with a balancing pole).

True somersault (feet to feet), frontward or backward (the principle exercise of low-wire artists and ropedancers, but unthinkable for a wire walker of great heights without protection).

The caboulot (backward roll with a balancing pole). Crossing the wire with caboulots.

The reverse (a caboulot without the balancing pole in which the acrobat takes hold of the cable behind him from a lying position and pulls, which rolls him over backward and puts him in a sitting position).

The human load (carrying someone on your back); the "baptism of wire" (taking someone from the audience and putting him on the wire for the first time); pushing a wheelbarrow with someone in it.

Falling astride the wire (usually to initiate a series of caboulots).

Spinning around the wire, starting from a straddling position.

Balancing a perch on the forehead, with crossing.

Hanging: from the knees, ankles, or toes.

Tightrope acts on a slack wire attached below the main cable.

The high-bar catch-and-swing. (After a real or reigned slip, the wire walker, hanging by his hands, gets back onto the wire by flaring out his legs over it; as soon as his feet catch hold of the wire, he turns around it, before springing to a standing position.)

Fireworks shot off on the wire (knapsack filled with sand in which fuses have been planted; helmet with a pinwheel; balancing pole adorned with flares and Catherine wheels—lighted with a cigarette at the middle of the wire). This exercise is often fatal.

Jumping on one foot, with crossing.

Crossing a burning wire (with boots and asbestos clothes).

"True" crossing on a motorcycle (holding the balancing pole, with no counterweight under the machine).

"False" crossing on a motorcycle (with a trapeze that works as a counterweight and holds the machine on the cable).

Exercises with a partner, group exercises:

The human column, either stationary or advancing along the wire (two, three, or four people on the shoulders of the under-stander).

The human column on a unicycle, on a bicycle (with two or three people).

The bicycle with trapeze hanging below the wheels (one or two trapezes).

The human pyramid (metal bars—"forks"—create a scaffolding for three, four, five, six, seven, eight, or nine people).

A pyramid of three bicycles, with crossing.

Two people passing each other from opposite directions, without a balancing pole, by "ducking" (without touching), by "embracing" (grabbing the partners' hands and turning while leaning outward).

Passing the sleeper. (You cross your partner, who is lying down on the cable, by placing your foot on his stomach.)

Passing the sleeper by jumping over him.

Jumping over the seated partner.

Passing with a balancing pole (with the partner seated, or lying down).

Climbing on the partner's back, then shoulders, and leaping forward, to land feet first on the wire.

Backward somersault (*salto mortale*) from the shoulders of an under-stander to the shoulders of another (never done without a safety belt).

Jumping from a springboard or teeterboard attached to the cable and landing on the under-stander's shoulders.

The Ladder of Death. (In the beginning, a simple ladder was placed flat across the wire, with one acrobat at each end. Today, the ladder is solidly attached to the cable and can freely pivot around it.)

The human belt. (The body of the rider is wrapped around the waist of
the under-stander.)
The human wheelbarrow. (The rider has his legs attached to the waist
of the carrier and holds a wheel in his hands that he guides along
the wire.)
Head to head.
Head to foot. (The top mounter stands on the under-stander's head.)
The wire walker's somersault (forward caboulot) over one, two, three,
or four people.
Working with several wires at different heights and angles.
Working with a wire that changes heights and angles during the act.
Working with animals as partners (bears, monkeys, birds).

It is also important to mention the roles of the various kinds of wires:
There are exercises for low-wire artists and ropedancers that
cannot be done on a high-wire walker's cable; others can be done on
any kind of wire. It is obvious that an acrobat on a slack rope one and a
half meters from the ground can raise his eyes for a long time to keep
an object balanced on his forehead or to juggle; the high-wire walker,
on a cable without elasticity or movement, can do no more than attempt the same exercise without a balancing pole. He will never succeed, however, unless he has immense talent.

The high-wire walker must be an inventor.
Jean-Francois Gravelet, a.k.a. Charles Blondin, prepared an
omelette on the wire; he also opened a bottle of champagne and
toasted the crowd. He even managed to take photographs—from the
middle of the wire—of the crowd that was watching him cross the
rapids at Niagara Falls.
Madame Saqui created historical frescoes to the glory of Emperor Napoleon, all by herself on the tightrope.
Rudy Omankowsky, Jr., set off numerous fireworks from his
cable. He specialized in somersaulting from a bicycle over four people
(the bike would fall into the net at the moment of takeoff). His father,
"Papa Rudy" Omankowsky, taught him the extraordinary dismount
from the giant unicycle: jumping forward onto the cable. He himself

was the master of a series of caboulots—his legs now shooting out to the right, now to the left, now on either side of the wire—and performed a dramatic crossing in a sack that ended with straddle falls and a series of rolls.

The ventriloquist Señor Wences has told me that on the tightrope, "facing the audience," Miguel Robledillo initiated a staggering drunk.

Francis Brunn, the legendary juggler, remembers admiringly how Alzana would jump rope on wet cables and continue to jump even after he had lost balance and was being carried away from the axis of the wire.

I myself have witnessed the delicate crossings of Sharif Magomiedoff several times: he placed the tip of his wife's foot on his forehead and walks along the wire while keeping her balanced—she herself is protected from falling by a safety belt. My friend Pedro Carillo goes down the steepest walk by jumping without a balancing pole and, almost in total darkness, slides down—sometimes backward—to reach the ground.

As for myself, I am endlessly hunting for new exercises—like throwing away the balancing pole; the half-turn with balancing pole sweeping through space; walking on tiptoe so as not to wake up the sleeping circus; bouncing a ball on my forehead; and other juggling acts directly inspired by Francis Brunn.

And, lest I forget the masters of us all: the high-wire animals. Artists have painted them with great enthusiasm, and photographs have allowed us to know the truth that lurks behind the legends.

★★★

Walking in wicker baskets is an old and very pleasant exercise. A great family of wire walkers robbed a cigarette manufacturer in this way.

It all happened long ago, so perhaps the story can now be told.

Once, while performing outdoors, they attached one end of their rope to the window of a cigarette warehouse. Having come to the basket exercise in their performance, the wire walkers repeated it so many times that the audience, which did not share this excessive passion for baskets, began to hoot with impatience.

The baskets were being systematically loaded at one end of the wire and then carefully emptied at the other. In this way, the family managed to steal enough cigarettes to fill a hay cart.

Without a Balancing Pole

This is the foundation of the art of high-wire walking.

For safety reasons, however, the high-wire walker has forgotten it.

It is rare to see a high-wire walker at great heights without a balancing pole.

It is, however, the purest image of a man on a line.

In a crossing without balancing pole, we see the qualities of an acrobat; in a true performance without balancing pole, we salute the blood of the high-wire walker.

The succession of balancings—first on one foot and then on the other—that allowed you to move along the wire with skill must now be developed into a controlled walk. The crossing must be made at an even speed, without the slightest loss of equilibrium.

If before you had to fix your eyes on the cable several yards in front of you, now you must look all the way to the end. This connection with the "target" is obligatory, and more than once it has saved a life.

Running without a balancing pole can be attempted only after your walk has become infallible. You can master it with constant and devoted work over a number of years. Like a juggler, you must practice fiercely and without distraction. Otherwise, your attempts on the wire will remain attempts, and you will always lose.

For example, consider the half-turn:

You can have an exact idea of it without ever being able to do it successfully.

Create a vertical motion in the wire; the moment to attempt the half-turn is when the wave is at its maximum height; the body will be lighter, the feet will turn more easily. This wave is imperceptible. Press down harder with the back foot; it will serve as a pivot. Remember that the feet never completely leave the wire during a half-turn.

To turn around on both legs at once, you must raise yourself slightly on the balls of your feet; the heels swivel one hundred and eighty degrees to meet up with the wire again at the same time as the front part of your feet. The half-turn can be done to the right or the left, after coming to a full stop or in the middle of a walk. This last will come as a surprise—like a sleepwalker suddenly changing direction.

If I had to present myself in the Paradise of Rope Dancers by doing one walk, and one walk only, I would make my entrance without a balancing pole. I would walk as naturally as possible, my arms at my sides, letting them sway slightly to the rhythm of my step. I would walk straight ahead without thinking for a single moment that I was on a wire: like some passerby receding into the distance.

And my salute would be a one-knee balancing without pole—which I believe is something no one has ever done before.

The King Poles

The high-wire walker no longer lives among the low branches of the trees. A new wire is waiting for him.

A solid guy wire, perhaps fifteen meters long, stretched out six or eight meters above the ground between two poles painted in the performer's favorite color. On these poles the wire walker can rest, place his different balancing poles, store his chair or his bicycle, as well as his juggling clubs and unicycle. The platform floor should be a square of wood strong enough to support all the equipment and the aerialist himself. It is positioned below the cable. The platforms of low-wire artists and ropedancers are positioned above the cable. They step down onto their cable. The high-wire walker, however, steps up onto his. Along the vertical axis of the walk cable, and on each side, an ungreased cable is stretched down to the ground. One of these inclined cables is drawn out to maximum length for the Death Walk. It is along this path that you will climb up to the installation, unless you have the patience to build a hemp-rope ladder with oak rungs.

Each pole is held vertically by the "obseclungs"—two thin cables attached to the top of the pole that come down perpendicular to the walk line and form a forty-five-degree angle with the ground. These guy wires are pulled into place by pulleys attached with "beckets" to "stakes." The whole installation is thus anchored by the stakes, thick steel bars—formerly wooden bars—that are driven into the ground with sledgehammers. These in turn have a sling of steel or hemp attached to them. This is called the becket.

Putting up the king poles will be your first great joy as a high-wire walker.

You measure the terrain. In the designated spots you lay out the pole sections that you will later fit together; these are hollow tubes or trussed pylons. Then you proceed to the "dressing": one by one jibing the platforms and poles with all their cables, in an order so complicated that the neophyte will have to go through it several times before he can assume sole responsibility for it. It goes without saying that you must have won the friendship of an old high-wire walker who will share his rigging secrets with you, and that he is with you now. If not, you will have to go about it according to your own ideas, and sooner or later you will pay for it with your life.

When the equipment is ready, you drive in the stakes. If five men produce a series of strokes in rapid succession—"a flying five"—watch out for the pieces of steel that whistle down, to land in a tree trunk twenty feet away, or in the flesh of a man who was not paying attention.

You raise up the king poles. One after the other. With the aid of a six-sheave block and tackle. Then you attach the tightening device: a heavy chain hoist or a giant turnbuckle. This latter should not be used for a big installation if the longitudinal section of the screw forms a series of triangles, for it wears out and gives way. The screw should have a square shape so that it will never loosen. This is the king of turnbuckle used for coupling railroad cars.

The curvature of the wire changes according to the height. Soon it will trace a straight line that seems rigorous; you then attach the cavalletti to the blocks and give a final turn to the tightening device—the "pull to death"—just before beginning your work.

To give your routines on the wire an aspect of perfection and to execute highly delicate balancings, the cable must not buckle or sway between the two poles. To avoid this, you attach a thin plate of light metal over the walk cable at appropriate intervals. These plates will fit snugly over the wire. To each flap you attach a length of hemp, the same thickness as the walk cable, that will be drawn down to the ground from various points on the wire at the same angle as the obseclungs. These are the cavalletti. The shape of the plates allows a bicycle rim to pass over them without jumping off tracks; because of the thickness of the ropes that secure them, you will not find yourself on the ground looking at your own severed arm after an accidental slip—which happened to an artist who had chosen to use a thin steel wire.

At times the cavalletti require these plates; at other times they do not. The cavalletti area necessary for great crossings and preferable for "high work" between the poles; in the open air, they are generally spaced fifteen meters apart. But Blondin, who worked on rope, placed them at every two meters for difficult crossings.

For a fifteen-meter wire between two poles, two cavalletti will be acceptable. Obviously, when there are too many cavalletti or when they are too close to one another, we sense the amateurism and cowardice of the performer. If you want to avoid the slightest jolt on the cable, if you want to be certain that it will not vibrate as you go over the cavalletti, at the end of each rope you must use a pulley and attach a counterweight—a bag of sand or a bucket of water. The rope crosses through the pulley, which is attached two meters from the ground by a brace anchored to a chain that in turn is tied to a stake. The wire will then breathe with each of your steps without giving way or turning.

All this must be learned. You cannot make it up.

There are some high-wire walkers who would rather die with their knowledge than let newcomers learn it. Besides, circus people distrust anyone who does not "live on the road," and how could it be otherwise?

The length of the walk cable should always exceed ten meters; the length works as a function of the height of the poles. For six-meter poles a good length is twelve meters. A number of aerialists would say fifteen meters; this makes the installation easier, since the circus ring measures thirteen and a half meters in diameter and the poles are always placed just outside the ring. The more one stretches the line without raising the height, the lower the installation will seem. And vice versa.

The high-wire walker eagerly carries his balancing pole to the foot of the king poles. With a smile he abandons the "little wire" of his first crossings. From now on, he will return to it only to learn new exercises or to throw himself into some whirling caper he hopes to invent. He puts his foot on the inclined cable and scales the sky, where the motionless birds are waiting to meet him.

Alone on His Wire

Up above, about to begin a long acquaintance with his new territory, the high-wire walker feels himself alone. His body will remain motionless for a long time. Grasping the platform with both hands behind him, he stands before the cable, as if he did not dare set foot on it.

It looks as though he is idly basking in the setting sun.

Not at all. He is buying time.

He measures space, feels out the void, weighs distances, watches over the state of things, takes in the position of each object around him. Trembling, he savors his solitude. He knows that if he makes it across, he will be a high-wire walker.

He wants to line up his doubts and fears with his thoughts—in order to hoist up the courage he has left.

But that takes too much time.

The cable grows longer, the sky becomes dark, the other platform is now a hundred meters away. The ground is no longer in the same place; it has moved even lower. Cries come from the woods. The end of the day is near.

At the deepest moment of his despair, feeling he must now give up, the high-wire walker grabs his balancing pole and moves forward. Step by step, he crosses over.

This is his first accomplishment.

He stands there trying to absorb it, his eyes blankly staring at this new platform, while darkness skims over the ground.

With the tops of the trees he shares the day's last light, a light softer than air.

Alone on his wire, he wraps himself more deeply in a wild and scathing happiness, crossing helter-skelter into the dampness of the evening. He attaches his balancing pole to the platform before settling down at the top of the mast. There, in a corner of dark and chilly space, he waits calmly for the night to come.

Practice

The sock of it lasted several days.

Every morning he ran to his wire, leaping over the grass so the dew would not weigh him down. Distracted by so much happiness, he would let himself simply walk back and forth, again and again. There are those who think this coming and going will turn them into high-wire walkers. The true man of the wire, however, cannot accept this horizontal monotony for very long: he knows that the path he is about to take has no limit. In remembrance of his recent birth, he stops short and sets to work. Silent and alone, he brings to the high cable everything he has learned down below. He discards the movements space will not support and gathers up the others into a group that he will polish, refine, lighten, and bring closer and closer to himself.

Each day he adds another mastered element.

Soon he goes out on his wire with only one goal: to discover new ideas, to invent a combination of unexpected gestures. He goes out hunting. And what he catches he hangs on his wire. Then he distracts himself with inconsequential walks, whimsical postures, exercises with no future, like a bear wallowing in his pool at the zoo. And if he loses his taste for movement to such an extent that he loses control, better that he should rest on the wire than stop and climb down. For you must reach some apex before stepping to the ground, no matter how small it is: your existence as a high-wire walker is at stake. You must leave the wire in triumph, not out of weariness.

Now that he knows how to go about practicing, each session will be longer, more fruitful, and the day will be meaningless unless it bears the shape of the wire.

Then the music starts!

For stimulation, he turns on the brassiest Circassian marches; he draws courage from Spanish bullfighting music; and, with exquisite ardor, he surrounds himself with the sound of a full orchestra.

The Wire Walker at Rest

At the time when wire walkers stretched their ropes between two X's of wood, one of the X's was always reserved for resting.

There was a simple hemp line stretched between the tops of the two beams, high enough for the dancer to lean the small of his back against it. It was covered by a large cloth decorated in the artist's colors and embroidered with fine gold threads. Leaning against it in this way, the acrobat could indifferently let his eyes wander down to settle on the rope.

As his name indicates, the wire walker of great heights is a dreamer: he has another way of resting. He stretches out on his cable and contemplates the sky. There he gathers his strength, recovers the serenity he may have lost, regains his courage and his faith. But weariness is necessary: you must not treat resting as an exercise.

Sit down. Fold one leg on the cable and then lean backward until your head touches it. A moment later the foot will begin to slide, and the leg will stretch out completely; the other leg will hand down and sway. Sometimes one hand lets go of the pole; sometimes it retrieves it. You want to feel the line of the wire. It will become your spinal column.

Each passing second shrieks like a grindstone. An endless pain takes hold of your body and breaks it down muscle by muscle. If you resist and cross the threshold of what is bearable, the torture will extend into your bones and break them one by one across the wire. You will be a skeleton balanced on a razor blade. Beyond this limit, millions of terrifying enchantments await you. Beyond this limit, breath and confidence go together. And still further beyond, a patience without desire will give each of your thoughts its real density.

Then be lazy—to the point of delirium!

With your back on the wire, you feel the vastness of the sky. To be a wire walker in its profoundest sense means to leave the wire behind you, to discover the cables that have been strung even higher and, step by step, to reach the Magic Wire of Immobility, the Wire that belongs to the Masters of the World. The earth itself rests on it. It is the Wire that links the finite to the infinite: the straightest, shortest path between one star and the next.

Now close your eyes.

The cable is limpid. Your body is silent. Together, they are motionless. Only your leg quivers. You would like to cut it off, to turn your body into a single human wire. But already it no longer belongs to you, is no longer a part of you. Like the chess player who closes his eyes and sees a whole plain of black-and-white squares passing under his feet, you close your eyes and see only a magnificent gray wire.

The silent wind of your eyes inhabits it.

A silence invaded by light.

Penetrate this luminosity by seeking out its source. Plunge down to find the place where nothing breathes, into the blackness that is hidden inside it. Keep going until you reach the other side of the light. It is a dazzling clarity, a clamorous splendor: wet, whirling, often colorless. As if through a black mirror, you will see a gleaming, untouched wire. That is the image you are looking for. It will quickly be jumbled together with the fireworks of new impressions. Once this image has come, however, the high-wire walker can live in space. For whole hours, for portions of entire days, as if time had come to a halt. No one else will ever notice.

You must throw yourself into this meaningless search for rest—without hoping for a result.

Here is the wire walker stretched out on his gigantic antenna, listening to the world. He can feel the noise of the city rise up to him; he can distinguish among the thousand sounds that fill the silence of the countryside. He starts at the whistling of shooting stars.

And all that puts him to sleep.

A deep breathing invades him.

Each time he draws in his breath, he hears noises; each time he exhales, he hears nothing. Then, during the space of several heartbeats, he forgets everything. He begins to snore. But between his sighs, what silence!

Below him, nothing. Neither dogs nor people. Nature has gone to sleep as well, so that the wire walker, balanced on his huge tuning fork, can at last begin to dream.

The Blindfolded Death Walk

You have no idea what's in store for you.

A cable inclined at a thirty-degree angle. From the ground to the top of the pole or the church bell tower. Three hundred meters. Guy-lined at intervals by a few lengths of hemp. Swaying in the face of a drowsing sun.

Despite all the care that has been given to its installation, the wire will never demark an evenly ascending line. It will dip into space, become horizontal at low altitudes, gently raise its head, lift up its nose, and with growing malice mime a venomous verticality in its last section.

When a blindfolded Death Walk takes place, it is always announced as an "attempt."

Step by step you will climb up, your eyes pressed against the black cloth, your face buried in the suffocating sack. Blind, deaf, and dumb, you will doubt you can reach the end of the wire.

The sun, which has been beating down since dawn, has drawn out the grease hidden in the soul of the cable. With your first steps, the whole installation will begin to move. Each cavalletti will pull on its area—which will amplify the wire's oscillation, as if it were now trying to throw you off. Without ever knowing where they are, your feet will unexpectedly touch an oily spot—and you will advance by millimeters, your hands clutching the balancing pole. The one you have chosen is long and heavy, and with each step forward it will grow even heavier. You will be at the end of your strength when the abrupt angle of the last steps begins, and the wind will be waiting in ambush for you there. You will think you are in the middle of the wire, so you will kneel down for an impeccable aerialist's salute, which will be ridiculous, for in fact you will be only ten meters from your starting point. You will lengthen your strides with the thought that you are half finished with the crossing, and you will bang your body into the pole or a stone of the building, for the walk is over. Then, with a superb gesture, you will tear off the blindfold and the hood, almost falling with the last step, for your vertigo will be total as you stand in the sudden dazzling light of the sun.

The first ascent will remain the most vivid sensation in your life as a high-wire walker. You will think: My shadow was faithful, it has led me this far, and if by chance courage fails me, I will throw the corpse of my memories helter-skelter on the wire, and in this way each the heart of a storm that will allow me to scale these ferocious heights.

Fakes

I know a man who sells himself body and soul to the highest bidder.

He uses a blindfold with holes in it, an immense balancing pole that hangs over both sides of his overly guy-lined wire, and presents his exercises above a net. He has learned how to walk on the cable with an "extension cord"—a second wire that runs parallel to the one he walks on. It is just above his head, and he can grab onto it whenever he wants.

Over the circus rings where he works as a so-called high-wire walker, he uses a "mechanic." This is an almost invisible cable attached to a safety belt that has been sewn into his costume. His assistant, who stays on the ground during his performance, manipulates the string with tiny, discrete movements, as though he were controlling a puppet. As a result, this equilibrist is able to do stunts that no wire walker could ever attempt, much less accomplish. Three times I saw him do a backward somersault on an inclined wire: this is impossible. Three times I saw him fail to gain his footing. Three times I saw his body fall to one side of the wire—although this was imperceptible to the crowd—and three times I saw his balance righted by the safety line. The rest of his performance was punctuated by cries, feigned slips, and pretend falls. From the simplest, most limpid exercises he knew how to extract interminable difficulties, which he mimed in the most grotesque fashion. Before he stepped onto the wire, he would take great care to rub the soles of his shoes with resin powder. Thus, his feet were not placed on the wire, they were glued to it. When I had the chance to walk on his wire, I could not take a step: my feet got stuck. I am used to wearing old and extremely smooth slippers so my walks will be as lithe and graceful as possible.

The terrain of the high-wire walker is bounded by death, not by props. And when a wire walker inspires pity, he deserves death ten times over.

Anyone can use a net, an extension cord, a blindfold with holes in it, a trick balancing pole, resin, cavalletti that touch each other, and a mechanic. To make life even sweeter for these people, I would advise them to practice falling as well. In the realm of the Absurd, they would become the masters of every artifice.

True high-wire walkers do not do such things.

But I know another aerialist.

He often appears on the wire of my dreams.

He is immense in his red-and-black cape—which he throws down to the crowd with a giant's laughter following his first crossing. At times he is majestic. He does the simplest exercises, even the ones that other artists disdain. But he performs them with such finesse, such cunning and ease, that everything about them seems difficult. At other times, he acts like a clown, makes false steps, tangles his feet, and stops in the middle of a move to strike a comic, ridiculous pose. At still other times, he is wild, throwing himself into mad stunts without even trying to succeed. He attacks the wire, slips, catches himself, bangs his head and howls, foams, springs back.

He is alone, like a flame, and the music of his blood silences all our cheers.

But he can hear what the people in the first row are whispering:

"Isn't he charming?"

"Do you think he's going to fly?"

Murderers!

At that point, he wipes off his sweat with the back of his arm and spits into the arena.

The customer is always right!

With dash and daring he responds disdainfully by pretending to slip with each step, stunning the many spectators who have no idea what he is doing. Then he reaches his platform with classic grace, the perfection he can achieve whenever he wants to.

Laughing, I stand up to applaud him.

I allow him everything. Whatever he does I will accept.

And if he would like to start working with a net, well, maybe I wouldn't disapprove.

The Performance

As the days went on, I found that I could repeat the same steps, the same movements.

My work was becoming serious.

I would begin with several crossings "to build confidence." But I was eager to get to what I love to do best: the slowest walks; the simplest, most delicate routines.

It was in a meadow at the end of a day of hard training that I found my first spectator, who had no doubt been attracted by my silence.

Before leaving the wire, I had allowed myself to do a crossing with one foot dragging behind me, thinking of all the things that foot might be able to do.

Suddenly, the tall hedge behind me opened.

A huge cow's head had just placed itself noiselessly on a row of brambles, its muzzle calm, its eye friendly.

Bashful at being surprised during my exercises, I withdrew very softly to the platform and then set out straight and erect to the middle of the cable, where I performed a mathematically exact half-turn and kneeled to my visitor in the most perfect fashion.

I continued to do the best and most beautiful things I knew. I did the exercises in the order I had prepared them during my practice sessions; I added what a man of the wire thinks he possesses: the expansiveness of movement, the steadiness of the eye, the feeling of victory, the humor of gestures. I climbed down from the wire, covered with sweat, unable to remember having once taken a breath, while the enormous animal turned around, chewing slowly, and went back to her pasture.

Since then, I have added much to this improvised group of exercises, and I have eliminated much. With great effort, I have tried to get rid of everything superfluous. With great regret, I have kept only one salute for every ten I have practiced. I have dressed myself in white, I have had multicolored music played that was originally composed for old circuses; I have invited concert pianists to perform. My act lasts twelve minutes, even though my head is filled with centuries of wire walking.

But when I present myself on the ground and grab hold of the rope ladder or cross a public square to begin a Death Walk without a balancing pole, when I see all the equipment on the ground ready to serve me, when I see the orchestra conductor waiting for my signal, I already feel myself to be a wire walker. From that point on, it is a piece of my life that I give or abandon—it depends. The only things I ever remember are walking on the ground, taking hold of the balancing pole for the first crossing, the moment of doubt, and the final salute. I prefer the ground to be flat, uniform, uncluttered, and clean; and I make sure that the spectators have been moved out of the way.

The rest does not belong to me.

It lives in the thousands of hands that will applaud. When I hear the sound of those hands, I am the only one who knows that in the middle of my performance, when I lie down without my balancing pole, my chest in a sky of spotlights, or my heart open to the wind in an outdoor theater, I am next to the gates of Paradise.

Rehearsal

Stop your normal practicing.

Keep doing walks until you leg breathes and your foot becomes a part of the wire.

Break down each element of your performance in any order you choose and examine it harshly. If the quality is good, repeat it simply as many times as necessary: you must imprint an irreproachable movement on the cable.

Make even the slightest gesture important; do not dawdle over something that seems right. Forget no part of the act.

You are now ready to rehearse.

Go down and rest. Change your costume. Prepare the music. Decide whether you want a few people to watch. Then, as if someone has just announced your entrance, walk toward the wire quickly and with a sure step.

Give your performance.

Go down, and that's it.

Do not do one more thing after that; do not amuse yourself.

Rehearse your act every day, at the end of each practice session.

And go home looking at the ground, thinking of nothing, nothing at all.

Struggle on the Wire

You must throw yourself onto the wire.

Robledillo became one of the great ropedancers at the end of a whip. His father attached little bells to the wire and would come running whenever it became silent.

The glory of suffering does not interest me.

Besides, I don't believe in anything. Uselessness is the only thing I like.

Limits, traps, impossibilities are indispensable to me. Every day I go out to look for them. I believe the whip is necessary only when it is held by the student, not the teacher.

When you train, you should be outside, on a rough coast, all alone.

To learn what you must, it is important to have been treacherously overturned by the ocean's salty air. To have climbed back up to the wire with a wild leap. To have frozen yourself with rage, to have been hell-bent on keeping your balance in the claws of the wind.

You must have weathered long hours of rain and storm, have cried out with joy after each flash of lightning, have cried cries that could push back the thunder.

You must struggle against the elements to learn that staying on a wire is nothing. What counts is this: to stay straight and stubborn in your madness. Only then will you defeat the secrets of the wire. It is the most precious strength of the high-wire walker.

I have kicked off snow with every step as I walked along a frozen cable.

In other seasons, I have run barefoot over a cable burning with sunlight. I have worked without cavalletti on a big cable. I have continued walking on a cable that was progressively loosening with each step. I have tried to cross a completely loose wire, forcing myself to abandon my great assurance. I have even asked people to shake the installation with ropes, to strike the wire with long bars. . . . With complete horror and shame I have fought not to find myself hanging by one hand from the wire with the balancing pole in the other.

I have put on wooden shoes, boots, unmatched pairs of shoes. I have held my balancing pole at my side like a suitcase; I have weighted it down, lightened it, cut it in half, used it with its point off-center in order to walk leaning to one side. I have waited for darkness, so my balance would be disturbed. I have tried Death Walks that were too steep, I have groped along a greasy cable, I have played with telephone wires and railway cables. I have forced myself to rehearse with music that disgusts me. In secret, I have practiced naked to learn how the muscles work and to feel my own ridiculousness.

And, drunk with alcohol, I have proved that a body that knows what it is doing does not need a mind to lead it. . . . I have picked myself up from each of my experiments even more savagely determined. And if I fell, it was silence. I did not wait for my shoulder wound to heal to go on with my backward somersaults—again and again and again.

I was not possessed. I was busy winning.

You do not do a true *salto* on a very high cable. You do not wear a blindfold or raise your eyes to the sky without using a balancing pole. You do not do a headstand on a great cable without a balancing pole.

Impossible?

Who is smart enough to prove it?

I tell everyone that I will attempt a crossing from the American to the Canadian side of Niagara Falls—where the water actually falls—and not over the rapids, where all previous crossing have been made. But once on that mile of unknown cable, shaken by the wind that does not stop, wrapped in a cloud of vapor that must be pierced little by little, over the whirlpools of the cataracts, listening to all that infernal noise, will I dare? Will I dare to be harder than the sun, more glacial than the snow? Will I dare to enter these pages on high-wire walking without knowing the way out? It is one thing to talk about my controlled experiments. But this?

Man of the Air, illuminate with your blood the Very Rich Hours of your passage among us. Limits exist only in the souls of those who do not dream.

The Wind

If this man standing at the edge of the seawall has not moved for such a long time, it is because he is looking out at the raging sea and watching the birds attempt to fly over the narrow passage—for no other reason than to intoxicate themselves with pleasure.

The harbor is deserted. The hurricane is approaching.

A mass of liquid wind, engulfed between the two towers, carries everything along with it.

The birds that cross from one wall to the next are sometimes assaulted by gusts that shut their wings with a sudden dry noise, hurling them and crushing them against a rock, where they remain until a higher and blacker wave comes to peel them off and wash them away.

The terns, the gulls—excellent sailors with voices so powerful they can hear each other through storms—have taken refuge high up in the green sky and remain silent.

Why do some of them dive down and pierce the smoking sea water that has now risen up in furious columns?

Why do they clamor and brush against the havoc of wind, dust, and foam—which they know is deadly?

Who urges this cruel-eyed animal to test himself against the storm?

One of them has almost managed to get through the forbidden passage on his back; the torrent pursues him and brings him down with a volley of hail.

Only one has made it. The gale has stripped off a few of his feathers, but he rejoins his companions, and they will make him their leader, crying out his victory until nightfall.

But he, the wire walker of the waves, knows that he was granted a miracle, and he remembers that moment with fear, for tomorrow he will be the one day they discover stretched out on the seawall.

His dust feeds the wind that little by little wipes him away. Nothing is stronger than the wind. No one is stronger than the wind.

Not even the courageous bird.

Falls

A fall from the wire, an accident up above, a failed exercise, a false step—all this comes from a lack of concentration, a badly placed foot, an exuberant overconfidence.

You must never forgive yourself.

The high-wire walker becomes the spectator of his own fall. With wide-open eyes he whirls around the wire—until he is caught by an arm or finds himself hanging by a knee. Without letting go of the balancing pole, he must take advantage of this motion to stand up again and continue the interrupted movement with rejuvenated energy.

More often than not, there will be applause. No one will understand what has happened

The mistake is to leave without hope, without pride, to throw yourself into a routine you know will fail.

Every thought on the wire leads to a fall.

Accidents caused by equipment must not happen.

Many wire walkers have died in this way. It is stupid. But sometimes the wire slips away from you, because you have put yourself outside the law, outside the law of balance. At such moments, your survival depends on the strength of your instinct.

There are those who allow themselves to be carried away without a struggle. Let them fall!

Others continue to flail their arms and legs above the wire, to beg their eyes not to lose sight of their target. With an avid hand they latch onto the cable at the last instant. Have you ever made a leap of faith toward a distant rope, grabbled hold of a cavalletti in midair?

I waited for my first slip in public. It fortified me, it flooded me with a joyous pride, in the same way a solid clap on the shoulder encourages more than it hurts.

The second slip made me think; I found myself below the wire after completing a movement I had mastered long ago. The third incident was terrifying: I almost fell.

Nevertheless, in my dreams I pursue legendary aerial escapes that will finally do my justice. I, who have everything to lose. For when a man begins to tremble for his life, he begins to lose it.

I demand to be allowed to end my life on the wire. I have the patience of those who have fallen once, and whenever someone tells me of a high-wire walker who fell to the ground and was crushed, I answer:

"He got what he deserved."

For that is clearly the fate and the glory of the aerial acrobat.

Great Crossings

For two weeks, the high-wire walker has been camping at the top of the mountain.

It is decided. Today he will determine the anchor points.

Eagles wheel around in the lukewarm air of the gorge. They can see this little character on the peak, pointing to a spot on the facing mountain.

An enormous roll of cable is on its way. The special convoy has reached the first steep curves. It will arrive tomorrow. A thousand meters of degreased, twenty-five-millimeter wire: discovered by miracle. It is the most beautiful thing I have ever touched. It weighs three tons. I am happy.

On one side I will encircle an outcrop of rock that stands as solid as a mill.

On the other side there is no protruberance. I will have to dig a hole and then pour a broad and deep column of concrete, around which the wire will be coiled and then fastened for safety to three large trees lined up behind it.

The reel has been solidly rooted to the ground.

A team of twenty men hauls up the wire, chanting as they pull. The cable advances a few inches each minute.

It snakes along the side of the mountain. It clears the road and passes over the telegraph lines. It must be taken across the lake by high-wire methods, for no motorboat would be strong enough to pull it from one shore to the other. If the cable touches bottom, you can forget about your crossing, since it will wedge in among the rocks and catch hold of the weeds so diligently that even the most powerful machines or the most expert divers will never be able to dislodge it. It is cruel for a high wire to drown. Eventually, it will be dragged down through the forest, where each tree is an obstacle; then it will climb, foot by foot, minute after minute, toward its anchor point. At last, everything is ready.

The cable is fastened on each peak. That takes a day. It runs along the valley floor, imprinting its weight on dead leaves, drawing an almost invisible boundary. This becomes alarming at the edges of the lake. You see the black serpent dive into the water and find it hard to imagine that it will emerge on the other side, coming up into the grass and continuing on its way, marking this corner of earth with the disagreeable stamp of its metal skin. Like an immense trap, waiting to snap.

You begin to pull, aided by the largest hoist in the world—or several strategically placed pulleys—and you see a long gray line lift itself from the ground and rise up, swaying. The wire suddenly stops. A small branch somewhere is blocking it.

When you have moved the branch aside with your hand, the cable will jerk up violently another five yards. Everything will go well until the next incident. If you must go through a pine forest, you can expect an additional ten days of installation work. You will have to bend back every branch of every tree the wire gets tangled in.

Finally, the cable is over the valley. It rises up in stages. You must load the motorcycle-trapeze with two thousand pounds of cavalletti and put them astride the cable one by one, while the wire sways back and forth over a radius of ten meters.

"Tighten it to death," your ears open to every sound. Then collect your thoughts.

On the day of the crossing, you will assign each volunteer his rope— which he will have to hold and pull on with all his strength when you are above him, and which he cannot release until you have come to the next cavalletti.

Even so, the cable will move so much that you will see undulations up ahead of you in the distance. You will have to wait for each one of them to come to you before going on with your walk: feet planted, on the alert.

The sun will draw the grease out of the cable.

The wind will pick up the moment you begin.

You will have forgotten to bring socks for the end of the walk, and so you will have to go barefoot, trying to complete the crossing by grasping the wire between your first two toes at every step.

But you will not be aware of anything that is happening. You will be completely engrossed in your crossing.

Only a man who is a high-wire walker to his very bones would dare to do this.

Once on your way, you are becoming the Man of the Wire, the Magician of High Altitudes: the length of your path will be sacred to you.

When you are above the lake, do not look at the surface of the water, for the movement of the waves will make you lose your balance.

If you manage to succeed, don't boast of it. What you have done is enough in itself.

Triumph by seeking out the most subtle difficulties. Reach victory through solitude.

The high-wire walker must rest in the way I have described—and fight in that same way.

Never break the rhythm of a crossing. The cable would start to tremble. For high-wire walking does not mean breathing in unison with the rope, but making sure that this joint breathing does not hinder the breath of the one or the palpitation of the other.

Finally: never fail to attend the performances of high-wire walkers.

★★★

Make up your own symbol of perfection. For me, it is throwing away the balancing pole.

With a long and endless gesture, the high-wire walker throws his metal pole far across the sky so that it will not strike the wire, and finds himself alone and helpless, richer and more naked, on a cable made to his own measure. With humility, he now knows he is invincible.

A red velvet wire will be unrolled for him in his dreams. He will move along it brandishing his coat of arms.

Perfection

Attention! You own the wire, that's true. But the essential thing is to etch movements in the sky, movements so still they leave no trace. The essential thing is simplicity.

That is why the long path to perfection is horizontal.

Its principles are the following:

If you want the High Wire to transform you into a high-wire walker, you must rediscover the classic purity of this game. But first you must master its technique. Too bad for the one who turns it into a chore.

Above the crowd on your wire you will pass. Pass above and no more. You will be forgotten.

You must not hesitate. Nor should you be conscious of the ground. That is both stupid and dangerous.

The feet are placed in the direction of the wire, the eyes set themselves on the horizon.

The horizon is not a point, it is a continent.

In walking, it is the wire that pushes you. You offer your balancing pole to the wire, perfectly horizontal, arms spread wide apart.

Like a bird, a man perches on the wire; he does not lean forward, ready to fall. On the contrary, he must make himself comfortable.

Learn your body: the movement of your arms, the breathing of your fingers, the tension of your toes, the position of your chin, the weight of your elbows. Leave nothing to chance.

Chance is a thief that never gets caught.

Eliminate cumbersome exercises. Keep those that transfigure you.

Fear

A void like this is terrifying.

Prisoner of a morsel of space, you will struggle desperately against occult elements: the absence of matter, the smell of balance, vertigo from all sides, and the dark desire to return to the ground, even to fall.

This dizziness is the drama of the rope dance, but that is not what I am afraid of.

After long hours of training, the moment comes when there are no more difficulties. Everything is possible, everything becomes easy. It is at this moment that many have perished. But that, no, that is not at all what I am afraid of.

If an exercise resists me during rehearsal, and if it continues to do so a little more each day, to the point of becoming untenable, I prepare a substitute exercise—in case panic grabs me by the throat during a performance. I approach it with more and more reluctance, come to it slyly, surreptitiously. But I always want to persist, to feel the pride of conquering it. In spite of that, I sometimes give up the struggle. But without any fear. I am never afraid on the wire. I am too busy.

But you are afraid of something. I can hear it in your voice. What is it?

Sometimes the sky grows dark around the wire, the wind rises, the cable gets cold, the audience becomes worried. At those moments I hear screams within myself. The wire has stopped breathing. I, too. It is a prelude to catastrophe—like a drumroll announcing the most difficult exercise. In waiting to fall in this way, I have sometimes cursed the wire, but it has never made me afraid.

I know, however, that one day, standing at the edge of the platform, this anguish will appear. One hideous day will be waiting for me at the foot of the rope ladder. It will be useless for me to shake myself, to joke about it. The next day it will be in my dressing room as I am putting on my costume, and my hands will be wet with horror. Then it will join me in my sleep. I will be crushed a thousand times, rebounding in slow motion in a circus ring, absolutely weightless. When I wake up, it will be stuck to me, indelible, never to leave me again.

And of that, dear heaven, I have a terrible fear.

To imagine that one evening I will have to give up the wire in the same way that so many bullfighters have given up the ring and disappeared into life; that I will have to say, "I was afraid, I met Holy Fear, it invaded me and sucked my blood"—I who hope to give the greatest gift a high-wire walker can give: to die on my wire, leaving to men the insult of a smiling death mask; I who shouted to others on their ropes: "Remember that life is short! What could be better than a happy man in flight, in midair? Think of all the things you've never done!"; I, the fragile walker of wires, the tiniest of men, I will turn away to hide my tears—and yes, how afraid I am.

Vary, France, winter 1972

The Other Side
of the Circus

BY EDWIN P. NORWOOD

The other side of the circus is the side you don't see. Or most people
don't. Too bad really, because many people hold the world of the backlot to be the most interesting aspect of the whole show. These people
were always trying to get on the lot and most of the time we'd shoo
them away. The trick was to catch them on the perimeter and turn
them away there. Once they got well inside it was trickier to shift them.
On our circus you had to actually know somebody on the show to be
allowed. Otherwise—sorry. And we were pretty strict about it. We felt
that if we once relaxed the rule, or showed the slightest forbearance, in
no time at all there'd be rubes (I never actually heard the word used in
my time on the show. Not once.) wandering all over the lot, pestering
the animals—to say nothing of the artists—and sticking their hands
into the cages of the big cats. But you can understand the other side's
allure. And it really doesn't matter, if you're a hayseed, just come to
town, or an inner-city slicker, you still can't help but ask yourself: how
does this behemoth work, and who are these wondrous folk who make
it go? Often as not, they aren't even circus fans. You see folk all the time
come by to watch the tents go up who have no plans to see the show.

The conceit in Norwood's small masterpiece here is that a little
boy named John accompanies Circus Boss Happy Jack Snellen, as he
sees first to the raising of the big top, and then as he inspects the workings and other various goings-on on the other side of the circus.

○ ○ ○

I t was still black night and so too dark to see things with any distinctness. But, as the men piled down from behind and moved into the path of the truck's headlights, John saw that what he had taken for arrows were only iron rods, and the things at their hilts, small bits of cloth. Those carrying them slung the bundles to their shoulders and tramped through the gloom toward the center of the lot.

Already Willie Carr and Happy Jack Snellen were walking in the same direction. John followed at their heels.

"There's a world of room, Happy," the former was saying, "though, as I figure it, you'll have to throw the back end of the big top pretty much over to the right to avoid a swampy spot."

"We'll soon find out. Plenty of room for the front here?"

"All kinds."

"Good. Then we'll tackle the big top."

"There are more ways of laying out a show lot than there are of skinning a kangaroo," Happy Jack confided to John, as they picked their way across the pasture, "for pretty nearly every one is of a different shape and size. Still, there are certain rules that you've always got to bear in mind. First place, you've got to have a good front—that's where the side show, ticket wagons, candy stands, and big show main entrance are located. Second place, you've got to have wagon room in which to store your wagons once they're emptied. Third place, you've got to be all-fired careful not to bottle yourself in. For when night comes, some parts of the show have to be pulled off the lot ahead of other parts. And you can't be dragging wagons through the big top while the clowns are kicking up. No, sir; you've got to get 'em off by going around it, or out some back road—if there is a back road. How about it here, Willie?"

"There's a sort of trick one—turtle back and gumbo, though. We'd be stuck in it until Christmas if it ever rained. I've figured pulling off through the front. Here's the back and upside of the lot now; here where this fence runs."

"Fair enough," returned Happy. "Now we can get to work."

He put one heel against the shadowy boards and then counted his paces outward.

"That's for wagon room and a road," he said. "Hey, you, Red! How about a pin?"

"Right here," answered a man from the darkness. He handed him one of the arrow-like rods. Happy pushed its pointed end into the ground.

"This is what we call locating the center lacing in the big top round end," he told John. "Now for the tape line."

Already another assistant was drawing yard after yard of line from a flat, nickel-plated box. The one called Red held the free end of the tape against the top of the upright pin, while the laying-out boss took the bulk of the line and struck off through the dark. As he strode along, he watched the figures on the tape by the light of an electric pocket lamp. When it showed "152 ft.," he stopped. Another pin man handed him a rod with a ribbon of white cloth tied to its ringed top.

"Now, let's have a squint at your old white-eye," Happy Jack bawled back.

A platinum-like spot wavered in the darkness and then steadied.

"Red's roosting his pocket torch on the top of the first pin," he explained. "This is the way we line up the centers."

He passed the pin he was holding a little to the right, then to the left, as if aiming, and then thrust it well into the ground. "That marks the first center pole. . . All right, Red! Let go the line! That's One! Meaning," he added to John, "Center pole No. 1."

He wound part of the tape back into its box.

"Get hold the end as it creeps up and lay it at the top of this pin, Joe," he instructed.

He and John again moved forward, this time for a distance of sixty feet by the line. Here Happy Jack once more reached for a white-flagged pin.

"Lights!" he called.

In answer two "white-eyes" settled into position, one at the top of each of the pins left behind. A moment of sighting, and the boss had stuck still another pin, adding,

"That's two! Not pins, mind you, but center poles."

Another dragging of the tape through the lush grass of the pasture to the point where it again read "60 ft." A repetition of the sighting along the row of lights. Another pin jabbed firmly in the earth. Then:

"That's three! There are six center poles, each sixty feet apart," he told John, as they again moved forward, "and it always pays to call 'em off as you plant the rods, especially when you're laying out in the dark. Of course, in the early summer, or when we arrive late, there's daylight to help. But when it's a firefly layout like this, it's best to play safe."

It did make you think of firefly time John thought as he peered about. For now electric torches were winking in still other directions. Or it was like being on a hillside and looking down on a town at night.

"Nor do we always lay out the same way," Happy Jack continued, as he sunk another pin. "For instance, at the beginning of a season when the big top's brand new, the length over all is as much as twenty-five feet shorter than it is now. That's because the ropes and canvas stretch that much after we've been out awhile. Or suppose a hard rain was setting in at this very minute and she promised to be soaking wet in the course of the next several hours. If you didn't take that into consideration in advance and lay out the centers accordingly, the old top would plumb pull herself to pieces when she started to shrink.

"I recollect"—and the boss chuckled at the thought—"I recollect a fellow who came to me all het up one day. Wanted to sell us a tent that wouldn't have to be laced. All we'd do would be to 'zip' the middle pieces and quarters together like when your sister closes the front of her zippers. Huh! Why, not having any play, that sort of a top would have more skylights in a week than a hot-house roof!"

"But how do you know just exactly how much to measure off at different times?" John asked.

"There's no special rule. You just keep your old guessing machinery well oiled. Same way when setting the first pin and starting to line out through the dark. Ten to one an old hand will come out right. You see, after you've tramped over show lots in the soot o' night for thirty or forty years, you sort of develop eyes in the bottom of your feet."

By this time the last center pole pin had been set. Then came the business of locating the lacings and the stake lines. An assistant held the free end of the tape against the top of the sixth center pin, while the laying-out boss began to describe an arc with the line, much as you would by fastening a string to a piece of chalk, pressing your finger against the string's end and then drawing the half of a circle.

At every given number of feet along the arc he set a pin. Those with red flags indicated where the big top stakes were to be driven. Others designated the lacings.

"Know the principle of a big top?" Happy Jack inquired. "Not likely. No way of finding out. I never could figure the chaps that lay out the dictionaries. They pack 'em full of drawings that tell all about the different parts of ships, castles, and such like; but nary a word on circus tents. Now, what you might call the roof of this big top is made up of eighteen pieces. When we take down at night each section is rolled into a bale and loaded into the big top canvas wagons. When the wagons pull on to the lot, there's got to be something to show where to drop each of the bundles so's they can be spread and laced together before raising. That's one of the reasons for the lacing pins."

The last of the big top pins in place, Happy Jack and his crew started on the menagerie layout. As with the larger tent, pins with white flags marked the menagerie center poles. But those used to indicate its stake line were topped with blue; because, as the boss pointed out, the two lines of stakes ran fairly close together and confusion might result were both the same color.

When it came to laying out the main entrance, or "marquee," at the menagerie front, the men set pins that bore double colors of red and blue. Yellow flagged pins were used to mark the position of side-show stakes and poles.

"Always the same colors, season in and season out," Happy Jack said. "And not just a happenstance either. Naturally, the centers and the lacings are the most important points. And at break of day, white can be seen farther than any other color. In a very bright sun, white's of no more use than a nickel on a railroad train. Red is the best then. See those white babies beginning to show up?"

So interested had John been in the work of laying out that he had forgotten to notice that day was breaking. Now the stars were gone, and the "old white-eyes" stowed away in twenty pockets.

As the pasture grayed with the dawn, he suddenly realized that for a half hour or more his ears had been partly conscious of muffled

290 . The Greatest Circus Stories Ever Told

sledge thumps and the deep rumbling of wagons moving in the lower half of the pasture. Now a film of light fog lifted to disclose a tent half built at the foot of a gentle slope. Near it, a dozen wagons were grouped, and from the top of one, a stack sent out a plume of smoke to blend with the lazying mist. The cook house, of course!

The show was beginning to take form.

From the higher ground on which he stood, John saw still another crew of men laying out the big horse tents in a more distant part of the pasture. Near them the blacksmith shop was going into the air.

At the "front," where the big Mack truck had drawn up less than an hour before, a score of wagons were pulling on to the lot.

"The dens will stand there until we get the menagerie up and ready for them," Happy Jack Snellen remarked. "That's always one of the first jobs of the morning—to get roofs over the animals and horses so's they can be fed and bedded down. The horse tents have their own crew and boss who lay 'em out and put 'em up. My crew lays out the big top, menagerie, and side show, puts up the menagerie, and sees to the driving of the big top stakes. Driving the big top stakes readies things up for Jim Whalen and his men, who arrive on the second section, so that they can dig in soon's they've had breakfast. Here comes thirteen now. It carries menagerie stakes—or staubs, if you want the slang of it."

A red, boxed wagon drawn by six dapple grays was heading toward them.

"All right, driver! Come along! More around this way—pull on your left hand!"

Next came wagons loaded with bales of menagerie-tent canvas, which men rolled to the ground as the heavy vans moved from lacing pin to lacing pin.

Then the menagerie-pole wagon.

Meanwhile, sledge gangs were driving stakes in pairs at each point where the white-topknotted pins marked a menagerie-tent center pole.

"Those deuce stakes will be for leverage in raising each of the six poles," Happy Jack explained. "Ever see a center pole and its fixings?

Got more parts than a dollar watch. First place, clap your eyes on that hunk of wood that Shorty's bringing over here now. It's what we call a mud block. There's one to set under every center pole so's the weight of the canvas won't sink the pole butts into the ground once the top is up.

"The first operation is to set the rounded bottom of the mud block against the two leverage stakes—the way Shorty's doing now. See the iron spike that's fixed into the face of the block? We call that the horn. Now, take a peek at the bottom of the center pole that's just been brought up. Hole in it, you say? That's the grummet—iron lined and made to receive the horn from the mud block."

Near the butt-end of each center pole the canvas men were placing huge coils of rope fitted with pulley-blocks. Others brought heavy hoops, made of rounded iron as thick as a broom handle. They dropped one beside each of the six piles of tackle.

"That's a bail ring," Happy Jack said, nudging the one which lay nearest them with the tip of his toe, "and a bail ring is about the most important article around a show lot.—Slip it on, men!—Of course," he added, "it has to be shoved over the pole butt before the mud block goes on. Now, then—see this bunch of tackle with the blue pulley blocks? It's the main falls; called that because it's got the mainest job of the several that are rigged to the pole. The mainest job owing to the fact that it pulls the canvas into the air.

"The down end of the main-falls rope hooks into the bail ring like this." The boss stooped and made it fast. "Then the rope runs up the pole and goes through the pulley block that Shorty's just hooking into the iron at the skyward end of the pole. Follow it with your eye and you'll see that after passing through that top-side pulley it returns down the pole to where we're standing and goes under this pulley wheel that's set in this slit made in the butt of the pole.

"Now, then," Happy Jack concluded, "once the pole is raised in place, all you have to do is to pull on this lower end of the falls rope to cause the bail ring to slide skyward up the pole—a good deal like you'd hoist a mainmast boom on a sailing vessel. Only, before this and the other five bail rings are raised, the canvas must be tied to 'em."

"Gee, they've got to be strong, all right!" John said.

"Pshaw, lad, these are only finger rings compared to those you'll see Jim Whalen using on big top. His weigh a hundred and thirty pounds apiece. And the load they carry is heavier than forty elephants. It's so heavy that the main falls double up and down the center poles six times in order to get sufficient purchase on the lift. There in the big top the bail rings take the canvas skyward and hold it. Besides that, they support the weight of the electric lights, the chandeliers, and all of the rigging used for the big flying numbers and every other act that goes in the air. I tell you, boy, the longer you troupe the more respect you have for a bail ring."

There did, indeed, seem to be an amazing number of parts to a center pole. For now that the bail ring had been adjusted, the mud block attached, and the main falls hooked in place, the light falls which would later handle the gas and electric lamps had to be rigged. Then, while the pole still rested on the ground, the "raising guy," the "lowering guy," and the "short guy" were looped over its skyward end. Lastly, the flag-staff was inserted in the "staff iron," and the lanyard, which would later spread a fine pennant to the breeze, attached to the staff head.

"And now it's ready for raising," Happy said. "Come on with you, boys!"

A dozen pairs of hands lifted the tapering end from the ground. Then they pushed it high over their heads until, passing the angle of resistance, the raising guy, manned by still other workers, stationed well out beyond the stake line, gained a purchase and brought it upright. That it might not slough to left or right, men slowly paid out the supporting guys. Then, the pole finally in position, these cables and the raising guy were made fast to deeply driven stakes.

The first center pole was in place. Quickly the gang tackled the next.

Meanwhile, others of the menagerie crew were distributing smaller poles of different lengths and color.

"Including the center poles, this and the big top have four kinds," the boss said. "Naming them outward from the centers, there first comes the circling row of blue quarter poles, next the red quarter poles and last, around the entire edge, the side poles. See the stripes painted midway along the heaviest ones? That's the point of balance, put there so's when a man picks one off a wagon he knows just where to glue his shoulder. Otherwise, he'd have to fiddle around and so lose time. And now, all six centers up, we're ready to spread the muslin.

"What do you say?" he called to the crew. "Let's open up these bundles men, and see what's inside. Quarters first!"

Then to John,

"That's what we call the V-shaped pieces that form the round ends."

An assistant boss began a running fire of orders:

"Roll it! Roll it! Head over! Hit it hard! Over again! . . . Pull it out and shake it up! Take it this way!—take it that! Open your hands and let it down!"

Then the next quarter until the "V's" of canvas patterned the ground like great gray fans.

"Now to the middles! Hit it!—Hit it again! Ro-o-o-oll it! Out to the borders.—All right!"

So, from bale to bale, until the entire canvas had been spread.

"'Middles' is short for 'middle pieces,'" Happy Jack interpreted. "A middle piece is always rectangular in shape while a quarter is always in the form of a triangle. If you took the four quarters of this top, laced 'em together, and hoisted 'em on a single center pole, you'd have a perfect round top just like the old one-ring shows used to use. But nowadays we need a whole lot more room. So we get it by splitting the round top, setting one half of it to the left and the other half to the right, and then filling in the gap between with a roof made up of middle pieces."

"But the big top's lots longer than the menagerie, isn't it?" John asked.

"Pretty nearly twice as long; though the number of center poles is the same. The trick's turned by using a bigger round top, larger poles, and wider middle pieces. Besides, as you'll see later on, each of the big top's round ends has four 'quarters' instead of two. I suppose they really should be called 'eights,' though, for some reason or other, they've always been spoken of as 'quarters,' same as here in the menagerie."

As they looked toward the big top layout, John saw that a miniature pile driver, set on a wagon, was following along the red-flagged stake line. At each point marked by a pin, a man placed the nose of a staub against the ground, while another, who operated the chugging engine, set the mechanical hammer in motion, to send it deep into the earth. They were, as the laying-out boss had promised, "making things ready" for Jim Whalen and his crew.

By now, the menagerie tent middle pieces and quarters had been laced into one vast "roof." Canvas men were busy fastening it to the bail rings. Care had been taken to stretch the ground end of the main falls well out across the pasture floor before the canvas had been spread over them.

The last lashing made, men laid hold of the falls. Six different gangs, grasping as many different cables, lay back from them as men about to engage in tug-of-war.

"Walk away with 'em!" sang a voice.

The workers put their weight to the falls. The pulley wheels at the pole butts creaked into motion. The bail rings slid upward, and with them the menagerie roof.

"That's what's called 'raising the peaks,'" Happy Jack told John. "Here we do it by man power, but only horses will do on the big top."

When the bail rings had lifted the roof a third of the way to the top, the main falls were tied off until the side poles were set. Yet another raising of the peaks, and then came the work of putting the quarter poles in place.

This was done by thrusting the horn that sprouted from the top of each pole into the grummet sewed in the tent top to receive it. The last one shoved home, the peaks were drawn into final position at the tops of the centers. Finally the side wall was hung.

Around the entire tent, men were tightening the guy ropes that ran down to the circling rows of stakes. The menagerie had taken definite shape. The waiting cages began to move in under the roof.

Then, suddenly, from somebody, somewhere, came the shout: "She's in the air!"

John heard a dozen voices repeat the cry.

He thought the announcement came a trifle late, for most certainly the peaks had been guyed skyward fully five minutes before.

"Come along, John," Happy Jack Snellen called across to him. "Here's where we scoff."

Then he knew the meaning of the shouts. Looking out over the lot, his eyes found the cook tent.

The flag was up!

○ ○ ○

As the boy and Happy Jack descended the slope, a breeze carried whiffs of frying bacon toward them. It seemed to John that he had never smelled anything half so good.

From the horse tents and blacksmith shop men were hurrying in the same direction as themselves. Others, from the menagerie, passed them as they went.

At the entrance of the cook tent, a man was taking tickets and dropping them into slits in a box.

"All working men must have tickets for every meal," Happy Jack said. "They get them from their different bosses just before the flag goes up. That's so ringers can't impose on the show. But the bosses, staff, and performers pass on their face, so to speak.

"O. K. for my assistant here, Doc?" he asked the doorman, as they passed.

"As if you didn't know," answered the other, grinning at John.

"We'll eat at the bosses' table here in the long end," Happy Jack decided, once they were inside. "Whatever you've got, and the same for my friend here," he told the waiter.

First there were grapefruit and cereal, then the bacon that had smelled so delicious, with eggs fried along with it, boiled potatoes fairly bursting from their jackets, coffee, of course, and bread and butter.

"Only don't tip yourself off as a greeny by taking the top slice," Happy warned, as he handed John the bread. "The open air hardens it a bit, and besides, when there's wind, it's liable to have sand in it. Just lift it up and take one from underneath."

The tables used by the bosses were located next to the red curtain that separated the long end from the short end of the dining tent. Running in rows from them were other tables occupied by the working men. John saw that the men were given exactly the same food as was served to Mr. Snellen and himself.

"Never any difference," Happy Jack said. "Everybody eats alike, and what's more, eats all he wants. Why, on a cold morning, and especially when we're late, I've seen some of those huskies put away three steaks at a sitting. And bread!—Oh, Ollie," he called to a man who had just come in.

"This is Mr. Webb," he said, as the other came toward them. "I was just trying to tell John Foster here how much bread a good healthy canvas man will eat."

"Ask me something easy. A loaf apiece, maybe. I'll tell you one thing, though: When we first come out under canvas, our bread bill will run twenty-five percent higher than it does a little later on."

"Go 'way!"

"Never fails to. That's because a lot of the men haven't done so well during the off months and so have to get fattened up. After a couple of weeks, they begin to ease off and the orders grow normal again."

"There's an item for you," Happy nodded to John.

"Oh, so it was you who helped Willie Carr wake us up this morning!" the commissary exclaimed. "Well, don't be afraid to ask anything you want to know about the cook house. After breakfast, I'll show you the kitchen. Getting plenty to eat? Here, Frank! How about some cakes?"

"Coming up, bossman," a voice replied. Then when, a minute later, its owner came with two stacks of smoking buckwheat cakes, he ejaculated, "Well, boil me if it isn't the buddy who dug me out of the clover this morning!"

"Gaze on him, John!" proclaimed Willie Carr who had just come in, "Mister Frank Detre, of Worcester, Mass. Headwaiter in the long end and champion long-distance sleeper of seventeen states."

"Introduced by Mister Willie Hollow-legs Carr," came back Frank, "who can see the flag farther and eat more than any agent ahead of the show."

"They're always abusing each other," Happy Jack confided to John, as he passed him the maple syrup. "And Willie's been routing Frank out for going on twenty years now."

Others came to sit at the bosses' tables. There were Art Rooney, boss of the menagerie; "Old Andrew," who had charge of the giraffes;

Jim Doyle and Blackie Diller, assistant boss hostlers, and others whose names John did not remember.

"There's Ollie Webb back in the kitchen," Happy Jack said, as they rose from their last hot cake. "This will be a good time to catch him."

"Come on over to the menagerie after while, and I'll show you how we brush the hippo's teeth," invited Art Rooney.

"I will," promised John.

The circus kitchen was located a half dozen steps back of the cook tent.

"Just in time to see a fine mess of peas," the chief commissary called, as John came inside. "How'd you like to shell what's in there?"

A pan so heavy that it took two men to lift it to the top of a cask greeted John's eyes.

"Once they're washed, they'll be dumped into one of those big copper caldrons, and the steam will do the rest. Steam is the principal fuel around here. See that donkey-engine-looking affair out there? That's what we call the steam-boiler wagon. It's the first to be fired of a morning. Pipes laid from it along the ground hook up with this row of copper kettles, the steam passes into open spaces between the kettle walls and so cooks vegetables, stews, soups, coffee, and the like."

"Will the others that come have peas for breakfast?" asked John.

"Oh, no. This stuff is for dinner. You see, as soon as one meal is well on its way, we start preparing for the next. When there are upward of sixteen hundred people to be fed three times every day, we've got to do it that way to keep up. Of course, some things have to be served right off the fire. Others can be cooked ahead of time and then kept hot in the steam boxes over at the left."

They passed the boxes and turned to where the pastry cooks were mixing piecrust.

"Apple pie for supper," Ollie Webb said. "How many are you making for tonight?" he inquired of the head baker.

"Figuring on a hundred and fifty, boss."

"Well, better increase it to a hundred and fifty-one," the commissary chief directed with a wink toward John. "Got an extra boarder today. Now," he added, "maybe you'd like to see how those potatoes you had for breakfast were cooked."

They walked past the score of white-coated chefs to the boiler wagon. A man dressed much like a locomotive engineer was raking the fire box.

"That's Hank Hill," Ollie Webb said, as they approached, "and he knows more about steam and boiling potatoes than any trouper alive. Got a good scald on those spuds this morning, Hank."

"Wall, the steam was exactly right," drawled the grimy-faced engineer. "Gimme right steam in this old tea kettle o' mine, and I'll bile 'em to a turn any time."

He squinted at the water gauge.

"Thar's as much difference in steam as there is between a couple o' strange bulldogs," Hank went on, now addressing his remarks to John. "You see, the way I do it is thiswise: I sinks the perf'rated boxes holdin' the taters in this iron-lined pit at the back o' the b'iler. Then I takes the steam-hose nozzle and shoves it in and shoots. Got to know just how your steam is when you do it, though. Leave 'er blow too long, and the jackets'll peel plumb off. Hold 'er in just long enough and they'll come out prettier'n a rosebud touched by the sun. Get the p'int?"

"Yes, sir."

Hank eyed him approvingly.

"You're a smart hombre. Anybody can see that with his lashes singed. Well, come back whenever you're a mind. Can't tell you much about any other part of the show. But I know steam—shucks a'mighty, I know steam."

"Hank ought to, if anybody does," Ollie Webb said, as he and John skirted the edge of the kitchen. "He's been a trouper for going on fifty years. And he won't allow anybody to touch that boiler wagon but himself. Watches it like a cat watching kittens. Even has all his meals alongside the fire box."

"I saw a cat in the cook house," John volunteered.

"Mother, like as not. She's traveled a hundred thousand miles since she joined out one morning, some four or five years back. She was only a kitten then. Wandered in from nobody knew where and curled up behind one of the ranges to get warm. That night the boys made a house for her out of a vegetable crate and lashed the crate to the grocery wagon. She's had a slather of kittens since then, and stalked field mice in most every state in the Union. That's one of her babies now—just skinning up that side pole.

"The cook-house boys are always carting pets along. We had a duck one season. Called him Moocher. Might have him yet, only one of the flunkies put him in a stream alongside of the lot one day. Remember Moocher's get-away, Grant?" the commissary called to a man who was passing.

"I should say I do! You couldn't have caught him with a motor boat."

"But the star was Cocky, the bantam rooster," laughed the boss.

"He certainly was a darb," agreed Grant. "Trouped with us three seasons, and if ever there was a cock of the walk, he was it. Never did like Andrew, the dwarf. Used to try chasing him. And whenever a town chicken showed up—good night! Remember the time, boss, when the cook house was butted up against the hen yard in Newark? Naturally enough, the gillie roosters and hens came around looking for chuck. It kept Cocky busy giving 'em the bum's rush. By the time we packed up he was all in."

"What became of him?" John wanted to know.

"Had to get rid of the little rascal," Ollie Webb said. "Got so spoiled that he thought he owned the show. Flew right into a midget's face one day and took a nip out of his ear. That was too much of a good thing. Plenty of meat around without using up our actors. Speaking of meat—cast your eyes over this."

They had come to the circus butcher shop. Like the kitchen, it was roofed with canvas, but instead of requiring center poles, its top was spread over a big wagon and the eaves extended outward to supporting side poles. Under this shelter John saw blocks strewn with knives, saws, and cleavers. Shoulders and entire quarters of beeves lay on long tables. Two men were engaged in cutting chops and tossing them into a pan that was even larger than the one that had been filled with peas.

John lifted one side of it.

"Some chops !" he said.

"Some chops is right," laughed Ollie Webb. "Here's still more stuff in the cold storage compartment."

He swung open a door at the front end of the wagon. John caught a glimpse of dressed porkers hanging from hooks, and the plump breasts of chickens piled on big cakes of ice.

"In every town played for but one day—and that's eighty percent of those visited in a season—we buy enough supplies for dinner, supper, and breakfast," John's guide explained. "The dinner and supper stuff is served in the town where it is bought, but the breakfast is carried along to the next stand so as to be ready for cooking immediately upon arrival. We store it in the forward end here, which is why we call this the grocery wagon."

On the side opposite to the butcher shop were dozens upon dozens of boxes and crates filled with oranges, apples, grapefruit, fresh vegetables, and bread. Besides, John saw stacks of sacked potatoes, flour, and three huge cans of honey.

As they walked toward the cook tent he noticed heavy wooden chests with hinged lids.

"Dish, glassware, and silverware boxes," Ollie Webb pointed out. He lifted one of the lids. "The dishes are placed in the slits. Other boxes have openings like pigeonholes in a desk. A drinking glass goes into each one of the holes. Then everything is loaded at night aboard what we call the crockery wagons. Oh, yes, a dish breaks now and then, but the average loss isn't much greater than in your kitchen at home."

"Don't forget to give the spud pile a visit," Grant called to John. "Come along, and I'll join you out right now."

"Go ahead," Ollie Webb advised. "You'll see quite a sight there this morning."

Permissions Acknowledgments

"Fifty Years with a Menagerie" by Dan Rice from *52 Stories of Animal Life and Adventure,* edited by Alfred H. Miles, London: Hutchinson & Co., 1903.

"Those Press Agents!" from *Under the Big Top* by C. R. Cooper. Boston: Little, Brown and Company, 1923.

"Toby Tyler chapters 1–7," from *Toby Tyler—Or Ten Weeks With a Circus* by James Otis. New York: Harper Bros., 1880.

"Peck's Bad Boy with the Circus" by Hon. George W. Peck, Chicago: Thompson & Thomas, 1906

"The Circus Lady" by Josephine DeMott Robinson, New York: Thomas Y. Crowell Company, 1926.

"Razorbacks and Skin Games" from *Here We Are Again* by Robert Edmond Sherwood, Indianapolis: The Bobbs-Merrill Co., Inc., 1926.

"When the Animals Escape" from *Under the Big Top* by C. R. Cooper. Boston: Little, Brown and Company, 1923.

"Circus Day at Mancos" from *The Red-Blooded Heros of the Frontier* by Edgar Beecher Bronson. New York: George H. Doran Company, 1910.

"Inside the Training Den" from *Lions 'N' Tigers 'N' Everything* by C. R. Cooper. Boston: Little, Brown and Company, 1924.

"The Elephant People" from *The Ways of the Circus* by George Conklin. New York: Harper & Brothers, 1921.

"Albany, New York" from *Cat Man* by Edward Hoagland, 1955. Used by permission of the author.

"On the High Wire" by Philippe Petit, translated by Paul Auster, 1972. Used by permission of Paul Auster.

"The Other Side of the Circus" by Edwin P. Norwood. Garden City, New York: Doubleday & Page, 1926.